PRAISE FOR

GRANT *and* TWAIN

"Cleverly conceived and brilliantly written . . . Perry has breathed life into this tale of two remarkable men."
—*The Philadelphia Inquirer*

"A very good short narrative of a fascinating period in American history."
—*Lincoln Journal-Star*

"*Grant and Twain* casts a full light on a moment that is little more than a footnote to history, a brief partnership between warrior and scribe that became history's greatest publishing triumph."
—*Times Record News*

"An excellent . . . account of this coincidence, thoroughly researched, closely considered . . . Perry gives you the great Grant that enthralled Mark Twain."
—*The Buffalo News*

"The story of . . . how Twain aided Grant in writing and publishing is highly absorbing."
—*Chicago Sun-Times*

"The two men had much in common, including roots in the frontier, strong ambition and persistent financial difficulties."
—*The Washington Post Book World*

"Perry's narrative is a double biography emphasizing the overlap between the two . . . men's lives and consistently implying the consequences this friendship had on America."
—*Booklist*

"Perry chronicles the hardships . . . that provoked Grant to complete his memoirs hurriedly and the perspicacity that motivated Twain to act on his friend's behalf. . . . A glimpse into the development of cultural history in late nineteenth-century America."
—*Library Journal*

"Mark Perry uncovers a crucial sliver of American literary and cultural history: the little-known connection between Grant and Twain, who, in the twilight of the old general's life, formed a friendship that is both interesting and important."
—JON MEACHAM, bestselling author of *Franklin and Winston*

"Mark Perry engagingly intertwines the lives of two near opposites, Mark Twain and Ulysses S. Grant, revealing how in a stunning burst of creativity the two friends produced works of genius that would lead America to find its distinctive literary voice."
—JOSEPH E. PERSICO, bestselling author of *Roosevelt's Secret War*

"Exploring how each man dealt with his America, particularly the questions of slavery and race, Perry illuminates not only their views, but also the America of their time."
—WILLIAM J. COOPER,
award-winning author of *Jefferson Davis, American*

"This slender book by Mark Perry tells a large tale about two misfits turned American giants turned friends and grand collaborators. *Grant and Twain* is a charming and evocative story."
—JAY WINIK,
bestselling author of *April 1865: The Month That Saved America*

GRANT
and
TWAIN

Also by Mark Perry

LIFT UP THY VOICE

CONCEIVED IN LIBERTY

GRANT

and

TWAIN

THE STORY OF AN AMERICAN

FRIENDSHIP

MARK PERRY

RANDOM HOUSE TRADE PAPERBACKS   🏠   NEW YORK

For Nicholas S. Mikhalevsky

2005 Random House Trade Paperback Edition

Copyright © 2004 by Mark Perry

Published in the United States by Random House Trade Paperbacks,
an imprint of The Random House Publishing Group, a division of
Random House, Inc., New York.

RANDOM HOUSE TRADE PAPERBACKS and colophon are registered
trademarks of Random House, Inc.

Originally published in hardcover in the United States by Random House,
an imprint of The Random House Publishing Group, a division
of Random House, Inc., in 2004.

Library of Congress Cataloging-in-Publication Data
Perry, Mark
Grant and Twain: the story of an American friendship / Mark Perry.
p. cm.
Includes bibliographical references and index.
ISBN 978-0-8129-6613-8
1. Grant, Ulysses S. (Ulysses Simpson), 1822–1885—Friends and associates.
2. Grant, Ulysses S. (Ulysses Simpson), 1822–1885—Literary art. 3. Twain, Mark,
1835–1910—Friends and associates. 4. Twain, Mark, 1835–1910—Literary art.
5. Presidents—United States—Biography. 6. Authors, American—19th century—
Biography. 7. Friendship—United States—Case studies. 8. United States—
Race relations. 9. Race relations in literature. I. Title.
E672.P47 2004   818'.409—dc22 [B]   2003066678

Printed in the United States of America

Random House website address: www.atrandom.com

Book design by Joseph Rutt

To the irresolute the victor came
and as he came it seemed to Soliman
he in his fury and his speed and frame
surpassed the semblance of a mortal man.
He put up little fight, but as he died
did not forget he was a noble man;
he gave no groans, but met the blows, uncowed.
To the last all he did was great and proud.
—*Gerusalemme liberata*
Torquato Tasso

ACKNOWLEDGMENTS

My appreciation is extended to my editor, David Ebershoff, at Random House—whose support for and attention to this book has been gratifying—and to my agent, Gail Ross, whose unerring faith in my work remains a source of strength.

This book could not have been written without the encouragement of my wife, Nina, and my children, Cal and Madeleine.

I wish to thank those librarians, archivists, and researchers, numbering in the hundreds, whose tireless work to provide history to historians too often remains unnoticed. The staff of the Library of Congress, the Chicago Historical Society, the New York State Historical Society, the New York Public Library, the Mark Twain Papers & Project at the University of California,

Berkeley, and the Mark Twain House were selfless in their time and effort in aiding this work.

This book is about two men who led lives of great honor and dignity, and so it is dedicated to another man of great honor and dignity, Nicholas S. Mikhalevsky.

CONTENTS

CONTENTS

"HE FIGHTS"

He wasn't much to look at—this "Hero of the Union," this "Savior of his country." As he alighted from his carriage at the Wall Street offices of the investment firm of Grant & Ward and tipped his hat to passersby, Ulysses S. "Sam" Grant remained as he had ever been: slight, compact, even forgettable. If now, in May 1884, he had rounded out a bit, he was still modest and soft-spoken. Girth did not come with fame: This tanner's son from Georgetown, Ohio, by way of Galena, Illinois, weighed all of 117 pounds when he entered West Point, in 1839; 140 pounds when the Confederates fired on Fort Sumter, in 1861; and not much more when he accepted Robert E. Lee's surrender, in 1865. When his wife saw him at the end of the war, he was so skeletal that she thought he was ill. His demeanor reflected his size. If he had not become "Unconditional Surrender Grant" and then been elected, twice, as president of the United States, he might have been remembered as he was in the late 1840s: as "the little man with the large epaulets."

Still, there was something about Grant that people noticed. The tanner's son had a hard-nosed quality that allowed him to get his way and a quiet ambition that, as his friend William Tecumseh Sherman had once said, was like a little engine, churning ceaselessly. When he left Galena, carrying a carpetbag in the wake of the resplendently blue-clad and recently recruited boys of the Twenty-first Illinois Volunteers, the townsfolk tittered at his appearance: There is Sam Grant, they said, going off to war. God help us. Four years later these same people celebrated his return with a parade, speeches, and a new $16,000 home. In the intervening four years he received the surrender of three rebel armies (including, of course, Robert E. Lee's), captured Vicksburg, Chattanooga, and Richmond, and reached the rank of lieutenant general (once reserved only for Washington). Soon he would be rewarded for his triumph by a landslide victory as the Republican Party's candidate for president. The people of Galena said then what historians have said about him ever since: His was a quintessentially American story, of a poor pioneer boy who led the nation and mastered the world. But it was that other pioneer boy, Abraham Lincoln, who described him best: "He fights."

There were other things. Back during the Wilderness Campaign—the tangled slaughter that he had inaugurated exactly twenty years before the day he alighted from his Wall Street carriage—a common soldier marching south in the hushed Virginia moonlight noticed Grant riding nearby. "He looks as if he meant it," the private said. A more expansive declaration was offered by a man who attended a White House reception in Grant's honor, just after he was placed in command of the Union armies: "He habitually wears an expression as if he had determined to drive his head through a brick wall, and was about to do it." James Longstreet would have agreed. The commander of the First Corps of the rebel Army of Northern Virginia, Robert E. Lee's vaunted "warhorse," and Grant's best man at his wedding to Julia Dent was once asked what the rebels could expect from Grant. Longstreet knew Grant well and hesitated for only a moment before answering: "We must make up our minds to get into line of battle and stay there," he said, "for that man will fight us every day and every hour till the end of the war."

That was Grant: a fighter. As the blood of thousands was spilled in the underbrush of the Wilderness and Robert E. Lee assailed both of his flanks with headlong charges, he sat—with his staff standing uneasily nearby—on a tree stump, whittling and whittling. When the battle lagged and Lee moved off, Grant, who should have known he was beaten and should have retreated (as so many of his predecessors had done before), mounted his horse and trotted off south—to fight again. His staff followed, wondering when he would issue the orders for a retreat. "Ulysses don't scare worth a damn," one Union soldier commented. Indeed, the man would not quit. Which is exactly the one quality that he needed now, on May 5, 1884, as he walked slowly into No. 2 Wall Street, the building housing the offices of the investment firm that carried his family's name. Now his personal appearance, his reputation, and his past made not one whit of difference; Grant needed all the tenacity he could muster. For on the previous morning, a bright New York Sunday, he had been visited at his home on 66th Street by the head of the firm, Ferdinand Ward, and told that they (Grant, Ward, Grant's son "Buck," and investor James Fish—the firm's four partners) desperately needed $150,000 to keep their business solvent. Grant was worried, but Ward's feigned indifference reassured him. Grant borrowed the money but soon found that Ward was lying. Grant & Ward did not need $150,000; the firm needed more than that, *much* more than that. In fact, Grant learned, Grant & Ward was bankrupt. He awakened the next morning determined to ask Ward what had happened. But Ward was nowhere to be found.

⊶⊷

ULYSSES S. GRANT's financial partner Ferdinand Ward was one of Wall Street's rising tycoons who epitomized the go-for-broke character of what was already known as "the Gilded Age." After arriving in New York City from the small upstate town of Genesco in 1875, he met and married the daughter of the head of New York's prestigious Marine Bank. His new family introduced him to his father-in-law's boss, the Marine Bank's president, James D. Fish, who was a highly respected New York financier. Ward cultivated Fish's friendship, and the two were soon inseparable. When Fish recommended that Ward buy a seat on the lucrative produce exchange, Ward was only too happy to comply, and, as they said then, "the young man made a great success." Ward's cut was impressive: easygoing, handsome, personable, and now powerful (with his marriage to the vivacious Henriette Green and his burgeoning friendship with Fish), Ward invested in transportation securities. He quickly made a tidy sum for himself and his new wife. By 1881 he was known as "the Young Napoleon of finance."

Ulysses S. Grant Jr.—Buck to family and friends—was quite different. While less dashing than the evanescent Ward, Buck had brains. Rotund but tall, Buck was always smiling; he had none of his father's guile, but all his ambition. Of all Grant's children, he was the best educated. He attended Exeter, then Harvard, received his law degree from Columbia University, and married Fannie Josephine Chaffee, the daughter of Jerome B. Chaffee of Colorado, an imposing, gruff westerner inured to the rough-and-tumble of frontier politics. Chaffee made millions from his investments in Colorado's silver mines, which he then translated into a seat in the U.S. Senate. Buck's marriage to Fannie sealed the Grant family's future: They could now take their place in New York society as rich, powerful, and prestigious— something not necessarily assured by the fact that Buck just happened to be the son of America's greatest general.

The financial marriage between Buck Grant and Ferdinand Ward seemed just as auspicious. Buck was entranced by Ward, as was the former president. For them, Ward symbolized America itself: self-made, outgoing, confident, relentlessly expansive, and experienced in the ways of Wall Street. Ward had an unerringly keen sense, Grant and Buck believed, of when to buy low and sell high. "There's millions in it," the hero of Mark Twain's *The Gilded Age* repeated in a phrase that came to symbolize America's fast-money mentality. It was a phrase Ward himself might have repeated—and often. Everything he touched turned to gold. "Some men worship rank," Twain had once written, "some worship heroes, some worship power, some worship God, and over these ideals they dispute and cannot unite—but they all worship money."

Ward worshiped money. It was precisely with this in mind that Ward courted Buck Grant, finally proposing to him that together they open a Wall Street investment house. Buck had the brains and the name, Ward said, and Ward would invest his own hard-earned millions to make the firm successful. With his experience and connections, Grant & Ward would be the most successful firm in American financial history. Ward proposed that they add two additional partners: Buck's father, Ulysses S. Grant, and Ward's longtime colleague James B. Fish, president of the Marine Bank. After several days of discussions, Buck and his father agreed: They would be equal partners with Ward and Fish, both of whom they trusted.

Fish had underwritten part of Grant's postpresidency

world tour, was a respected businessman, and could cover any shortfalls the firm might incur. Of course, neither Buck nor his father thought this would ever be necessary, but just to be sure, Grant invested $100,00 of his own money in the business, Buck borrowed $100,000 from his father-in-law to ensure that he was Ward's partner, and the aging Senator Chaffee, in a sign of confidence in his son-in-law, invested a further $400,000. Together, with Ward and the Marine Bank, the initial investments would more than capitalize any shortfalls in the highly unlikely event (Ward said expansively) there were any. Ward was also betting that the Grant name would bring business to the firm—and if investors did not realize that the "Grant" of Grant & Ward was Ulysses S. Grant Jr. and not his father, it hardly mattered: The former general and president had his own offices on the second floor and arrived at work promptly each day to lend his weight, and handshake, to Ward's numerous transactions. This is just what Grant, at the age of sixty-two, had always wanted. Having been a captain of armies, he was now a captain of industry, mimicking in his dress and demeanor the worldly mien of those he admired most. He was finally, as William Henry Vanderbilt (that scion of Wall Street, that pillar of New York finance, that builder of financial empires) described it, "one of us."

The arrangement worked well. Within three years, Grant's initial investments were worth $750,000 and he could indulge his tastes. They were modest enough. Grant gave his wife, Julia, $1,000 a month (an enormous sum for the time) to spend in any way she saw fit. He kept a lavish home on East 66th Street, bought boxes of expensive cigars, and purchased and rode the best horses. If he had any questions on Grant & Ward's investments, or if ever a nervous investor approached him with worrying questions, Ward was ever present, smiling and helpful, leading Grant and the customer through the maze of investments he had made and which, he continually pledged, were making Grant rich. In truth, Grant came to expect such results. Since his retirement from the presidency he had been showered with gifts: the $16,000 home in Galena, a home given him by the people of Philadelphia, a home on "Eye" Street in Washington, D.C., and, finally, the New York home—given to him by an old friend, George Childs of Philadelphia, who raised a subscription ($1,000 from each of twenty millionaires) on his behalf. A portion of the mortgage was paid by the subscription, but, as Grant decided, the remaining money would buy "premium" securities offered by Grant & Ward.

There was in all of this, however, a whiff of deceit, of easy money made too easily. By the beginning of 1884, there were rumors on Wall Street that Ward was mishandling his investors' money and that Grant & Ward, far from being the meteoric success that Ward claimed, was fast failing. The firm's profits, Grant's profits, were not worth the teetering pile of gilded paper they were printed on. If Grant noticed the eyes that followed him on the street, the titterings and whispers (not unlike those that had once followed him as he trailed the Twenty-first Illinois Volunteers through the streets of Galena), he did not show it. Ward, he told his friends and family, had a sure eye for investments, and the firm was sound—which is pretty much what Ward had told him. In all, Ulysses S. Grant remained what he had always been: modest, proud, and confident. All of that changed, however, on May 4, when Ward visited him at his home on 66th Street.

∞

WARD ARRIVED AT THE Grant home at midmorning on May 4 and stayed for just over one hour. His message was a strange combination of hope and dread: Grant & Ward was solvent and healthy, he reassured Grant, but the Marine Bank was not. The city chamberlain of New York, Ward explained, had made a sudden and unexpected withdrawal from the bank. Since Grant & Ward's cash reserves were held by the bank, the withdrawal imperiled their investments. The bank needed an immediate cash infusion of $150,000—"and only for one day"—to meet its debts. Could Grant help?

The former president listened closely to Ward and sensed the dread in his voice. The firm was in the midst of a crisis, his good name was in question, and he needed to act. Immediately. That afternoon, Grant visited the home of an old friend and political supporter, the president of the Pennsylvania Railroad—William Henry Vanderbilt. The plain-speaking self-made financial titan shook his head knowingly; he had warned Grant that Ward's business practices were risky. But he was willing to help. "I care nothing for the Marine Bank, General Grant," he said. "To tell the truth I care very little about Grant and Ward. But to accommodate you personally, I will draw the check for the amount you ask. I consider it a personal loan to you and not to any other party."

The next morning Grant delivered the check to Ward, and the crisis seemed to pass. But that afternoon, Ward told Buck that the $150,000 secured from Vanderbilt was not nearly enough to ensure the firm's survival. Grant & Ward needed $600,000 to meet its creditors' demands, he said. Buck, a good lawyer and a dutiful and loving son, did not tell his father about this new crisis but instead visited the redoubtable Jay Gould, New York's leading financial tycoon and the nation's most admired business mind. Gould looked over a list of Grant & Ward's holdings, then issued his judgment. The securities were virtually worthless, he said. Knowing now that Grant & Ward was facing bankruptcy, Buck visited the offices of his law partner Stanley D. Elkins, who also represented his father-in-law, Senator Jerome Chaffee. Elkins, a lawyer with a rapier mind, acted swiftly. He told Buck that they should pay a visit to Mr. Ward to hear his explanation of why the redoubtable Jay Gould would think his securities worthless.

That evening, Elkins and Buck Grant arrived, uninvited, at the Ward home at 181 Pierrepont Street in Brooklyn. Henriette Ward answered the door and told them that her husband was not at home and would not arrive for some time. "We'll wait," Elkins said, and he and Buck deposited their hats and coats and were seated. Five hours later, just after midnight, Ward appeared, suddenly, to confront his guests. He waved aside their concerns: The firm was solvent, the crisis was temporary, the securities of the firm were not worthless, he said. Elkins was not impressed. He said that while he appreciated Ward's candor, it would be helpful if he wrote a check to his client, Senator Jerome Chaffee, to cover the $400,000 investment the senator had made. Ward was irritated but said that if this was absolutely necessary, he would comply with the request. The check would be available in the morning, he said. With that Buck and Elkins thanked Ward for his hospitality and left. Outside, in the chill New York spring, Elkins turned to Buck. "The whole thing is suspicious," he said. "Did you observe Ward had his slippers on? He was in the house all the time and was afraid to come down and see us."

The next morning Buck wrote a check in the firm's name for $400,000 and sent it to the Marine Bank. He intended to give the money to his father-in-law as reimbursement for his investment in the firm. The bank refused to honor the check and, later that morning, closed its doors. A bank official announced that the institution had suspended all payments. An angry crowd gathered at the bank, demanding admittance. Trouble was averted, finally, with the appearance of the police. One hour after this, the First National Bank followed the Marine Bank's lead and announced that it would not honor any checks drawn on Ferdinand Ward's account. Checks in the amount of $85,000, $80,000, and $25,000 were not honored. Furthermore, a bank officer announced, Ferdinand Ward had a total of $1,000 in his account.

Shortly before noon, General Grant arrived at No. 2 Wall Street to begin his day. An angry crowd—depositors at the Marine Bank—greeted him on the street, demanding their money. Grant surveyed the scene and walked slowly into the firm's offices. "The Marine Bank closed this morning," his son told him. "Ward has fled. We cannot find our securities." Grant nodded, looked around for a moment, then wordlessly made his way through the crowd to the elevator and ascended to his office. Later that afternoon, he listened as Buck briefed him on Grant & Ward's future. The firm's securities were worthless, Buck confirmed. The firm could not pay its debts and would have to close its doors. They were broke. Visibly shaken, Grant turned to the firm's bookkeeper. "Spencer, how is it that man has deceived us in this manner?" he asked, but he did not wait for an answer. "I have made it a rule of life to trust a man long after other people gave up on him. I don't see how I can trust any human being again."

<hr />

ON THE SUNDAY MORNING that Ferdinand Ward was asking Ulysses S. Grant to find $150,000 for Brooklyn's Marine Bank, Samuel Clemens ("Sam" to his closest friends, "Mark" to his admirers, and "Mark Twain" to his readers) was at home in Hartford, Connecticut, planning yet another grand speaking tour—and cursing fellow author George Washington Cable. Like Grant, Twain felt the irresistible pull of wealth and was forever concocting schemes that would line his pockets. Just months before, he had urged Cable to join him in a lecture tour that would publicize their books and add to their bank accounts. It was to be a grand event, national in scope, that would be a celebration "of our great century." Cable readily agreed, in part because he was no longer welcome in the South (where his views on black emancipation made him a pariah) and in part because, like Twain, he badly needed the reinvigoration such a tour offered. So the two had planned and planned. But they never planned on a Sunday. The Sabbath had a special meaning for the devout Cable, who would not go anywhere on the day of rest, let alone plan a tour that bowed to mammon. Cable's devotion more than annoyed Twain. "He has taught me to abhor and detest the Sabbath-day," he harrumphed to coauthor William Dean Howells, "and hunt up new and troublesome ways to dishonor it."

Given to exaggeration, Twain would later tire of Cable's eccentricities, calling him "that louse" while admitting privately to his wife, his "beloved Livy," that Cable had taught him much over the years. For while Twain struggled with the issue of race, Cable attacked it head-on, writing and speaking about black equality before audiences that booed him regularly. It was for this reason alone that Twain remained Cable's friend and admirer. They had even seen Grant together, paying him a visit on a cold winter's day just months before Grant's bankruptcy, to obtain his blessing for their tour and to delicately suggest that perhaps he would add his endorsement to a special project they had concocted "for the relief of the Ohio River overflow sufferers." Cable was properly impressed by Twain's friendship with Grant ("whom Mark knows well," Cable had portentously written to his family), and he basked in the glow of Grant's fame. As did Twain.

Twain worshiped Grant. In the words of biographer Justin Kaplan, he was "a Grant-intoxicated man." While seemingly so different in temperament and outlook, they had much in common. Like Grant, Twain grew up on the frontier, the son of a successful father who expected much. Like Grant, he had failed, at least in his early years, to live up to those expectations. What Clemens said of his father might have been said by Grant of his. "My father and I," Clemens wrote, "were always on the most distant terms when I was a boy—a sort of armed neutrality, so to speak." Not much was expected of either Sam Clemens or Sam Grant. They were just boys with dreams. And if the tittering crowd in Galena had prayed that Sam, the son of the town tanner, would not do anything to embarrass them, so too the people of that other river town—Hannibal, Missouri—had hoped that their Sam, the son of the town judge, would never embarrass *them*. Sam Clemens an author? God help us.

So Sam Clemens struck out on his own, as Sam Grant had, and struggled to find his way. Though much younger, Clemens had yet to find his first great success when Grant was already celebrating his. Grant and Clemens first shook hands at a Washington reception in the winter of 1866, but they did not exchange a word. Both remembered the handshake and commented on it during a second meeting, which took place at the White House during the first term of Grant's presidency. Twain, under the guidance of Nevada senator Bill Stewart, greeted the president politely, and then they stood, awkwardly, searching for something to talk about. "I shook hands and then there was a pause and silence," Twain later recounted. "I couldn't think of anything to say. So I merely looked into the General's grim, immovable countenance a moment or two in silence and then I said: 'Mr. President, I am embarrassed. Are you?' He smiled a smile which would have done no discredit to a cast-iron image and I got away under the smoke of my volley."

Twain was then "very thoroughly notorious," as he said, to the point where, ten years after his first meetings with Grant in the White House, he was asked to prepare a toast to honor Grant at the Palmer House in Chicago. As Grant sat, impassively, listening to the round of testimonials, Twain vowed to break his iron demeanor. He accomplished his mission by recalling a poignant moment in Grant's infancy when "the future illustrious commander-in-chief of the American armies" gave his entire attention "to trying to find some way to get his big toe into his mouth." The crowded room, pale with the clouds of cigar smoke and raucous just a moment before, was stunned by this. All present knew that Grant was returning a hero from a world tour that had been a kind of exile. After all, some of his political enemies noted, Grant had spent as much time as president trying to pull his foot *out* of his mouth as he had as a baby (as Twain would have it) trying to get it *in*. But Twain had taken Grant's measure and broke the embarrassed silence by finishing with a flourish: "And if the child is but the father of the man there are mighty few who will doubt that he succeeded."

The joke has paled over the years, but in 1879 it was the talk of Chicago and the nation. Twain was exuberant. "I fetched him up," he wrote to his wife, "I broke him up entirely. The audience saw that for once in his life he had been knocked out of his iron serenity." Unable to contain himself, Twain next scribbled off a note to Howells, describing the speech, the crowd, and the banquet. "Grand times, my boy," he wrote, "grand times." Twain's triumph over Grant complete, the two worked diligently to cement their friendship; they stayed in close touch after the Palmer House banquet, and when Grant moved to New York, Twain came often to see him and they spent a number of afternoons talking about the war, mutual friends, and Twain's writing career. Twain brought his friends to see Grant, as much to entertain Grant as to show off to them that he could call the former general a friend. Like Cable, William Dean Howells (then the most powerful arbiter of American literature) was awed by Grant when Twain introduced him at Grant's New York home in October 1881. Howells requested the meeting because he wanted Grant to help his father gain appointment as American consul in Toronto. Grant said he would forward a recommendation to President Chester A. Arthur.

Howells was suitably grateful, but Grant was modest. He said that he was more than happy to do what he could, and he started to talk about the war. It was his favorite topic. He went on for many minutes, with Twain and Howells listening politely, and he might have gone on for many more, but Twain had other ideas. During a pause in the conversation, he turned the subject to writing. Intrigued by this, Grant suggested the three continue their discussion over lunch, and he ushered them into a nearby family room to enjoy ample helpings of bacon, baked beans, and coffee—battlefield food. Twain would later cite this conversation as the first he had ever had with Grant about Grant's own writing, about his need to set down on paper the story of his life, his battles, and his presidency. Twain was blunt, argumentative. It was time for Grant to write his memoirs, he said. Grant listened silently and politely, but he shook his head.

Grant "wouldn't listen to the suggestion" and added that he had no confidence in his ability to write. He was "sure that the book would have no sale," and he would feel embarrassed to see a book published under his name. Twain attempted to dampen these fears. "I argued that the book would have an enormous sale," he recounted, "and that out of my experience I could save him from making unwise contracts with publishers, and would have the contract arranged in such a way that they could not swindle him, but he said he had no necessity for any addition to his income." Grant would not be swayed. No, he said, he would not write his memoirs, and he changed the subject.

But that was in 1881, three years before Grant's bankruptcy.

We cannot know for certain when the former general and president began to rethink his position on writing his memoirs, but it would not be surprising if the thought first occurred to him on the morning of May 5, 1884, when his son told him that they were bankrupt and that the man who had swindled them was nowhere to be found. Deceived and downcast, Grant called his carriage and returned home. There, on the front table, lay the daily newspapers. The *New York Sun* recounted the firm's collapse with a headline that slapped at its most public partner: IS GRANT GUILTY? The *New York Post* was even more biting. "The conclusion is irresistible," the paper editorialized, "that a large number of persons were drawn into the maelstrom by a belief held out to them that General Grant's influence was used in some highly improper way to the detriment of the government and the benefit of Grant and Ward."

This was not true, but the criticism hit hard. After reading the papers, Grant vowed that he would repay every penny of the debt he owed and pledged that before his death, he would find a way to provide for his wife and children. He started by taking account of everything he owned: a farm in Missouri, his remaining homes in Galena and Philadelphia, and two undeveloped parcels of land in Chicago. He needed $150,000 to repay William Henry Vanderbilt, and all of the properties he owned would not come near to doing that or begin to repay the debts owed by Grant & Ward. So Grant collected his wartime mementos—his swords, campaign maps, cigar boxes, gold medals, honorary commemorations, letters, notebooks, papers, uniforms, and boots—and put them all in a pile. It was still not enough. So Grant and his wife, Julia, added to the pile: all of the cabinets, gold coins, jade, porcelain vases, teakwood cabinets, jewelry, and mementos (including two elephant tusks, gifts from the king of Siam) they had received during their world tour.

All of this was piled high in the front room at Grant's 66th Street home and shipped off to Vanderbilt the next morning. This embarrassment of riches (calculated at precisely $155,417.20—that is, $150,000 plus interest) greeted Vanderbilt when he returned from a trip to Europe. Horrified and annoyed, Vanderbilt insisted that all of it be returned. Instead, Grant demanded that Vanderbilt lodge a judgment against him for the amount of the loan. Vanderbilt grudgingly agreed, but more to satisfy the former president's honor than to honor the debt. The two appeared in court, and the judgment was entered. Vanderbilt was more embarrassed than Grant: He would much rather have forgiven the loan than have Grant repay it. Which is what he told Julia Grant in a letter dated shortly thereafter. "Now that I am at liberty to treat these things as my own," he said, "the disposition of the whole matter in accord with my feelings is this: I present to you as your separate estate the debt and judgment I hold against Grant; also the mortgages upon his real estate and all the household furniture and ornaments coupled only with the condition that the swords, commissions, medals, gifts from the United States, cities and foreign governments and all articles of historical value and interest shall, at the General's death, or if you desire it sooner, be presented to the United States government at Washington where they will remain as perpetual memorials of his fame and of the history of his times." So it was done. Grant had at least satisfied his friend and debtor William Henry Vanderbilt. All that was now left to do was to retrieve his personal fortune.

Vanderbilt's generosity showed Grant that he had friends who remembered his service, who celebrated his modest judgment, who valued his companionship. But what was most stunning to Grant was not that a person like Vanderbilt would come to his aid in time of need, but that people he had never met, from every part of the country, would interrupt their lives to remember what he had done. In the midst of his financial crisis, Charles Wood, an aging veteran who had fought with Grant in Virginia, sent him $1,000 from his home in Lansing-burgh, New York, "on account of my share for services ending April, 1865." Grant was overwhelmed and vowed that he would repay Wood. For now, the money was needed, and desperately. An old friend closer to Grant, Mexican ambassador Mathias Romero, left $1,000 in neatly stacked bills on the front bureau of Grant's home on 66th Street. Romero knew that if he pre-sented the money to him in person, Grant would have rejected the generosity. Romero had been overwhelmed, in 1866, when Grant befriended him. As a new ambassador in Washington, Romero was regularly snubbed by other diplomats until Grant introduced him to Washington's social and diplomatic commu-nity. Grant took Romero's money, but hesitantly. Other friends also helped: Julia sold the two small homes they owned in Washington to a family friend, W. J. McClean, who paid their full value—$3,000 each.

Watching this from afar, from his ornate steamboat-shaped home on Farmington Avenue in Hartford, Mark Twain was saddened by the precipitous fall in his friend's personal for-tunes. It was not just the loss of money that obsessed Grant. The president's pride had suffered a grievous wound. That he could be shown to be so gullible, so eager, to have so willingly pranced and prattled with the barons of Wall Street, to have pretended to be one of them, and to have fulfilled his dream of being not simply a successful soldier but now a man of means . . . to have accomplished this and then, at the pinnacle, to see the eyes of those he admired averted when he appeared on the street—this, more than any debt, was a wound that would not heal.

Twain knew this about Grant, perhaps, better than anyone. For while these two men were so different in appearance and so seemingly different in interests, they had this in common: They both believed that when all the books were written and the battles fought, it was the men of means—the financial barons of the Gilded Age (those whom Twain lampooned but admired)—who mattered most. Both believed that in the America of the 1880s it was money (and men of money) that ruled the world. Both Grant and Twain had said this themselves. So it was that Twain, while saddened by Grant's fall, began plotting to reengage him in a discussion of how he might retrieve his fortune and pride. What Twain had in mind was a return to the discussion that he and Howells had had with Grant back in 1881—"before Ward." Grant would write his memoirs and retrieve his fortune; of that, Twain was certain. The only question that remained was whether Twain would publish them or not.

⚬⚬⚬

THIS IS THE STORY of a friendship. Over a period of just fifteen months, from Grant's bankruptcy in May 1884 until the former general and ex-president died in July 1885, Ulysses S. "Sam" Grant and Mark Twain—Samuel Clemens—became the best of friends. Seemingly so different and yet with so much in common, Grant and Twain would, in that short time, transform the world of American writing. For as Grant was struggling to write the story of his life, he was helped in his final battle by a man who had just completed the story of his. Within that single fifteen-month period—perhaps the most creative in American literary history—Grant would not only write his *Personal Memoirs*, Twain would reach the peak of his career with the publication of *Adventures of Huckleberry Finn*. Those two books, perhaps the finest work of American nonfiction ever written and the greatest of all American novels, defined their legacy. In the end, the struggle of both men—Grant's struggle to retrieve his fortune and Twain's to make his—was not about wars or books or even money. Over a period of fifteen months, Grant and Twain wrote the story of their country and ours.

GRANT AND TWAIN: A CHRONOLOGY

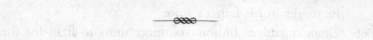

1822: Hirum Ulysses Grant is born on April 22, in Point Pleasant, Ohio.

1835: Samuel Clemens is born on November 30 in Florida, Missouri.

1839: Grant is appointed to West Point as Ulysses Simpson Grant.

1839: The Clemens family moves to Hannibal, Missouri.

1843: Grant graduates from West Point—twenty-first in a class of thirty-nine.

1847: Grant is recognized for bravery during the Mexican War and promoted to captain.
Clemens leaves home and begins a career as a printer.

1848: Grant marries Julia Dent on August 22.

1852: Grant's unit is transferred to the West, and Grant and Julia are separated.

1854: Grant resigns from the army on April 11 and begins life as a farmer in Missouri.

1859: Clemens receives his license as a pilot of steamboats on the Mississippi.

1860: Near bankruptcy, Grant moves to Galena, Illinois, where he works in his father's store.

1861: Grant organizes Illinois volunteer units to fight for the Union.

1862: On February 7, Grant captures Fort Henry; on February 16 he captures Fort Donelson.
       Grant fights and wins the Battle of Shiloh, April 6 and 7.
       Samuel Clemens works as a miner and reporter in Nevada, and adopts the name Mark Twain.

1863: Grant accepts the surrender of Vicksburg on July 4.
       Grant lifts the siege of Chattanooga in late November. He is promoted to lieutenant general and given command of all the Union armies.

1864: Grant commences the Battle of the Wilderness, May 5 to 7, 1864.

1865: Grant accepts Lee's surrender of the Army of Northern Virginia on April 9.

1866: Twain meets Grant, for the first time, at the White House.

1867: Twain publishes *The Celebrated Jumping Frog of Calaveras County.*

1868: Grant is elected president of the United States in a landslide victory.

1869: Twain publishes *The Innocents Abroad.*

1870: Twain marries Olivia Langdon on February 2.

1871: Twain moves, with Livy, to Hartford and lives next door to Harriet Beecher Stowe.

1872: Twain publishes *Roughing It.*
       Grant is elected to a second term as president of the United States.

1873:   Twain publishes *The Gilded Age.*

1876:   Twain publishes *The Adventures of Tom Sawyer.*
Twain begins *Adventures of Huckleberry Finn* but, after chapter sixteen, lays the manuscript aside.

1877:   Grant and his family begin his two-year world tour.

1879:   Twain toasts Grant in his "to the babies" speech in Chicago on November 13.

1882:   Twain revisits the Mississippi, his tour beginning on April 17. He visits Vicksburg and completes "Old Times on the Mississippi" upon his return.

1883:   In midsummer, Mark Twain once again begins work on *Adventures of Huckleberry Finn.*

1884:   The firm of Grant & Ward collapses and Grant is bankrupted on May 4.
In June, Grant notices a sharp pain in his throat.
Twain completes writing *Adventures of Huckleberry Finn.*
In July and August, Grant discusses publishing his memoirs with the Century Company.
In October, Grant is diagnosed with cancer.
On November 5, Twain begins his "Twins of Genius" tour, with George Washington Cable.
On November 19, Twain offers to publish Grant's memoirs.
Adventures of Huckleberry Finn is published in December, but the first copies are not circulated until February of 1885.
In December, William T. Sherman visits Grant and attempts to raise a subscription for his financial relief.

1885:   In January, reports circulate on Grant's poor health and reporters mount a death watch outside of his New York home.
On February 21, Grant signs a publishing contract with

Twain for Charles L. Webster and Company to publish his memoirs. On that same day, New York newspapers report, incorrectly, that Grant does not have cancer.

Grant's health deteriorates and, on April 1, he is close to death, but recovers and continues to write his memoirs. On April 29, the *New York World* reports that Grant is not the author of his memoirs. In the days that follow Grant repudiates the report.

On June 8, Grant tells Twain that he has completed volume two of his memoirs

In mid-June, Grant's health deteriorates and, on June 16, Grant and his family travel to Mt. McGregor, in northern New York, to spend the summer.

Ulysses S. Grant dies at 8:08 on the morning of July 23.

Ulysses S. Grant is buried, in Riverside Park in New York City, on August 8.

Personal Memoirs of U. S. Grant is published on December 10. It sells 312,000 copies over the next three years and saves the Grant family from penury.

1889:   Mark Twain publishes *A Connecticut Yankee in King Arthur's Court.*

1894:   Mark Twain publishes *Pudd'nhead Wilson.*

1896:   In August, Susy Clemens dies while Twain is returning from a European tour.

1897:   Mark Twain publishes *Following the Equator.*

1904:   Olivia "Livy" Langdon Clemens dies on June 5.

1910:   Mark Twain dies on April 21 and is buried in Elmira, New York.

GRANT
and
TWAIN

"A MAN WITH FIRE"

Ulysses S. Grant never understood how to handle money. That was not true of his father, Jesse, who understood it so well that he became a successful and affluent businessman. A tanner by trade, Jesse Grant came to the Ohio country and opened a business in Point Pleasant, a small trading town on the Ohio River. Tanning is a dirty and bloody business, but it's honorable and ancient: The apostle Paul was a tanner, a fact undoubtedly pointed out repeatedly by Jesse's devout and dour Methodist wife, Hannah. Hannah Simpson was a strong-willed Pennsylvania woman who believed that work could save souls and who told people (apparently with some repetition) that she wanted to live "unspotted from the world." People noted that she meant what she said. Hannah worked from sunrise to sunset, like her husband, Jesse, whose face was pockmarked by tannic acid but whose biceps were as hard as iron cannon—the result of throwing ungainly pickled hides out to dry.

Ulysses was Jesse and Hannah's first child, born with the name Hiram Ulysses Grant in a single-room clapboard shack at Point Pleasant on April 27, 1822. Jesse worked hard for his new

family, and eight months later the shack was replaced by a two-
room house at Georgetown, twenty-five miles to the east. The
move reflected Jesse Grant's rising status and unerring business
sense. Georgetown was not only on a major highway leading
from Pittsburgh west into the rich farmlands of Illinois and
Wisconsin, it was also in the middle of one of Ohio's most expansive oak forests; oak bark, when mixed with water, makes
tannic acid, the potion that produces tanned hides. Within five
years, Jesse Grant had transformed his business from a small
one-man operation into a burgeoning enterprise employing five
workers and dozens of returning satisfied customers. With his
profits Jesse acquired fifty acres of prime forest land, two small
farms, and a two-story brick house. The house was sparsely
furnished, as Hannah insisted, and over the next years she gave
birth to five more children, two boys and three girls: Simpson,
Clara, Virginia, Orvil, and Mary.

Just five years after coming to Ohio, Jesse Grant was a success. He not only owned a profitable tanning business, he was
one of Georgetown's most important citizens. He ran for office
(as an abolitionist), participated in town meetings, and was a
regular and outspoken contributor to the town newspaper, the
Castigator. He designed and built the town jail and even started
another business, opening a carriage service to western Ohio
and points south. But Jesse was not well liked: He argued heat-
edly with Georgetown's pro-southern elite (who were enriched
by the region's slave-dependent tobacco-trading industry), became a "Clay man" (and voted repeatedly for Henry Clay, that
most eloquent of voices for the Union), shouted down his op-
ponents at town meetings, and regularly and vocally prosely-
tized for the Whig Party. As his employees were busy slinging
hides, Jesse Grant stood in front of his store and argued about
slavery. Jesse hated slavery: Before he came to Ohio, he was an
apprentice tanner in Kentucky but left the state because, as he

said proudly, it was poisoned by "the slavocracy." It was his obsession with slavery and his sour personality that made Jesse disliked: His first son once commented that in that part of Ohio, antiabolitionist sentiment was so strong that Jefferson Davis might have been elected president.

That Jesse Grant could see the coming conflict was certain. He was ahead of his time. Though the nation was not yet divided by the slave question, the first cracks in the foundation of the Union were beginning to show. In the year that Ulysses S. Grant was born, Denmark Vesey was put on trial and executed in Charleston for plotting a slave uprising. Two years before, Henry Clay—then a rising young politician from the same Kentucky that Jesse abhorred—authored the Missouri Compromise, which saved the Union. The debate over slavery deepened in 1828, when Ulysses was just six, when John Quincy Adams signed the "Tariff of Abominations," which favored the business interests of the North and the West over those of the South. South Carolina threatened secession. Two years later, Daniel Webster of Massachusetts and Robert Y. Hayne of South Carolina debated the question of slavery on the Senate floor. The compromises and debates of the 1820s carried over into the next decade. In 1831, Nat Turner launched a bloody and unsuccessful slave rebellion in Virginia. In the years that followed, new "slave laws" were enacted throughout the South, and the trickle of African Americans that traversed the underground railroad, many of them through Ohio, became a torrent.

Jesse Grant was proud of his son Ulysses and showed him off to anyone who came into his store. The boy was strong and smart and understood more about horses than anyone Jesse knew. Horses came to Ulysses like money to Jesse. Throughout his life, Grant had an affinity for horses and could gentle the wildest in any herd. His gift with horses was obvious from an early age. When his mother was warned that her three-year-old son was crawling in the yard beneath horses' hooves, she dismissed the danger. He will take care of himself, she said, and went back to her washing. Ulysses Grant found in horses a silent trust and compassion that was nonexistent at home. His mother never kissed or hugged him ("Well, Ulysses, you've become quite a great man, haven't you," she said coldly after his return from the war—and then went back to her work), and his father, while bragging about his son's strength and spirit, rarely showed any affection. Jesse was self-made, pugnacious, outspoken, and hardworking, and he expected his son to be the same, so he demanded that Ulysses help in the shop at a very early age. Ulysses abhorred the backbreaking work and the animal blood, but he did it. At the age of fifteen, after his father suggested that he might follow him in the business, Ulysses told him he never would. "I'll work at it though, if you wish me to, until I am twenty-one. But you may depend on it, I'll never work a day longer at it after that," he said.

Grant's personality was formed in opposition to his father. Where Jesse was outgoing and outspoken, Ulysses was shy and contained. He grew up to be a man of few words, though those few, when spoken, were well chosen. His beliefs were held deeply, like his father's, but his aversion to argument was developed at a very young age. While he served two terms as president, he was arguably the least political of any of our presidents, and while he enjoyed those most common of pleasures, smoking cigars and reading, he was nearly an ascetic. He bore the casual hooting and indiscreet bullyings of childhood, most of them the result of his father's outspoken (and often obnoxious) personality, without complaint, as he would later bear the privations of soldiering. He was as fearless in battle as he was beneath the hooves of those horses in his mother's yard, and several times during the Civil War he would look up, surprised, to see his staff scattering before the onslaught of an artillery barrage.

All of this might have come from his mother, Hannah Simpson, except that unlike her, he was never devout and viewed religion as he might have looked at cannonballs—a curious nuisance that caused more fear than harm and simply had to be tolerated. That he was intelligent was never in doubt, but he lacked scholarly brilliance. He mastered mathematics, as a child, simply by working at it. He worked diligently, but without remarkable insight. That perhaps was Grant's most sterling quality. While not the tallest, or strongest, or brightest, or even the most insightful of men or generals, Grant brought a singular concentration to everything he did. When he failed, he would pick himself up and start again. As a child and later as a soldier, he was undeterred, unfazed, and unafraid. This might well have come from working in his father's business, with older and stronger men, or perhaps from those he met on the road—as he drove his father's hides to Cincinnati or farther south or west. His only truly unique and eccentric quality was his inability to turn back, to literally retrace his steps. If lost, he plunged on rather than retrace where he had been, and he sometimes went miles out of his way rather than return along a well-worn road. He commented on this himself, often, and admitted that it was an obsessive quirk that he simply could not correct. That oddity defined his life: He would set out to do something and would not stop until he got it done—and he would go someplace and get there.

If Jesse and Hannah were unaffectionate, they still placed great hope in their oldest son. His mother insisted that he receive a better education than his playmates, and while Ulysses was in his teens, Jesse told him that he would be expected to go to college, a privilege reserved for only the most well-educated, and affluent, children. Jesse made enough money to enroll his son in a number of private schools, including a "village school" run by Thomas White, a strict disciplinarian who gave his students a book, a desk, and little else. White expected his pupils to teach themselves, emphasizing the point by keeping at hand a switch made of hard cane bundled together. At the insistence of his parents, Grant next attended a private school in Maysville, Kentucky. He left home for Maysville at the age of thirteen and lived there with an aunt. He attended school during the day and studied at night. One year later, he was enrolled by his father at a private academy in Ripley, on the Ohio River, where the academic work was more difficult than any he had ever had. "They taught me that a noun was the name of a person, place or thing so often that I came to believe it," he later said.

Jesse Grant's son had big ideas. From the moment he began to lead his father's buckboards out of Georgetown, Grant dreamed of becoming a river trader. He admired the well-dressed men striding onto the steamboats of Cincinnati, bound for those exotic river towns of St. Louis, Natchez, and New Orleans. He also thought of becoming a farmer, though this was far less romantic. But farming was a thing he could do, and it didn't involve dipping his hands in animal blood. And that was good enough for him. It was not good enough for Jesse, however, or for Hannah, who had definite opinions about what their son could become. Downriver traders, Jesse thought, were thoroughly disreputable. Being one would not likely bring honor to the Grant family, and as for being a farmer, well, anyone could be a farmer—and most people were. The Grants, as Jesse would say, were not most people. In 1838, Jesse wrote to Ohio senator Thomas Morris about Ulysses, asking that Morris appoint his son to the U.S. Military Academy at West Point. Morris replied that he did not then have an appointment to give, but that Congressman Thomas Hamer did, if Jesse was willing to write to him.

It was an audacious request. Jesse had not thought of sending his son to West Point until his wife had suggested it, and she did so only after hearing that a neighbor's son had failed the entrance examination. More important, Hamer and Jesse Grant were political enemies. While Jesse had campaigned for Hamer when Hamer ran for a seat in Ohio's legislature, the two had had a bitter argument over President Andrew Jackson's fiscal policies and had not spoken since. But Jesse swallowed his pride and wrote to Hamer, hoping that his former friend would remember how close they had once been. Hamer received Jesse's letter on the last day of his term and immediately filled out the application for Grant's admission. The application was to have lifelong ramifications for Grant: Struggling to remember the boy's full name, Hamer appointed him to West Point as Ulysses S. Grant, using his mother's maiden name as his middle initial. He then wrote to Jesse, burying the bitter feud: "I received your letter and have asked for the appointment of your son which will doubtless be made. Why didn't you apply to me sooner?"

But being appointed to West Point was one thing, passing the entrance examination was another. The people of Georgetown, many of them offended by Jesse Grant's presumption, believed that his son would never attend. "I'm astonished Hamer did not appoint someone with intellect enough to do credit to our district," one of the townsmen told Jesse. Ulysses knew none of this and protested the appointment when he heard of it. He told his father that he thought he would not go. But, as he later recounted, "My father said he thought I would, and I thought so too, if he did." Grant passed the entrance exam and, vowing secretly that he would never like West Point and that he would never be a soldier (no matter what his father thought), left for New York on May 15, 1839. He arrived, a little more than one week later, on the bluffs above the Hudson, to see his name posted with those of the others of the class of 1843.

◦◦◦

IT WAS THEN, and still is, a tradition at West Point that entering plebes receive a nickname. The West Point of Grant's era is famous for such names. William Tecumseh Sherman (one class ahead of Grant) became "Cump," while William Rosecrans (a devoted Catholic, gifted mathematician, and average general) became "Rosie." Winfield Scott Hancock (who was named for the old general, and who repelled Pickett's charge at Gettysburg) became "Win." All of that is predictable, but how do you explain James Longstreet, who was known ever after as "Pete," or George Pickett (a Virginian appointed by a then little-known congressman from Illinois named Abraham Lincoln), who was so dandified that he had no nickname at all (and who graduated dead last in his class), or Lewis Armistead, who became "Lo"—for "Lothario"—and who died in the charge that Pickett commanded? As Hiram Ulysses Grant became Ulysses Simpson Grant, so Ulysses Simpson Grant now became U. S. Grant or, more simply, "Sam." No protests that he (Hiram, or Ulysses, or even U. S. Grant) would ever issue would change that name. Among his closest friends, from his plebe year forward, Ulysses S. Grant was "Sam" Grant, and so he would forever remain.

Grant entered West Point as the smallest cadet in his class. He stood barely five feet one, and he weighed just 117 pounds. He was issued a uniform that, in using language his father would understand, he described as being "as tight to my skin as bark to a tree." It would have been easy to underestimate Grant. He struggled with his studies, but he rarely broke the academy rules, and he seemed to get along well with the upperclass officers. His class of seventy-seven comprised mostly boys from the South and the Northeast, with only a scattering of midwesterners. Grant endured his plebe year and stood aside when others protested, or openly rebelled, or were expelled for fighting or complaining. In that first year he never once received a demerit for disobedience or disrespect, a rarity among cadets in any age. He was well liked, but years later (when it would have been in people's interest to regale listeners with stories of the famous cadet Ulysses S. "Sam" Grant), he was not well remembered. Pickett, Rosecrans, Longstreet, Sherman, and even future Confederate general Jubal Early (called "my bad old man" during the war by Robert E. Lee were legends at West Point. Grant was a plodding enigma.

Grant finished his first year near the bottom of his class, but he had come further than anyone dared imagine. While the people of Georgetown, Ohio, might well have protested Grant's appointment, no one could argue with his ability to concentrate, to apply himself single-mindedly to his weaknesses and master them. All the while, amid the sometimes vicious physical hazing and challenges of West Point mathematics, Grant read the newspapers, carefully following the congressional bill aimed at closing the academy. The legislation was authored by those who thought the military academy an institution for the education of the effete and unmanly, a "breeding ground for snobbery and a waste of money." This would have shocked those who saw Grant, a slightly bow-legged rustic from the backcountry of Ohio with a shy streak. Grant hoped the bill would pass and that West Point would be closed. All he wanted to do his first year, as he later remembered, was go back to Ohio to become a farmer or, better yet, one of those worldly traders on a Mississippi steamboat.

This fantasy aside, by the end of his first year as a cadet,

Grant was beginning to like West Point. When General Winfield Scott came to visit, Grant was impressed, writing effu-
sively about the medal-bedecked American hero, and imagined
himself in his place, reviewing the Corps of Cadets. While he
found the constant drill and discipline "very wearisome and
uninteresting," he discovered that he had a facility for mathematics, which was often the one course most likely to lead
cadets to failure. Longstreet struggled with the academy's mathematics course (the primary reason he graduated so low in his
class) and swallowed his considerable pride long enough to
agree to after-hours tutoring from William Rosecrans. Grant
did not need help (it is unlikely he would have asked for it if
he had), and by the end of his first year he was mastering the
course and rising through the class ranks. "The subject was so
easy to me as to come almost by intuition," he later remembered. As a result of his strong academic standing, Grant could
now and then take some time to reflect on his surroundings and the history that filled the Hudson Valley, whose river
shone from his room. "I do love the *place*," he wrote in one letter home. "It seems as though I could live here forever if my
friends would only come too." Ulysses S. Grant was not his father; he was lonely, but he wasn't shunned. Rather, his natural
shyness meant that he had trouble making close friends, so he
spent much of his free time reading novels from the academy
library—an eclectic mix of James Fenimore Cooper, Washington
Irving, and Walter Scott.

Grant survived his first year and entered his second year at
the midpoint of his class. He excelled at mathematics and he
discovered art. His talent in this came as the result of his instruction in technical drafting, a requirement in the engineering-
focused academy where cadets were expected to know the
minute details of constructing and maintaining battlements.
Grant loved drafting and converted that love into drawings and

watercolors. He was an adept artist with a keen eye. He struggled in French, but he made it through the course as best he could, knowing that his scores in math would keep him near the middle of his class. By the end of his second year, it was apparent to everyone at West Point that while Grant did not stand out in any single subject, he was a solid cadet with an adept mind. He was also an exceptional horseman; he may well have been the best horseman to have ever graduated from West Point. His talent with horses became apparent his sophomore year, and his reputation grew, so that by the time he was an upperclassman, he would be called on repeatedly to show his skills. He held the West Point high-jumping record for twenty-five years. His classmates would later recall how Grant so mastered horses that it seemed as if "man and beast had been welded together."

Grant rose in his class during his third year, and he finally made some close friends, including future Civil War generals Samuel French (a Mississippian who fought at the Battle of Atlanta), William B. Franklin (who graduated first in Grant's class and commanded a part of the disastrously bloody federal attack on rebel lines at the Battle of Fredericksburg), Frank Gardner (a New Yorker who married into a Louisiana family; he later commanded the attack on Grant's lines at the Battle of Shiloh), and Frederick Dent, a Missourian and Grant's roommate. Grant and Dent became good friends, in spite of their often bitter arguments about slavery, and Dent invited Grant to visit him and his family after they graduated. Grant's academic standing continued to improve during his junior and senior years, but, surprisingly, his military standing deteriorated. The once shy boy from Ohio began to rebel and at one point was confined to his quarters for two weeks for disrespect. This only deepened his doubts about leading a military life, and he pledged that while he would fulfill his commitment, he would not stay in the military. Now, he said, he would quit the army and return to West Point as a professor of mathematics.

Grant welcomed the end of his time at the academy, and while his class is forever remembered for graduating the greatest leader of the Civil War (and two-time president), Grant himself later commented on the remarkable plebes who came to the academy when he was a senior. The class of 1846, which graduated three years after Grant, included among their number some of the most storied of Union commanders: General George McClellan (who fought the Battle of Antietam), Jesse Reno (who died leading his men at the Battle of South Mountain), Darius Couch (a corps commander in the Union Army), Truman Seymour (taken prisoner by the Confederates during the Battle of the Wilderness), and cavalry commander George Stoneman (who laid waste to large swathes of Alabama and Georgia). The southern contingent was nearly as legendary: George Pickett, John Adams (a brigadier general at the Battle of Franklin, where he died), Dabney Maury (who was dismissed from the army in 1861 for having Confederate sympathies and went on to become the Confederacy's greatest diplomat), Cadmus Wilcox (a division commander in Lee's army during the Wilderness Campaign), William Gardner (a Confederate commander at Bull Run, where his leg was shattered), and a lanky Virginian by the name of Thomas Jonathan Jackson, who became "Stonewall" Jackson and nearly destroyed the Union Army at Chancellorsville—where he was fatally wounded.

But all of this was in the future. For now, Grant had to be satisfied with a simple commission in the infantry. While he graduated twenty-first in his class, an extraordinary accomplishment for an undersized and indifferently educated boy from Ohio, Grant did not stand high enough in the class ranks to be able to choose his branch of service. He would have preferred the cavalry and requested that he be assigned as an officer in the dragoons but, in 1843, was ordered to serve as a brevet second lieutenant in the Fourth Infantry, which was commanded by Richard S. Ewell, a future corps commander in Robert E. Lee's Army of Northern Virginia. After a short time at home (Jesse had since moved his family from Georgetown to Bethel, a short distance away), he reported for duty at Jefferson Barracks, a sprawling and dusty military reservation just outside St. Louis. He had his sights set on the future, but it was not the future that the army intended: All through these first years in uniform, he pined for a simpler life—as a professor, or farmer, or river trader.

AS GRANT SUSPECTED, and feared, life as a brevet second lieutenant in the U.S. Army was not appealing; army officers were poorly paid, and Grant's duties took on a soul-killing routine of drill, paperwork, and more drill. Grant did the best he could to keep his mind focused on his work throughout the autumn of 1843, but he chafed at army regulations. Home seemed far away: The nation was at peace, and even the debate over slavery seemed to abate. If there was any solace in Grant's assignment, it was that Jefferson Barracks was only six miles away from the home of his former West Point roommate, Frederick Dent. While Dent was then assigned elsewhere, he had told his family about Grant and had urged his former roommate to ride over to the family home, White Haven, for a visit. At first Grant did so out of politeness, but as time went on he felt more and more at home. The large Dent family was led by the imposing, gray-haired, short-tempered, and garrulous "Colonel" Frederick Dent, who had fathered four strapping and hardworking sons and four young and pretty daughters. They welcomed Grant as a member of the family. Soon Grant was visiting Colonel Dent (this was a southern conceit, for Colonel

Dent was no more a colonel than, say, Jesse Grant) regularly. He was often accompanied by a friend from West Point, James "Pete" Longstreet, who was a distant relative of the Dent clan.

Grant was awed by White Haven and Colonel Dent. The plantation was set on over 950 acres of prime Missouri farmland, which was worked by a handful of slaves and supervised by the colonel and his growing sons. In the spring, Colonel Dent planted acres of corn and vegetables. Half of the corn was fed to the hogs, which were sold or slaughtered in great droves each year. There was a small herd of cattle and dozens of chickens, enough to feed the Dent family and provide a considerable extra income. When more land was needed for planting, the Dent slaves cleared out the lowlands, sold the lumber, hauled away the stumps, and put in more crops. Colonel Dent was a prodigious worker, but as a descendant of a well-known southern-sympathizing Maryland family, he was given to aristocratic sentiments. The Dents entertained often, holding dinners for their large group of nearby friends (who also owned large farms) and St. Louis merchants. White Haven was the center of a prosperous and growing Missouri community where the staid formalities of class and the customs of family were highly valued.

But Grant's visits were more than formally polite. While he enjoyed the company of the colonel (and talked politics with him incessantly), a visit to White Haven provided a welcome break from his work at Jefferson Barracks. Grant was well liked by the Dents and he liked them, so much so, in fact, that for a time he was coming to dinner twice each week. His visits were welcome, especially by the colonel's wife, Ellen Dent, who found favor with Grant's clear-eyed demeanor and soft but firm political arguments (like his father, he was an abolitionist Whig, Colonel Dent a pro-southern Jacksonian Democrat). Her husband, Ellen Dent believed, had finally met his match. "That young man will be heard from some day," she remarked. "He has a good deal in him. He'll make his mark." But it was soon obvious that while Grant enjoyed the society provided by the Dent family, he was increasingly turning his attention to the colonel's oldest and favorite daughter, Julia. Julia was intelligent, refined, petite, and pretty (except for the squint in her right eye, the result of a childhood illness). They had much in common: a love of reading, an unwavering sense of personal loyalty, and, perhaps most important, an affinity and love for horses. Julia also loved to dance, which the tone-deaf Grant hated—but he did it just the same, because she wanted him to.

There is a portrait of Grant from this time in Missouri, given to us by the colonel's youngest daughter, Emmy, who was as enamored of "my beau" as her sister Julia: "His cheeks were warm, and round, and rosy; his hair was fine and brown, very thick and wavy. His eyes were clear blue, and always full of light. His features were regular, pleasingly molded and attractive, and his figure so slender, well formed and graceful that it was like that of a young prince to my eye." That is what Julia also saw in Grant, and after a season of traditional disinterest (including her rejection of his class ring), she began to show an interest, in spite of her father's almost open disapproval "You are too young and the boy is too poor," he said. "He hasn't anything to give you." The two plotted on how to win her father's confidence, with Grant telling Julia that they simply needed to be patient. Many months went by as Grant leisurely but firmly attempted to ingratiate himself into the colonel's favor. But it was the news that his unit would be transferred out of Missouri that finally shook him into action. One evening, having been granted a special leave from his commanding officer, Grant rode through the night to White Haven to propose to Julia, fording a dangerously swollen river in the process. Julia, of course, accepted—though depressed by the thought that soon he would be gone. Overjoyed, Grant then took a train south, to Camp Salubrity, in Louisiana, to join his regiment. There was only one thing left to be done. During a furlough the next year, and despite the colonel's opposition, Grant made his intentions known to him. He expected that he would be denied, but he was prepared to argue his case.

"Colonel Dent, I want to marry your daughter Julia," he said.

Dent thought about this for a minute before responding: "Mr. Grant, if it were the younger girl, Nelly, you wanted, I'd say 'yes.'"

"But I don't want Nelly, I want Julia," Grant said.

"Oh, you do, do you? Well, then, I suppose it will have to be Julia."

❧

IN THE HISTORY of the Republic, 1844 stands out as a most unusual year. President John Tyler stood for reelection but dropped out of the campaign when it became clear that he could not win. James K. Polk took Tyler's place, while the Whigs nominated Henry Clay of Kentucky. James G. Birney, a former slaveholder, became the nominee of the antislavery Liberty Party. The stage was thereby set for yet another clash over slavery—in this case, as a part of the debate over whether Texas should be annexed to the Union. Polk won the election in a campaign that reflected the nation's division over this question. Polk's motto—"Fifty-four Forty or Fight" (with the emphasis on "Fight")—reflected his belief that America should consume and digest Oregon and then annex California and Texas, even if that meant going to war with Mexico.

Jesse Grant was horrified by this prospect. A Clay man, he saw the war coming, thought it immoral, and urged his son to leave the army. While Grant agreed with his father about Polk, he was beginning to enjoy his time with the Fourth Infantry, which was now encamped at Corpus Christi, preparing for war. He missed Julia. "In going away now I feel as if I had someone else than myself to live and strive to do well for," he wrote to her. "You can have but little idea of the influence you have over me Julia, even while so far away. If I feel tempted to do any thing that I think is not right I am sure to think, 'Well now if Julia saw me would I do so' and thus it is absent or present I am more or less governed by what I think is your will." Grant reassured her that there would not be a war, writing to her (with his unique spelling), "Evry thing looks beliggerent to a spectator but I believe there will be no fight." But in April 1846 a Mexican unit captured an American detachment near the Rio Grande, and Zachary Taylor marched his army toward Point Isabel, a Mexican stronghold. "Don't fear for me my Dear Julia," Grant wrote, "for this is only the active part of our business. It is just what we come here for and the sooner it begins the sooner it will end and probably be the means of my seeing my Dear Julia soon."

It began at Palo Alto, when the Mexican army bombarded the approaching American force (the soldier in the line next to Grant was hit, his brains spattered onto Grant's blouse—an incident Grant would remember for the rest of his life) and then withdrew. "It was a terrible sight to go over the ground the next day and see the amount of life that had been destroyed. The ground was litterally [sic] strewed with the bodies of dead men and horses," he wrote. Taylor chased the Mexican army farther south, then occupied Matamoros for the summer and waited for reinforcements. The lull gave Grant a chance to assess his commander. What struck him most profoundly was Taylor's outward calm. He rarely lost his temper, and he gave clear, simple instructions to his subordinates. Taylor's battle plans were the soul of simplicity: He believed the American army should always attack an enemy relentlessly and at his weakest point. He was a cool-eyed calculator of the enemy and almost cold and unfeeling in battle. He did not cavalierly send his men to their death, but he believed firmly that the more violent the battle (and therefore the shorter the battle), the more lives would be saved. More than any other soldier, Zachary Taylor provided a model for Ulysses S. Grant. "No soldier could face either danger or responsibility more calmly than he," he later wrote. "These are qualities more rarely found than genius or physical courage."

In August 1846, Taylor's army, with Grant as its new quartermaster, moved southwest, toward Monterrey, where the Mexican army awaited. Grant did not look forward to the coming battle. "Wherever there are battles a great many must suffer," he wrote to Julia. "If we have to fight I would like to do it at once and then make friends." The army knew that the assault on Monterrey would be costly, with seven thousand Mexicans behind strong fortifications facing six thousand Americans, long odds for Taylor's army. By the end of September, the American army was drawn up in front of Monterrey. Taylor planned a two-pronged envelopment culminating in an attack by General William Worth's division from the west. As a quartermaster, Grant watched from the rear as his brigade led the assault. But he was soon caught up in the action. He later explained that he joined the attack because he lacked "the moral courage to return to camp"; but the sound of battle clearly appealed to him—and he was anxious to get into combat. This was one of the first of his many lessons about war; the attack was bungled, and Grant's unit was cut to pieces.

Two days later, on September 23, Taylor ordered a new assault. This time Grant, recently appointed adjutant of Colonel John Garland's brigade, was in the thick of the fight, commanding forces that moved into Monterrey and then fought from house to house in a costly attempt to take the city. Grant showed his mettle as a soldier: In the midst of battle he volunteered to ride through the city to retrieve ammunition for his hard-pressed troops. As he galloped through Monterrey, Mexican soldiers fired wildly in an attempt to bring him down, but he arrived at his destination unscathed. It was a heroic deed, remembered and recalled by his fellow soldiers for years. But Grant did not mention his brush with death to Julia; he only commented in a letter he wrote that night that he was "getting very tired of this war, and particularly impatient of being separated from one I love so much." The next day, the Mexican army surrendered.

But the war was not yet over. After Monterrey, Taylor agreed to help General Winfield Scott take Mexico City. In January 1847, the Fourth Infantry returned to Palo Alto, and in March, in what was to be the culminating stroke of the war, Taylor's forces joined those of Scott (one of whose aides, Robert E. Lee, met Grant at the time) at Vera Cruz. The plan was for the two armies to march overland to the Mexican capital and, in a headlong assault, defeat the forces of General Santa Anna. Vera Cruz fell much more easily than either Taylor or Scott envisioned, and by early summer the American forces were making their way overland. General Santa Anna attempted to defeat the Americans at the Cerro Gordo mountain pass, but Scott's forces overwhelmed the poorly deployed Mexican army. Grant, watching from a distance, believed the battle would be bloody. "While it was a most inspiring sight," he said of the battle, "it was a painful one for me." In August, Scott moved his army west toward Mexico City while Grant (once again "with the mules"—as his brigade's quartermaster) looked for a way to command troops. "You could not keep Grant out of battle," his old friend "Pete" Longstreet later said.

Grant's chance to join the fight finally came during the

attack on Mexican positions at San Cosme, on the outskirts of the capital. In the midst of the assault, Grant was assigned as a scout for a brigade pinned down by Mexican fire. Making his way forward, he found a way to attack a vulnerable part of the enemy line, returned to the American position, and volunteered to lead a small detachment to make the attempt. As Grant led his men forward, his unit crashed through the Mexican position, only to be thrown back when, supported by raking artillery, the Mexicans counterattacked. Undeterred, Grant led his troops to the left, in a march around the Mexican lines. When he spotted a church, Grant ordered his men to disassemble an American cannon and lug it piece by piece into the belfry, where it brought a withering fire on the Mexican defenders. Recalled by his commander, Grant was praised for his initiative while a number of his colleagues (including John Pemberton, who would later surrender to him at Vicksburg, and Henry Hunt, the Union artillery commander at Gettysburg) worked to exploit his opening. The Mexican lines were breached, and U.S. troops poured into Mexico City. The war was over—won.

"There goes a man with fire," his commander, John Garland, later said. Others had noticed Grant as well, and he was cited for his bravery and promoted to brevet captain. Grant was circumspect. "The loss of officers and men killed and wounded is frightful," he wrote. But he had found something that he enjoyed and was good at.

In the weeks that followed the end of the war, Grant deepened his friendship with his fellow commanders and enjoyed the fruits of victory. It was then that the first report of his problem with alcohol surfaced—the result of Grant's reaction to army routine. "If you were here I should never wish to leave Mexico," he wrote to Julia, "but as it is I am nearly crazy to get away." Finally he did, in May 1848, when the Fourth Infantry was ordered home. Grant was overjoyed: He made it to St. Louis in July, where he saw the Dents and Julia. He stayed for only a short visit before traveling to Ohio to see his family. He returned in August, and on August 22, 1848, he and Julia were married.

<hr />

ULYSSES S. GRANT was devoted to Julia from the moment he met her. The difference that Julia had on his life was plain for all to see. "He came out of his shell in her presence," one of his friends noticed, while another reflected that Grant was, if anything, "overly attached to his wife." His loyalty was lavishly repaid. Through all the years ahead, including those that were the most difficult of his life, Julia never lost confidence in her husband's abilities, always believed in his greatness, and remained unerringly loyal. When Grant received orders to report to Detroit and then to Sackets Harbor in New York, Julia, who had never left home, was worried and nervous. Her father took advantage of the situation, suggesting that she stay with him. "You can get a leave of absence once or twice a year," he told his new son-in-law, "and run in here and spend a week or two with us." Upset by this and fearful that her new husband would be angry, Julia immediately rejected this advice. "I could not, would not, think of that for a moment," she reassured her new husband.

When Julia became pregnant, however, she decided to return to her father's house. Her decision, after the earlier pledge of fealty, caused tension in the marriage that was eased only when their first child, Frederick Dent Grant, was born. But the pattern was set: Whenever Grant was separated from Julia, he was uncontrolled and miserable. His greatest fear was that he would be separated from her for any length of time, for he thought himself weak and uncertain when he was away from her. When the Fourth Infantry was ordered to California, Julia said she would not accompany him. She was pregnant again, and her doctor told her not to make the journey. Grant was crestfallen, but in July 1852 he reported for duty with the Fourth Infantry in New York City, and on July 5 he left, with them, for California. "We sail directly for the Isthmus," he wrote to Julia. "I never knew how much it was to part from you and Fred. until it come to the time for leaving. Our separation will not be a long one anyway. At least let's hope so. Good buy dear dear Julia. Kiss Fred. a thousand times. A thousand kisses for you dear Julia."

Grant must certainly have suspected what it would be like to live without his wife, but he could not have predicted the string of failures that would greet him in this, his first extended time away from her. After arriving in San Francisco, Grant began to look for ways to supplement his meager income. He bought a farm, but it washed away in a springtime torrent. An investment in cattle and pigs actually cost him money, as did the meager amount he put in a brood of chickens, which all died. The thought of failure depressed him, but the fact that he was away from his family depressed him even more—as did news that, during his absence, a second son, Ulysses S. Grant Jr., had been born. He wrote to Julia constantly, underlining his efforts to arrange for her and their sons to come to California. "I am doing all I can to put up a penny not only to enable you and our dear little boys to get here comfortably, but to enable you to be comfortable after you do get here," he wrote. She did not respond and, despairing, he began to drink. "Liquor seemed a virulent poison to him," one of his fellow officers noted, "and yet he had a fierce desire for it. One glass would show on him and two or three would make him stupid."

In the fall of 1853, Grant and a small detachment of the Fourth Infantry were transferred to Fort Humboldt, 250 miles north of San Francisco on the California coast. It was a crushingly lonely assignment. He wrote to Julia often, wondering about his two sons, one of which he had not yet seen. Her only occasional letters embittered him: "You never complain of being lonesome so I infer you are quite contented."

It was in April 1854 that the crisis that nearly ruined him took place, though the exact details of what happened and why remain murky. We can only surmise what might have happened from Grant himself. On April 11, 1854, he sent two letters to Washington; in the first he formally accepted his long overdue promotion from brevet captain to captain, and in the second he tendered his resignation. Over the years that followed, rumors circulated that Grant had been forced from the army when his superiors found him drunk on duty. There is no evidence of this, though Grant was drinking heavily in California—a habit that would be repeated at various times in his future. But even if Grant was becoming "a drunk" (a claim that was to follow him the rest of his life), it was also clear that he could no longer live without Julia. He must see her, even if that meant leaving the army. He resigned and headed east. "Whoever hears of me in ten years, will hear of a well-to-do old Missouri farmer," he said.

Grant booked passage on a ship to New York, borrowed money from his old West Point classmate Simon Bolivar Buckner, visited his father in Ohio (where he borrowed more money), and returned to the Dent household in Missouri. Using what little money he had left, Grant joined the Dent clan, living with Julia and his two sons in a bungalow near the Dent house. When this proved difficult (for Grant did not like to be so close to his father-in-law), he bought his own farm equipment and set about plowing, seeding, and harvesting the parcel of land that Julia had been given by her father as a wedding present. He built a small home for his wife and two children and named it "Hardscrabble." He busted the sod the first year, put in a crop, and hoped for the best. But even in the best of the years that followed, Grant was regularly forced to supplement his income by selling cords of wood in St. Louis, which is where James Longstreet saw him on a chilly day in 1855. Grant put up a good front, but "ol' Pete" could tell he had fallen on hard times. Grant would not admit defeat. "Evry [sic] day I like farming better and I do not doubt but that money is to be made at it. So far I have been laboring under great disadvantages," he wrote confidently to his father, "but now that I am on my place, and shall not have to build next summer, I think I should be able to do better."

He did not. While tough and lean and weathered by the years in Mexico and California, Grant could not manage the farm, let alone the three slaves (assigned to him by Colonel Dent) who helped him turn the soil. "He was no hand to manage negroes," a neighbor remembered. "He couldn't force them to do anything. He wouldn't whip them." One of these slaves was Mary Robinson, who cooked for the Grants and maintained contact with them late into her life. "I have seen many farmers," she later recalled, "but I never saw one that worked harder than Mr. Grant. He plowed, split rails, and drove his own team." Robinson always enjoyed telling her friends about Grant and recalled and repeated one story in particular:

I could tell you enough about Mr. Grant to fill a good-sized book. He loved his wife and children, and was the kindest husband the most indulgent father I ever saw. At one time he was very poor, but both his wife and himself always looked on the bright side of things. One day—I will never forget the circumstances—Mrs. Grant was sitting in a large rocking chair talking to some of her relatives about family matters. She referred to the financial embarrassment of her husband and then added: But we will not always be in this condition. Wait until Dudy (meaning Grant) becomes President. I dreamed last night he had been elected President. The rest all laughed and looked upon it as a capital joke. The idea that her husband, who was then a very poor farmer, would ever become president of the United States. Mrs. Grant always had great confidence in her husband, and she never relinquished the belief that he was destined to become one of the greatest men in the nation.

In early 1858, finally defeated by the mounting bills, Grant quit the farm and went into business with a friend in St. Louis. But the business failed. With the birth of a third child, a daughter, Grant was desperate to make money, so he stood for election for the post of county engineer. He thought for a time he would get elected, and everyone predicted that he would win, but he lost the vote. So at the age of thirty-eight, Sam Grant swallowed his pride and agreed to work for his father, who had moved the Grant family to Galena, Illinois. It was a humiliating time, but Grant had no choice. In April 1859, the former captain of the Fourth Infantry and his family, which now numbered four children—Fred; Ulysses S. Grant Jr., called "Buck"; Ellen ("Nellie"), the only girl; and the new son, Jesse—arrived in Galena from St. Louis aboard a steamboat and rented a house on High Street. Grant went to his father's store each day wondering what the future would bring.

THERE HAVE BEEN STORIES of Grant told by dozens of historians through the years. These are not the well-known stories of battles and campaigns, but stories of Grant himself—of his character, of what made him tick. One of the most famous comes from the earliest days of the Civil War, just after Abraham Lincoln called on the people of the North to defend the Union. Grant answered the call by agreeing to train a company of recruits from Galena. The townspeople of Galena outfitted the recruits in new uniforms, and after being sworn to defend the Union, they marched proudly and smartly through the streets of the city. The old men cheered and saluted, the women wept, the children, awestruck, flitted in and out of the motley lines. And there was Grant, his uniform having not yet arrived, trailing after the regiment in his slouch hat. It was a slightly embarrassing spectacle—Ulysses S. Grant going off to war, carpetbag in tow—and the image of the slight and begrizzled man stayed in the memories of the people of Galena ever after.

Even Illinois governor Richard Yates thought Grant unimpressive, and when the former West Pointer and Mexican-war veteran arrived in Springfield, Yates refused to give him any duties. That did not last long. Short of experienced officers, Yates sent Grant off to recruit three regiments in downstate Illinois, and when an ill-disciplined rabble rebelled against their appointed colonel, Yates assigned Grant to bring them into line. Grant did this quickly by imposing a strict but fair discipline on the men and listening closely to their complaints. When the regiment was asked to enlist for three years, they did so just to be under Grant's command. Yates was impressed, as was Grant's first commander, General John Pope, who described him as "an officer of intelligence and discretion." When it came time for Illinois to nominate four officers as brigadier generals, Grant's name was at the head of the list.

Wherever he went Grant brought order out of chaos. In his first command in Missouri, he helped to clear the state of rebels. Called back to Illinois, he trained more troops and fortified positions on the Mississippi River ("What I want is to advance," he complained) and then marched his army south. Grant's superiors looked askance at his aggressiveness—what did this failed officer and store clerk know of strategy? In early 1862 Grant presented himself to Henry Halleck, commander of all the Union's western armies, and told him that he had a plan to capture three key forts on the Cumberland and Tennessee rivers, deep in rebel territory. Intimidated by Halleck, Grant stumbled through his presentation. "I was received with so little cordiality that I perhaps stated the object of my visit with less clearness than I might have done," Grant later wrote, "and I had not uttered many sentences before I was cut short as if my plan was preposterous." Under pressure from Lincoln to do *something*, Halleck finally gave Grant permission to assault the forts. In the first week of February 1862, Grant set off with his three divisions of slightly more than nine thousand men and five gunboats and plunged deep into rebel territory.

Grant's strategy surprised the rebels, who, after a desultory defense, abandoned Fort Henry. But Fort Donelson, deep in the Tennessee woods on the Cumberland River, was strongly defended. With his three division commanders, Generals John McClernand, Lew Wallace, and Charles F. Smith, Grant surrounded the fort, lofted shells at it from the five gunboats patrolling the river, and repulsed a Confederate attack aimed at breaking the siege. Finally, on a bitterly cold mid-February day, the garrison's commander, Simon Bolivar Buckner, who had loaned Grant $50 back in New York, wrote to ask what terms could be negotiated for the rebel surrender. Grant's answer became one of the war's most memorable moments. "Sir: Yours of this date proposing Armistice, and appointment of Commissioners, to settle terms of Capitulation is just received," Grant wrote back. "No terms except an unconditional and immediate surrender can be accepted. I propose to move immediately upon your works." Buckner's surrender (the next day) and

Grant's words *unconditional surrender* made headlines in the North. Hiram Ulysses Grant, Ulysses S. Grant, and now "Sam" Grant had suddenly become "Unconditional Surrender Grant"—and an icon for a northern population impatient for victories.

While Grant went on to other and even greater victories, at Shiloh, Vicksburg, Chattanooga, the Wilderness, Spotsylvania, and finally Appomattox, it would be more of what he said that would mark him as unusual. In the aftermath of the Battle of Shiloh, where his army was surprised and mauled, Grant reviewed the roster of the fallen, composed his report on the battle, resupplied his army, and set about planning his next campaign. The casualties at Shiloh were more than had been lost in all previous American wars combined, and the people of the North were stunned by the casualty lists. Grant was not. "I gave up all idea of saving the Union except by complete conquest," he said. Lincoln defended Grant against criticisms that he was a butcher, incompetent, and a drunk. Hearing this last, Lincoln said that whatever Grant drank should be sent to the North's other commanders. Grant conquered Vicksburg, the South's last bastion on the Mississippi, on July 4, 1863, and then allowed the southern commander's men to return to their homes in exchange for a promise that they would never again fight for the Confederacy. Grant's leniency led to a storm of protest, but Lincoln again supported his commander, calling his campaign "one of the most brilliant in the world."

When Lincoln appointed Grant commander of all of the Union armies, he reported with his thirteen-year-old son, Fred, to Washington in a simple army coat, shorn of rank, and checked into Willard's Hotel. Grant, the clerk later said, looked like a "short, round-shouldered man in a very tarnished major general's uniform who did, or once did, take a little too much to drink." Judging him of little influence, the clerk assigned Grant and his son a modest room. Grant nodded his compliance. He then signed his name—"U. S. Grant & Son, Galena Illinois"—and wordlessly gathered up his carpetbag. It did not take long for the clerk to discern his mistake. After an effusive apology, Grant was directed to "Parlor 6"—the best room in the hotel. Later, Grant walked the two short blocks to the White House, where he met Abraham Lincoln. After a short discussion, Lincoln introduced Grant to a roomful of dignitaries, who strained to catch a glimpse of Vicksburg's conqueror. In great discomfort (and much to Lincoln's amusement), Grant climbed onto a White House sofa so that everyone could see him. But he would not speak. Several days later, with Grant having taken command in Virginia, an unknown Union soldier best reflected the generally accepted view of Grant, both in the White House and in the army: "He's a little 'un," he said.

One of Grant's most memorable moments came during the Battle of the Wilderness. It was his first test against Confederate commander Robert E. Lee, a brawling fight amid the tangled central Virginia undergrowth just south of the Rapidan River. The battle started when Lee attacked Grant's right flank and continued nightmarishly on into the next day, when the woods caught fire, immolating those among both armies too wounded to move. Their screams could be heard throughout the night. On this second day, an overcast early spring day in May, Lee again attacked both of Grant's flanks. The battle roared on while Grant, seemingly imperturbable, sat on a stump, whittling away on an odd piece of wood. He moved only to give orders or fetch a cigar. But he lost his temper when a staff officer, unnerved by Lee's attack, advised Grant that he should do something to turn the tide of battle. "This is a crisis that cannot be looked upon too seriously," the officer said. "I know Lee's methods well past experience. He will throw his whole army between us and the Rapidan, and cut us off completely from our communications." That was just about enough for

Grant. Rising from his stump, he pulled his cigar from his mouth. "Oh, I am heartily tired of hearing about what Lee is going to do," he said, his voice a low growl. "Some of you always seem to think he is suddenly going to turn a double somersault and land in our rear and on both our flanks at the same time. Go back to your command and try to think what we are going to do ourselves, instead of what Lee is going to do."

Ulysses S. Grant's "Forty Days"—the time it took for him to lead the Army of the Potomac from the Wilderness to the outskirts of Richmond—is still viewed by military scholars as one of the most brilliant campaigns in military history. But it was not without cost: Tens of thousands of Americans lost their lives in a series of battles that forever changed the nature of American warfare. After the Battle of Cold Harbor, halfway down the road to Richmond, in which thousands were killed or wounded in just seven minutes (presaging the carnage of World War I on the western front), Grant never again launched a series of headlong charges. That Grant eventually cornered Robert E. Lee's Army of Northern Virginia west of Richmond, at Appomattox, might now seem inevitable. But for those who had suffered through four years of devastation, Grant's victory—during Easter Week 1865—seemed like a redemptive triumph. He was an immediate hero and, in the wake of the assassination of Abraham Lincoln, the nation's lone hope of an abiding peace.

THE QUALITIES THAT Grant brought to the Union armies did not transfer so easily to the presidency, but he spent two terms in the office. He was propelled there not simply because he had "organized victory," but also because the magnanimous surrender terms that he offered Confederate general Robert E. Lee at

Appomattox, in April 1865, reflected the will of the nation. America was shocked and saddened by Lincoln's assassination and exhausted by war, but it was poised to launch itself westward. While the North and the South continued to tussle in the immediate aftermath of Appomattox—and for three years prior to Grant's election—the nation made an astonishing leap into the future once the "Hero of Appomattox" took office.

Grant's two terms as president were marked by successive scandals that tarnished his reputation as a politician but did little to stain him in the eyes of a still grateful nation. While even his closest political advisers were accused (and often convicted) of massive corruption (and of taking advantage, it was said, of Grant's political naiveté), Grant himself remained above reproach. He once said that he could not ever remember having uttered a profanity. People believed that and knew while those around him might be lining their pockets, Ulysses S. Grant remained the modest soldier. The sting of innumerable scandals that marked his successive administrations never touched him. Grant left the White House as honorably as when he had entered it, accepted modestly the accolades of a grateful nation, and slipped quietly into retirement. But he was restless and so decided that he and Julia would tour the world. Much to his surprise, he was welcomed as a great hero wherever he went and was as lionized in Prussia, Egypt, and China as he ever was in New York or Washington. When he returned to America, he was given a hero's welcome as the nation's most effective and storied emissary. Dinners, tours, banquets, and veterans' reunions followed until Grant, wanting to accomplish even more, allowed his name to be used in connection with the Wall Street firm of Grant & Ward. That his good name could be so sullied now, in what would be his final years, hurt Grant more than even his family realized.

By the end of May 1884, the crisis that started with the bankruptcy of Grant & Ward had abated. The newspaper articles questioning Grant's honesty and intelligence slipped dimly into the recent past, though its humiliation was remembered by Grant every day. The strain of the bankruptcy and newspaper reports, his friends said, showed on his face—as did the worry over how, now that the scandal was behind him, he would care for his family. On May 26, Ferdinand Ward returned to New York, was arrested, indicted for fraud, and released on bail. On May 27, he came to see Grant at 66th Street, but he was not admitted. On May 30, Grant and his family left the city for their cottage at Long Branch, a beach resort town in New Jersey. There, Grant decided, he would rest and reflect on doing the one thing that he had told innumerable suitors, including Mark Twain, he would never do—write his memoirs.

TWO

❧

"A WOUNDED LION"

Samuel Clemens was not the
son of a tanner or a great commander in the Civil War, did not
serve as president or receive the accolades of a grateful nation.
But the similarities between Clemens and Grant are remarkable. Both were frontier boys and sons of proud, successful,
and often indifferent fathers. Both were quietly ambitious. Both
were intelligent, articulate, and well educated. Both became
doting fathers of admiring children and loyal husbands of hardworking, dedicated wives. Both were caught up in the errors
and triumphs of their time, both believed in America and its
freedoms. Both loved money. There were differences, of course:
Grant's father was a tanner, Clemens's a judge. Grant's father
was a business success, Clemens's father went bankrupt. Grant's
family was tied to the land, to the success of agriculture, Clemens's to small-town, middle-class America. Grant was reserved,
modest, and a man of few words. Clemens was anything but:
He was outgoing and ostentatious, and his love of words (and
lots of them seemed to pour out of him) defined his character.

There is this: As young men, Grant and Clemens had the

same dream, of traveling on the big steamboats of the Mississippi to make their fortunes. And this one difference: While Grant did not follow his dream, Clemens did. Samuel Clemens did not just love the Mississippi or simply become its most famous biographer, he understood the power of rivers. For him, rivers were the highways of America's first decades of economic growth and, therefore, a symbol of the nation's freedoms. Rivers brought settlers to the West, transported their harvests to market, conveyed finished goods from the cities, and served as a province and temporary home to that most romantic of all nineteenth-century figures, the riverboat captain. Samuel Langhorne Clemens, the sixth child of John Marshall and Jane Lampton Clemens, became a riverboat pilot in 1859 at the age of twenty-four. It had been an unexpected journey. After a childhood spent in the small river town of Hannibal, Missouri (described by Clemens as "a child's paradise"), a sojourn at his brother's failing newspaper, and a stint as a typesetter for a printer in faraway New York, Clemens decided to make his fortune in New Orleans. After serving as an apprentice and cub pilot, he received his license and served aboard over one dozen boats, including the *White Cloud*, the *Crescent City*, and the *City of Memphis*. "A pilot, in those days, was the only unfettered and entirely independent human being that lived in the earth," he later wrote. "His movements were entirely free; he consulted no one, he received commands from nobody, he promptly resented even the merest suggestion. . . ."

Clemens met freedom and tragedy on the river. He thought the job would be easy, but it wasn't: He was forced to memorize every bend and eddy, and the river changed constantly. As there was freedom on the river, there were also constant reminders of its treachery; wrecks and burned-out skeletons of ships, skiffs, rafts, and riverboats dotted its shores and sandbars. "Two things seemed pretty apparent to me," he later wrote.

"One was, that in order to be a pilot a man had to learn more than any one man ought to be allowed to know; and the other was, that he must learn it all over again in a different way every twenty-four hours." In 1858, Clemens signed his brother Henry on as a clerk on the *Pennsylvania*, and off they went, down the river. But Clemens argued bitterly with the *Pennsylvania*'s captain, so while Henry stayed aboard for the return trip north, Clemens decided to sign on with another riverboat. Two days later, and two days behind Henry, Clemens learned the *Pennsylvania*, nearing Memphis, had burst a boiler and exploded, killing 150 people. When he arrived in Memphis he found his brother alive but badly burned, with no hope of recovery. "For forty-eight hours I labored at the bedside of my poor burned and bruised but uncomplaining brother," Clemens wrote to his sister-in-law, "and then the star of my hope went out and left me in the gloom of despair." He blamed himself for his brother's death and remembered it long after—alluding to the destruction of the *Pennsylvania* in nearly all of his subsequent books.

The Civil War found Clemens a volunteer in the Marion Rangers, an irregular Confederate unit raised from his hometown of Hannibal. His enlistment did not last long. After spending several weeks as the unit's second lieutenant, Clemens decided he had had enough of war. "When I retired from the rebel army in '61," he later wrote, "I retired . . . in good order, at least in good enough order for a person who had not yet learned how to retreat according to the rules of war, and had to trust to native genius. It seemed to me that for a first attempt at a retreat it was not badly done." He wanted nothing of war, so he left for Nevada with his brother Orion and settled in Carson City. Soon Clemens was "smitten by the silver fever" and became a prospector. Silver was pouring out of Nevada and making men rich overnight. "I succumbed and grew as frenzied as the craziest," Clemens later wrote. By the time Clemens arrived in the silver fields, however, the great rush had all but ended, and after six months of failure, Clemens turned his sights on journalism. He became a reporter for the *Territorial Enterprise*, Virginia City's (and Nevada's) most successful newspaper.

On February 3, 1863, Samuel Langhorne Clemens became Mark Twain, a name he had inherited from his riverboat days. Ever willing to use his creative energies to tell stories when there was nothing to report, Twain tried his hand at fiction, and soon some of his writing began to appear in national newspapers—including one, a hoax, in which he reported finding a "petrified man" among Nevada's limestone outcroppings. An accompanying sketch showed the man winking and thumbing his nose at the readers, but the story was so odd (and so believable) that it was widely reprinted. Still, Clemens was restless. "I began to get tired of staying in one place so long," he later wrote. "There was no longer satisfying variety in going down to Carson to report the proceedings of the legislature once a year . . . I wanted to go somewhere. I wanted—I did not *know* what I wanted. I had the 'spring fever' and wanted a change." He moved to San Francisco and befriended Ambrose Bierce and Bret Harte, two rising stars of America's nascent literary tradition, and for a time became a muckraking journalist for San Francisco's *Morning Call*. He denounced mob violence against Chinese immigrants and attacked the San Francisco police, then went to California's gold rush hills and listened to the stories the miners told (including one about a man who would gamble on anything, even on his notorious jumping frog). But he still could not decide what to do. Finally, with the Civil War over, he determined to return to Missouri. "I am tired of being a beggar," he wrote to Orion, "tired of being chained to this accursed homeless desert, I want to go back to a Christian land once more."

Samuel Clemens may have begun using the pen name Mark Twain in 1863, but Sam Clemens actually became Mark Twain in late 1865, when the humorist Artemis Ward began to circulate his story "The Celebrated Jumping Frog of Calaveras County," which was reprinted widely in a number of newspapers. Twain was soon a popular, if puzzling, figure in the literary community of New York, where his humor and sketches were gaining increasing popularity. "The foremost among the gentlemen of the California press, as far as we have been able to judge is one who signs himself 'Mark Twain,'" a writer for *New York Round Table* reported. "He is, we believe, quite a young man, and has not written a great deal. Perhaps, if he will husband his resources and not kill with overwork the mental goose that has given us these golden eggs, he may one day rank among the brightest of our wits." Twain himself now acknowledged his calling. "I never had but two powerful ambitions in my life," he wrote to his brother, "One was to be a pilot, & the other a preacher of the gospel. I accomplished the one & failed in the other, because I could not supply myself with the necessary stock in trade—i.e. religion. But I have had a 'call' to literature, of a low order—i.e. humorous. It is nothing to be proud of, but it is my strongest suit."

Ever unsatisfied, and still honing his writing skills, he sailed to Hawaii, where he discovered he could hold an audience in thrall through the simple talent of telling a story. Like Artemis Ward, an old friend upon whom he patterned himself, Twain became a popular and appreciated public humorist, sprinkling his witticisms with cutting political commentaries. His old friend Bret Harte described his talent as "of the western character of ludicrous exaggeration and audacious statement"—but for Twain the "lectures" came to him as naturally as gentling horses did to Grant. After appearing to appreciative audiences in California and Nevada, Twain returned to New York and thence to the Midwest, where he gave more lectures as "the celebrated California humorist, and most extraordinary delineator of human character in America or upon the Continent of Europe."

Twain had never been to Europe, but he resolved this quickly enough by booking passage on the *Quaker City*, which was bound, with its retinue of devout passengers (enlisted for the voyage by no less a personage than the famous minister Henry Ward Beecher—who decided at the last minute, with profuse apologies, that he, alas, could not make the voyage), for the shores of the Mediterranean and the hills of Jerusalem. While his fellow passengers read guidebooks and attended lectures, Twain played cards in his cabin with a group of men who called themselves the *Quaker City* Nighthawks. But Twain was never so outlandish as his self-description as "the Wild Humorist of the Pacific Slope" promised. He befriended everyone and listened politely and closely to everything they had to say and promised himself he would put it all down in a book he would write when he returned to America. In the meantime, it would be far better, he thought, to put the journey's real goal in its proper perspective. "We wish to learn all the curious, outlandish ways of all the different countries, so that we can 'show off' and astonish people when we get home," he said.

∞∞∞

THE INNOCENTS ABROAD, Twain's account of his overseas journey, was published by Hartford's American Publishing Company in 1869. It was followed soon after by *Roughing It* and then by *The Gilded Age*, the signature book of the era and, at least in part, a condemnation of the economic policies of the Grant administration. Twain's reputation, already made through the lecture circuit and his legendary "Jumping Frog," was further enhanced by his decision to move to Hartford, which was then the unlikely center of America's literary community. Charles Dudley Warner, the editor of the *Hartford Courant*, became a good friend—and coauthor with Twain of *The Gilded Age*—and Twain rubbed shoulders with the great and near great, including the aging Harriet Beecher Stowe, author of *Uncle Tom's Cabin*. Hartford was not Hannibal. There was no big booming river roaring by, no town drunk, and no family bankruptcies. But Twain grew to love Hartford, and he spent much of his life there. In 1868, Twain met Olivia Langdon—"Livy"—the sister of a friend, in Elmira, New York.

The Langdons were a distinct shock to the red-haired Missourian. They were openly affectionate (Twain commented that he had never seen anyone in his family kiss anyone—except during funerals), but also opinionated, religious, abstemious, and affluent. The strongly abolitionist Langdons disapproved of Twain, but he would not be deterred in his pursuit of Livy. "I'll harass that girl and harass that girl," he said, "till she'll have to say yes." She did finally, and Twain approached her father, Jervis Langdon, to seek his permission. The older man was stunned to silence but soon said that he would give his permission only if Twain could provide him with the appropriate references ("from out west") attesting to his good character. Supported by this, Livy set out to "reform" her fiancé. She sent him to hear a sermon of a family friend, Henry Ward Beecher, who had organized the *Quaker City* expedition (to satisfy her, Twain received a copy of the sermon and read and reread it), made him promise that he would try to stop drinking, and urged him to give up cigars. He promised all of these things, and more, as his references had not done his cause much good. "They said with one accord that I got drunk oftener than was necessary & that I was wild and Godless, idle, lecherous & a discontented & an unsettled rover & they could never recommend any girl of high character & social position to marry me—but as I had already said all that about myself beforehand there was nothing shocking or surprising about it to the family."

The Innocents Abroad sold one hundred thousand copies. Roughing It, which recounted Twain's Nevada days consorting with whiskey-drinking adventurers and down-on-their-luck prospectors, was published three years later. Roughing It did not sell nearly as well as his first book, but it solidified Twain's reputation as a new and unique voice in American literature. It also established him in the eyes of Livy's family. On February 2, 1870, Livy Langdon and Mark Twain were married in her father's parlor in Elmira. Twain was overjoyed, and the Langdons, despite their skepticism, were gracious: Awaiting the new bride and groom was a house on Buffalo's Delaware Street, purchased and furnished by Livy's father. This might well have been the happiest time of Twain's life: "The fountains of my great deep are broken up, and I have rained reminiscences for four & twenty hours. The old life has swept before me like a panorama; the old days have trooped by in their old glory, again; the old faces have looked out of the mists of the past; old footsteps have sounded in my listening ears; old hands have clasped mine, old voices have greeted me, & the songs I loved ages & ages ago have come wailing down the centuries."

Such creativity as he had, Twain now believed, should be put to good use. He had been a typesetter, prospector, reporter, steamboat captain, and world traveler. Now he would be a writer, devoting his days to replicating the success of The Innocents Abroad. He could make a living at writing, he thought, and realized soon enough that he would have to. In 1870, Livy gave birth to a son, Langdon, who provided an incentive for not only writing but also selling his work.

In March 1871, Twain, Livy, and their new son sold the house in Buffalo and moved to the Nook Farm district of Hartford, the home of Charles Dudley Warner, Harriet Beecher Stowe, and Stowe's notorious and outspoken sister, Isabella Beecher Hooker. Twain immediately resuscitated his lecture series ("the most detestable lecture campaign that ever was," he said) to pay his debts, returning home only in time to celebrate the birth of his second child, Olivia Susan. "Susy is bright & strong & we love her so, no sacrifice seems too much to make for her." In June 1872, however, Twain and Livy's lives were blighted by the death of their son, who succumbed to diphtheria. For a time Twain was inconsolable. He blamed himself for Langdon's death, saying that he should not have taken the boy for a carriage ride, as it exposed him to the cold. But their son's death brought Twain closer to his wife, who now shared at least a part of his dark view of the world. "I feel so often as if my path is to be lined with graves," she remarked. She added that now she was "almost perfectly cold toward God."

Twain plunged on. After a tour of England and the publication of *The Gilded Age*, he designed and built the house of his dreams on five acres of land next door to Harriet Beecher and her husband, Calvin Stowe, outside Hartford. He hired architect Edward Tuckerman Potter to design a quirky three-floor nineteen-room home: It had jutting balconies, a wraparound porch, and a combination billiard room and study where Twain could work. This done, Twain decamped with Livy and his newborn daughter to Quarry Farm, his sister-in-law's spacious retreat in upstate New York. The Hartford home was a symbol of Twain's pride, a fitting monument to his success, but Quarry Farm was the place that made that success possible. Quarry Farm, Twain discovered, was "the quietest of all quiet places"— which was just what he needed to write. It was here, in June 1874, that a very healthy and pudgy Clara Clemens was born

(Twain called her "the Great American Giantess"), and it was here, that same summer, that Twain met John T. Lewis, a freeborn African American from Maryland. Lewis entertained Twain with his thick southern drawl, his innocent but profound simplicity, and the stories of his footloose childhood. Lewis's stories, Twain realized, were much like the stories he told his lecture audiences of his boyhood in Hannibal. It was to people like Lewis and places like Hannibal to which Twain was inexorably drawn, and they became the icons of his work. "I begin to write incidents out of real life," Twain once said. "One of the persons I wrote about begins to talk this way and another, and pretty soon I find that these creatures of the imagination have developed into characters, and have for me a distinct personality. They are not 'made,' they just grow naturally out of the subject."

Twain began to write a new book in the quiet summer of 1874 that reflected on his own childhood but included some of the characters with the drawling southern dialect provided by John Lewis. "Mr. Clemens was never so good and loveable as he is now," Livy said of him then, "we never were so happy together it seems to me—He is perfectly brim full of work, says he never worked with such perfect ease and happiness in his life. It is splendid to see him so heartily love his work, he begrudges every moment's interruption."

Twain called his new book *The Adventures of Tom Sawyer*. He labored diligently on *Tom Sawyer* all through the summer of 1874, hoping that the book would be published the next year. He also desperately hoped it would be a success, for while he had enjoyed the notoriety of *The Innocents Abroad*, *Roughing It*, and *The Gilded Age*, his expenses were mounting: They included everyday expenses for living at Quarry Farm and the upkeep for six servants (a nursemaid, housemaid, laundress, cook, butler, and coachman) at his home in Hartford. "We had a charming visit, not marred by anything," William Dean Howells wrote to his father after a visit to Hartford in early 1875. "The Clemenses are whole-souled hosts, with inextinguishable money, and a palace of a house."

But the money was not inextinguishable, which was why Twain worked so obsessively on his new book; as his expenses mounted, his writing routine became more and more demanding. In Hartford Twain would isolate himself in his billiard room for hours on end and complain bitterly about any interruption. Some days he would write twenty-five hundred to three thousand words (depending on the book) and then review his manuscript or read parts of it aloud to his family each night. The routine was no less stringent at Quarry Farm, where on a normal summer's day, Twain rose early, ate a breakfast of steak and eggs, and then set off for his study, perched in an isolated pavilion on a small nearby hillock with a sheaf of papers and a box of cigars. He composed until late in the afternoon. Twain did this every summer for twenty years, writing some of the greatest works of American fiction. *Tom Sawyer* was written at Quarry Farm, and when it was finally published, two years after its completion, Twain was proud of the book and gloried in the reviews he received. "The study is a wonderful study of the boy-mind which inhabits a world quite distinct from that in which he is bodily present with his elders," William Dean Howells wrote of *Tom Sawyer* in the *Atlantic Monthly*, "and in this lies his great charm and its universality, for boy nature is the same everywhere." For Twain the book was, simply, "a hymn."

But *Tom Sawyer* was *not* a success, and it did not begin to cover the mounting expenses of Twain's Hartford home. In the midst of this—the expenses, the constant dinners, the demands of groundskeepers and servants, the constant comings and goings of neighbors, friends, and visitors ("Just think of this going on all day long, and I a man who loathes details with all his heart," Twain wrote)—he struck on an idea that might solve all his problems at once. He would write not simply about Hannibal and its characters, but about the Mississippi River itself, of "old Mississippi days of steamboating glory," in a series of articles for the *Atlantic Monthly*. The work would keep him focused on a part of his life that was a constant inspiration at the same time that it provided him with the income he now so desperately needed. "What a virgin subject to hurl into a magazine!" he exclaimed. The first of seven installments of *Old Times on the Mississippi* appeared in January 1875. The pieces were a popular success and, at least for a time, eased some of Twain's financial worries. "The piece about the Mississippi is capital," the *Atlantic Monthly*'s Howells wrote, "it almost made the water in our ice-pitcher muddy as I read it."

BY APRIL 1875, Twain was considering a new book project that would build on *Tom Sawyer* and on the success of his *Atlantic Monthly* series. It would be "another boy's book"—beginning where Tom Sawyer had left off and telling a story about the river he loved. But it would be more. For over the last two years, and certainly since rubbing up against the problem in *Tom Sawyer*, Twain had been turning the issue of slavery over and over in his mind. His friendship with John Lewis solidified his thinking on the subject, but so too did his decision to make Hartford his home. Twain's relationship with his neighbor Harriet Beecher Stowe was at least part of the reason he kept thinking about slavery. Stowe was not only famous, she was famous for having written *Uncle Tom's Cabin*, the most successful American novel of its time. *Uncle Tom* was not simply a successful book, it had done more than any other book to solidify the nation's abhorrence of slavery. *Uncle Tom's Cabin* sold three hundred thousand copies in the first year after its publication and gave Stowe such notoriety that it was said that Abraham Lincoln greeted her with, "So this is the little lady that caused this Civil War," when she visited the White House. While the story is apocryphal, it contains a seed of truth. Harriet Beecher Stowe was viewed not only as the nation's preeminent expert on slavery, but as its most articulate critic.

The Stowes were one of the reasons Twain moved to Hartford in the first place. They—Harriet, her husband, Calvin, Harriet's sister Isabella Hooker, and her husband, John Hooker—formed the core of America's premier literary society. Then, too, Hartford was famous not only for its colony of writers, but also for its burgeoning commercial industries, including a number of major publishing houses. Isabella Hooker, known for her outspoken views on women's rights, was the acknowledged leader of Hartford's literary community, and invitations to her spacious and intellectually lively Sunday night dinners were coveted. Opinionated and passionate, Isabella Hooker delighted in the common flirtations of Hartford society and competed unabashedly for public attention with her sister Harriet: "You can have no idea of the pleasure of being admired and loved after having been shut out from the world as I have been," she once said. But for all their egalitarian instincts, Isabella and Harriet remained New England aristocrats. Isabella accepted Twain and his wife, Livy, but only because Harriet insisted; Isabella thought Twain a "parvenu"—her word for "southerner."

The Beechers were themselves among America's first families. Harriet's father, Lyman Beecher, was the nation's most famous minister. His message of renewal changed the face of American Calvinism—and, in the 1830s, led to his trial before a group of Presbyterian Church leaders on a charge of heresy. During the trial (which was suspended without a finding), Lyman stood with his son Henry at his side, defending himself in a booming voice, chin forward, fist upraised, like a latter-day Jeremiah. The stammering but handsome Henry Ward Beecher (the fourth of six sons) went on to become the head of Brooklyn's famous Plymouth Church and, following in his father's footsteps (and after losing his stammer), America's most fiery religious orator. Before the Civil War, Beecher was an outspoken abolitionist and even raised money to purchase rifles, called "Beecher's Bibles," to arm Kansas's abolitionist militias. His sermons were so overpowering that women for miles around would come to Plymouth Church just to hear him preach—and would swoon, and faint, in the aisles at the most emotionally appropriate moments. It was Henry (a thoroughgoing abolitionist and no pacifist) whom Harriet chanced upon in her kitchen during the Cincinnati race riot of 1837, pouring lead into molds to make "bullets to kill men with."

That Twain was now a part of Hartford society, and a regular visitor to Harriet's home and Isabella's Sunday night dinners, reflected his new position as one of America's leading writers. For a time, Twain acted the part. He was the young but rising writer who enjoyed the company of the anointed. But there was always a sense in Twain that while the Beechers represented the cream of American society, there was a certain aristocratic hypocrisy that marked the Beecher legacy: Isabella publicly questioned the manliness of her retiring husband (her brother Henry said that she was insane and should be put in a sanitarium), held strange séances in her home (the ghosts of which resulted less from transferences from the spirit world and more from the world of spirits), and publicly and embarrassingly derided Susan B. Anthony, her competitor in the women's rights movement. Far from being the aristocratic exemplars of moral rectitude that much of America believed them to be, the Beechers turned out to be as avaricious as any of Twain's *Gilded Age* characters. Henry Ward Beecher was discovered to have accepted $15,000 from financier and corporate mogul Jay Cooke in exchange for publishing glowing editorials about Cooke's business acumen (Cooke then promptly swindled thousands of his investors) and was later subjected to public ridicule for having an adulterous affair with Elizabeth Tilton, the wife of crusading journalist and publisher Theodore Tilton, who gained his reputation by being a constant critic of the Grant administration.

The resulting trial, in a civil suit brought against Henry by Tilton, caused a sensation. During the winter and spring of 1875, thousands of people crammed into a Brooklyn courtroom to view the proceedings. The black-suited Henry Ward Beecher appeared, upright, staid, with his grizzled and overwrought wife, Eunice (that "virago," that "griffon"—as the press pilloried her), on his arm. Eunice testified, Beecher testified, and dozens of character witnesses for both sides testified. In the end, the twelve jurors could not decide on the case and it was dismissed, a clear victory for the Beechers. But the scandal and trial, and the near bankruptcy of Brooklyn's Plymouth Church, ruined the Beecher family. When the scandal broke, Isabella broke ranks with her sisters and stated publicly that she thought her brother Henry had, in fact, committed adultery. Henry's response was savage, and Harriet refused to talk to Isabella, who was shunned in the family circles. Twain attended one of the court sessions in Brooklyn, shook his head despairingly, and pronounced his own verdict, condemning, in turn, preachers, politicians, journalists, and political bosses: "This nation is not reflected in [Massachusetts abolitionist] Charles Sumner, but in Henry Ward Beecher, Benjamin Butler, Whitelaw Reid, Wm. M Tweed. Politics are not going to cure moral ulcers like these, nor the decaying body they fester upon."

After a season of bright lights and Sunday dinners, Twain returned to his roots in *The Gilded Age* and his glib but razor-sharp cynicism of *The Innocents Abroad*. He was disappointed in what he had seen but reconfirmed in his belief that "the human being is a stupidly-constructed machine. He may have been a sufficiently creditable invention in the early and ignorant times, but to-day there is not a country in Christendom that would grant a patent on him." Seeing what celebrity and greed had done to the Beechers, he pulled Livy and his daughters more closely into his orbit and rededicated himself to his work. He also, as the Beecher trial was nearing its end in the summer of 1875, spent considerable time thinking about slavery. Harriet Beecher Stowe was a constant reminder to him of this, for she would occasionally amble by his home on a summer eve and wave to him. While Twain had little respect for her brother Henry, he always maintained a cordial and even affectionate relationship with Harriet, despite her eccentricities. The scandal surrounding her family had clearly taken its toll on her. At times, as Twain later testified, she would "slip up behind a person who was deep in dreams and musing and fetch a war whoop that would jump that person out of his clothes." As she grew older, Harriet Beecher Stowe was a constant reminder of what could happen to aging writers: She would knock on his door in Hartford with a gift of flowers for Livy, who would later find that Harriet had plundered them surreptitiously (dripping roots and all) from her own garden.

Mark Twain had read *Uncle Tom's Cabin*, and he admired it. But Stowe's portrait of slavery—the constant beatings and lashings, the deliberate but offhanded cruelties, the continual yearnings, escapes, captures, and night posses of slave hunters—was not familiar to him. Hers was the northern view of slavery, and he thought it simplistic, clichéd. For Twain, as for many southerners, slavery was a complex and nuanced evil (which is what *made* it evil) not given to melodramatic turns of phrase. The difference between Stowe's view and Twain's was that while

Stowe had seen slavery and the horrid cruelties visited upon the black community in the days before the Civil War, she had not actually *lived* among slaves. Twain had. For Twain that made all the difference. "In my schoolboy days I had no aversion to slavery," he wrote toward the end of his life. "I was not aware that there was anything wrong about it. No one arraigned it in my hearing; the local papers said nothing against it; the local pulpit taught us that God approved it, that it was a holy thing and that the doubter need only look in the Bible if he wished to settle his mind—and then the texts were read aloud to us to make the matter sure; if the slaves themselves had an aversion to slavery they were wise and said nothing. In Hannibal we seldom saw a slave misused; on the farm never."

It is little wonder that in the summer following the end of the Tilton-Beecher trial, in 1876, Twain thought he might put all of this—river, home, pride, avarice, slavery, and the human condition—in a single book built on the character of a young boy. Hannibal, Twain decided, would once again serve as the foundation for the book, for it was a perfect model of America. "In the small town of Hannibal, Missouri, when I was a boy everybody was poor but didn't know it; and everybody was comfortable, and did know it," Twain wrote. "And there were grades of society; people of good family, people of unclassified family, people of no family. Everybody knew everybody, and was affable to everybody, and nobody put on any visible airs; yet the class lines were quite clearly drawn, and the familiar social life of each class was restricted to that class."

Twain retreated to Quarry Farm, far from the everyday worries and scandals of Hartford, and set to work. He began writing in June 1876, and he wrote steadily into August. "Began another boy's book—more to be at work than anything else," he wrote to Howells. "I have written four hundred pages on it—therefore it is very nearly half done. It is Huck Finn's Autobiography. I like it only tolerably well, as far as I have got, and may possibly pigeonhole or burn the MS when it is done."

Mark Twain wrote sixteen chapters of *Adventures of Huckleberry Finn* during the summer of 1876, and then he stopped. The well had run dry. The slave Jim and his companion, Huck Finn, had escaped from Hannibal (St. Petersburg in the book) and were on the river headed south. They had made it to Cairo, Illinois, where the Ohio River joins the Mississippi. But they were lost. Reading and rereading what he had written during the summer, Twain realized that he had run into a nearly irresolvable problem. He had to decide whether he should carry Jim and Huck up the Ohio River, to freedom—which seemed natural—or leave them on the raft and send them deep into slave territory. But why would they do that? Why would two characters seeking freedom, one a boy and one a grown man but a slave, go south? At the end of August, Twain finished writing the end of chapter 16, looked it over for a time, then wrapped it up and put it away. He returned to it only in 1884, when, in the midst of his friendship with Ulysses S. Grant, he finally realized what *Huck Finn* was really all about.

THE MORNING OF JUNE 2, 1884, found Ulysses S. Grant and his family at their summer home on the beach at Long Branch, New Jersey. Their cottage, three stories high with an encircling balcony, provided a welcome respite for the general and former president. It was a place where he could relax and read. He was still, more than a decade after the end of his presidency, Long Branch's "first citizen" and a continuing and constant source of public speculation. The citizens of Long Branch and those enjoying a summer vacation there often took the opportunity to pass the Grant cottage in the hopes of seeing the great man. They were rarely disappointed. Grant loved to sit on his porch and read, and from time to time he would look up at the passing strollers, smile, and wave. The people of Long Branch reciprocated this courtesy by honoring his privacy. Though the Grants had many callers, they only rarely hosted an uninvited guest.

The Grant family had come to Long Branch during the first summer of Grant's first term as president, in 1869, as the guest of the publisher of the *Philadelphia Ledger*, George Childs. Childs was one of Long Branch's most important investors and took pride in the growing prestige of the resort. He became a close friend of Grant's and introduced him to his affluent circle of friends. It was at Childs's urging that Grant became a member of the Grand Army of the Republic (George C. Meade Post No. 1 of Philadelphia) and was invested during a ceremony in the Ledger building in Philadelphia. As a token of their friendship, Childs bought a cottage with two other investors—George Pullman and Moses Taylor—in Long Branch, and he allowed the Grants to use it, without charge, for the rest of their lives. In the first summer of his long tenure as Long Branch's most prominent citizen, Grant deployed secretaries and aides throughout the cottage's twenty-eight rooms, conducting the business of the government from his rocker. Reporters soon began referring to Long Branch as the nation's "summer capital."

Long Branch was popular, but Grant made it famous. Other presidents followed his example: President Rutherford B. Hayes spent nearly every summer at Long Branch, President James A. Garfield died of his wounds there (in 1881), and, later, Presidents Benjamin Harrison and William McKinley were often seen riding the Long Branch streetcar to the beach. But it was Ulysses and Julia Grant who first gave Long Branch its national reputation. They could be seen, nearly every morning, seated together on their porch. In the early afternoons Grant often rode a team of horses into the surrounding countryside, so often that he came to know the area of Long Branch nearly by heart. Some afternoons he and Julia took a box at the racetrack, an entertaining sidelight that titillated the townspeople. During his time as president, Grant's political enemies ridiculed this summer retreat and Grant's indulgences, but it did not stop him from spending as much time as he could, every summer, at the resort. Grant played poker with a group of friends every Friday night at Long Branch, and the games lasted into the early hours of the morning.

On Thursdays each summer, Grant and Julia would take one-day excursions into New York. Grant visited friends and political allies in the city, while Julia either accompanied him or visited her own friends. That changed after 1884, of course, as the Grants were forced to be frugal with their money. While Grant continued to play poker with his friends, Julia did all the cooking. Gone were the secretaries and assistants, the political advisers and government officials, and gone too were the one-day excursions to New York. Grant was now thinking about what he would do to rescue his financial position. He had decided, much against his own judgment, that he should write his memoirs, but he did not know how to start, and he did not yet know who would publish them. He was naturally reticent about his own writing abilities, for he was quick to point out that all he had ever written were military reports or dispatches. While he had written extensively as president, most of his work had been confined to editing, rejecting, or signing the work of others. Writing a memoir would be much different and, he supposed, much more taxing.

It was in the middle of such ruminations, on the morning of June 2, that Grant joined his wife in their pantry to share some fruit. They talked for just a moment before Grant lifted a peach and bit into it. After another moment he howled in pain. He looked up, shook his head, and told his wife what had happened. The pain in his throat had lasted for only a moment, he said, but it had been almost unbearable. When Grant took a second bite of the peach, however, the pain seemed to have subsided, and in the weeks that followed, it sometimes disappeared altogether. Even so, by July the pain in his throat was returning with greater frequency, especially when he ate. While he passed this off as a minor annoyance, Julia decided to call on a doctor. George Childs, who was visiting with the Grants at the time, said that Grant should be examined by a Philadelphia surgeon by the name of Jacob Mendez da Costa, who was then in Long Branch on a one-week vacation. Da Costa examined Grant and saw that the back of his throat was inflamed—he wrote a prescription and advised the general to see his family doctor immediately. The family doctor, Fordyce Barker, was in Europe, however, so Grant delayed a visit, and the pain in his throat seemed to subside for a time.

In mid-June, Grant attended a convention of army chaplains held at nearby Ocean Grove. This was his first public foray since the bankruptcy of Grant & Ward, and Grant was worried. But his fears were allayed when his good friend Dr. A. J. Palmer introduced him. "No combination of Wall Street sharpers shall tarnish the lustre of my old Commander's fame for me," he said, and Grant was given a standing ovation.

Palmer's accolade dampened Grant's fears about how he might be greeted by his old army comrades, so on June 11, he traveled to Brooklyn to attend the annual reunion of the Society of the Army of the Potomac. Once again he was greeted warmly and was even elected the society's president. Watching from afar, Richard Watson Gilder—the senior editor of the *Century* magazine, which was then one of the leading periodicals in the country—was heartened by the public show of support for Grant. Gilder, associate editor Robert Underwood Johnson, and Roswell Smith, the Century Company's president, had spent the previous year planning out what would become one of the most successful publishing ventures in U.S. history—a three-year project featuring articles written by Civil War participants. The articles would appear first in the magazine but then be put into book form. While the series was destined to become enormously popular, initial efforts by Gilder, Johnson, and Smith to recruit major military figures to write had been disappointing. Gilder and Johnson were convinced that if Grant could be induced to write several articles, his prestige would be enough to convince other commanders to contribute.

Johnson and Gilder allowed that they might be overly optimistic. They had first approached Grant about writing a one-time submission in New York in 1884, but he had turned them down. He explained that other writers, including his aide and close friend Adam Badeau, had already written extensively on the war. "It is all in Badeau," Grant said, referring them to his aide's highly successful three-volume *Military History of Ulysses S. Grant*. Grant added, unnecessarily, that he did not like to retrace his steps, a superstition that he had had since he was a boy. "I have frequently started to go places where I had never been and to which I did not know the way," he once said, "depending on making inquiries on the road, and if I got past the place without knowing it, instead of turning back I would go on until a road was found turning in the right direction, take that, and come in by the other side." But in the early summer of 1884, in large part because of his bankruptcy, Gilder and Johnson planned out a new approach to Grant. "Grant's recent election to the Army of the Potomac position may reengage his attention to military matters," Gilder wrote to Johnson. "He must be, this is [the magazine's] strongest hold." Much to their surprise, several days after this discussion, Gilder's hopes were confirmed by a note sent by Grant to the magazine. Grant said that he would welcome a visit from one of the editors to discuss what he should write.

Johnson visited Grant at Long Branch in mid-June and was surprised by Grant's candid explanation of his financial problems. Grant reviewed the bankruptcy of Grant & Ward and said that the scandal had plunged his family into a financial crisis. "He gave me the impression of a wounded lion," Johnson later wrote. "He had been hurt to the quick in his proud name and in his honor, and the man [who was] stolid and reserved showed himself to me as a person of the most sensitive nature and the most human expression of feeling." Grant then expressed his reticence in providing any articles for the *Century* series: He was not a writer, he said, and his campaigns had already been the subject of numerous articles and books. He was not sure that he was up to the job. Johnson worked to allay these fears: An article from the former Union commander and president would be more informative than any previously written, he said. Moreover, Grant would be free to write as many articles as he wanted and on any subject from the war that he had witnessed. The magazine, Johnson said, would accept all of them and work with him to make certain they received the attention they deserved. Johnson then suggested that Grant write four articles, one each on the Battle of Shiloh, the Vicksburg Campaign, the Battle of the Wilderness, and the surrender of Lee. Johnson said the magazine would pay him $500 for each article. It was an extraordinary sum for the time. Grant agreed to this arrangement.

Grant set to work on the Shiloh article almost immediately after Johnson's departure and worked diligently on it all through June, averaging four hours of work each day. To spark his memories of the battle, he referred to official reports and previous articles and often called on his son Fred to retrieve documents that he thought would be useful. On July 1, Gilder received a handwritten copy of Grant's Shiloh article in the *Century*'s New York offices. "Hurrah for Grant," he wrote to Johnson. "Now for [General Philip] Sheridan & [General William Tecumseh] Sherman. Gen. Grant on 'Shiloh' is decisive and soldierly but not picturesque. Hurrah!"

Gilder's jubilation was not misplaced—for a magazine to have an article from Grant on a major aspect of Civil War history was a publishing coup, and Gilder, Johnson, and Smith knew it. But the article itself was flat; it was written on four single sheets of paper and gave a workable account of the battle, but that was all. There was no color or life in the article and almost none of Grant: of what he was thinking, considering, or doing. Johnson visited Grant at Long Branch several times that July, tactfully praising what he had written but subtly and firmly coaching him to add personal anecdotes to his account. This was not supposed to be a battle report, he told Grant, but a story. It had to come complete with characters and a plot, and it should be written as if the reader had never even heard of Shiloh.

Grant, Johnson discovered, was actually much more talkative than the public realized. He was expansive in his description of other generals and had a good eye when it came to reporting details. Nor was he hesitant about describing his own feelings. During their several meetings together, Johnson applauded this, praised Grant's ability to remember the slightest detail, and said that if such details were included in his articles, they would be enormously popular. "I told him that what was desirable for the success of the paper was to approximate such talk as he would make to friends after dinner, some of whom should know all about the battle and some nothing at all, and that the public . . . was particularly interested in his point of view, in everything that concerned him, in what he planned,

saw, said, and did," Johnson said. Johnson also used some of
the tricks he had learned as an editor working with particularly
recalcitrant writers: During their sessions at Long Branch, Johnson would ask Grant about a particular incident from the war,
and when Grant answered him, often expansively, Johnson
would say, "Well, you should put that in the article."

Johnson's advice was a revelation for Grant, but once he
understood what the magazine wanted from him, he plunged
back into his work. By the end of August, he had completely
rewritten the article and produced a memorable account of the
battle. Starting in August, Grant's prose, much to the surprise
of Gilder, Johnson, and Smith, radiated confidence and had
a sense of immediacy that brought the reader into the action.
He had followed Johnson's advice, recounting small incidents
that gave color to the larger theme—and he had a prodigious
memory. At times his prose was almost electrifying. The key to
Grant's writing, it was plain to all, was his talent for understatement and his ability to explain the most significant events
through a simple explication of their core elements. Perhaps
most important, Grant had an eye for detail and was now willing, following Johnson's lead, to recount the simplest but most
human anecdotes.

> We were moving along the northern edge of a clearing,
> very leisurely, toward the river above the landing. There
> did not appear to be an enemy to our right, until sud-
> denly a battery with musketry opened upon us from
> the edge of the woods on the other side of the clearing.
> The shells and balls whistled about our ears very fast
> for about a minute. I do not think it took us longer
> than that to get out of range and out of sight. In the
> sudden start we made, Major Hawkins lost his hat. He
> did not stop to pick it up. When we arrived at a per-

fectly safe position we halted to take account of damages. McPherson's horse was panting as if ready to drop. On examination it was found that a ball had struck him forward of the flank just back of the saddle, and had gone entirely through. In a few minutes the poor beast dropped dead; he had given no sign of injury until we came to a stop. A ball had struck the metal scabbard of my sword, just below the hilt, and broken it nearly off; before the battle was over, it had broken off entirely. There were three of us: one had lost a horse, killed, one a hat, and one a sword-scabbard. All were thankful it was no worse.

GRANT'S ARTICLES ON SHILOH (which were in their final form at the end of August and published, to great acclaim, the next February) still retains the ringing quality that brought it so much notoriety over one hundred years ago. In many ways, what Grant did was revolutionary. No American soldier to that time had written about his experiences as a commander, and few soldiers in history had done so with as much success as Grant. His articles made the *Century* series one of the most popular (if not the most popular) magazine series of his, or any, time. But this was tough work for Grant. Getting the details correct (for Grant was a detail man, almost obsessively so) was difficult, almost exhausting. Grant had two helpers. The first was his old friend and former military secretary, Adam Badeau. The second was Grant's son Fred, who was an accomplished writer: He had written a book on the Yellowstone Expedition, undertaken when, in following in his father's footsteps, he served as an officer in the Fourth Infantry. "Never had a father a more devoted son," Johnson later remembered. "Indeed, if I may venture to say so, the whole family gave him a respect and tender care that were conspicuous and beautiful."

Gilder and Smith, the Century's senior editor and publisher, kept close tabs on Johnson's meetings with Grant, assessing Grant's willingness to write his memoirs and nudging him gently to put his Century articles together in a series that would tell the story of the entire war from his perspective. This was a "soft sell"—Roswell Smith was very aware of the possibility of public criticism if he were to pressure Grant, and he was also sensitive to Grant's recent troubles at Grant & Ward. He did not want to add to them. Even so, Smith, Johnson, and Gilder worked throughout the summer of 1884 and into the autumn talking about the idea with Grant. Roswell Smith, in particular, had concrete ideas about what the Century was willing to offer and what it would not. Smith was particularly disdainful of paying Grant an advance on any future sales of his memoirs, a policy that is now a tradition in publishing but was then just coming into vogue. "I said we do not want Grant's book unless he wants us to have it, nor unless the terms are equitable," Smith wrote to Gilder at one point. "I said bad policy for author to accept advances, but would make advances if need be on completion &c." Despite this, Smith desperately wanted Grant's memoirs, as it would add prestige as well as profits to his publishing enterprise. "I think well of the project of a subscription book by Genl. Grant on the war," Smith told Gilder. He gave the Century's editors the right to pursue it "at once."

Grant, meanwhile, had begun his article on the Vicksburg Campaign, and now that he was actually researching and writing, he found that he enjoyed what he was doing. "I have now been writing on the Vicksburg Campaign two weeks, Sundays and all, averaging more than four hours a day," he wrote to Johnson on July 15. "Only now approaching [the Battle of]

Champion Hill, I fear that my article will be longer than you want." On July 22, Johnson visited Grant in his library at Long Branch and had a long discussion with him about his articles, including his recounting of the Vicksburg Campaign. But Johnson's real intention was to engage the general in a detailed discussion about his memoirs. Grant was in a good mood and told Johnson a humorous anecdote about the siege of Vicksburg. Johnson was happy to see that Grant was working, for on previous visits he had found him deep in thought—apparently worried still about the effect of the Grant & Ward bankruptcy on his finances and reputation. Johnson's discussion with Grant, however, did not yield a final agreement on Grant's memoirs, though Grant now had told his family that he was seriously considering the project.

Of the three *Century* managers, Richard Watson Gilder was the most worried that other publishers might make Grant a better offer, so in August he approached Grant's friend George Childs to see if he would "say a good word" for the *Century* magazine. Childs was noncommittal. Gilder then pushed Smith to have the company make a firm offer to Grant. He emphasized Grant's international appeal: "Mr. Johnson understands the book situation, evidently with thoroughness," he told Smith. "If we take it, it would be good for the book to announce its appearance in England, France & Germany—simultaneously." He then added, unnecessarily, "We have never had such a card before as Grant, let alone the other papers in the series." Gilder's impatience prompted Smith and Johnson to visit Grant in Long Branch in early September. It was the end of the summer season, but the beach town was still crowded. Johnson noticed that while the day was warm, Grant had his throat wrapped in a scarf and his voice was raspy. After a midday lunch at the home of George Childs, Grant, Smith, and Johnson walked the short distance to the Grant cottage and sat in wicker chairs on

Grant's veranda. Finally, with these pleasantries behind them, the three talked about Grant's memoirs.

"Do you really think anyone would be interested in a book by me?" Grant asked.

The question came as a surprise to Smith. "General, do you not think the public would read with avidity Napoleon's personal account of his battles?" he asked.

Grant remained silent, but he was impressed. Smith then revealed that the Century Company would sell the book by subscription. Two days later, he summarized the conversation: "His ideas agree with ours—to make a good book, manufacture it handsomely, sell it at a reasonable price and make it so commanding that we can secure competent agents at a fair commission." Smith was confident that the Century Company would get the book. The day had been a success. "When the book is ready he is to come to us with it."

Grant had finished the first draft of his article on the Vicksburg Campaign at the end of August and spent all of September drafting his article on the Chattanooga Campaign. The work was going well, and Grant was enjoying himself. He took satisfaction in what he had done so far. At the end of October, the Grants left Long Branch to return to New York. He was not only intent to continue his work, he had appointments in the city, including one with the Grant family doctor, Fordyce Barker. The pain that he had first noticed in his throat, in June, had returned.

THREE

"THE SMALL ROOM AT
THE HEAD OF THE STAIRS"

In 1884, the Republican Party candidate for president was Maine senator James G. Blaine, while the Democrats nominated Grover Cleveland. The campaign was scandal ridden: Blaine was accused by the Democrats of profiting from the Credit Mobilier scandal involving the building of the Union Pacific Railroad, while Cleveland was forced to admit that he had fathered an illegitimate child. Democrats chanted, "Blaine, Blaine, James G. Blaine, the continental liar from the State of Maine," while ministers campaigned nationally against Cleveland's lasciviousness. The election was decided on October 9 when the Reverend Samuel D. Burchard called the Democrats the party of "Rum, Romanism, and Rebellion." The Catholic vote in New York swung that state into Cleveland's column and propelled him into the White House.

Less than two weeks after Burchard's speech, Ulysses S. Grant walked into the offices of his family doctor, Fordyce Barker. Grant told Barker that he had a nagging pain in his throat that made it difficult for him to eat. Barker conducted a cursory examination of Grant's throat and immediately noticed a swelling on the back of the general's tongue. Barker would not give an opinion on Grant's malady but instead sent him to see Dr. John Hancock Douglas, the foremost throat specialist on the East Coast. Grant and Douglas knew each other; Douglas had served on the U.S. Sanitary Commission during the Civil War and had met Grant during his march on Fort Donelson in 1862. Douglas was something of a medical genius: He had discovered a remedy for scurvy during the war (recommending that all Union soldiers add sauerkraut and pickles to their diet), and he was instrumental in introducing a number of hygienic regulations into the Union Army. He gained his reputation while supervising field hospitals at the Battles of Shiloh, Fredericksburg, Gettysburg, and the Wilderness.

The general entered Douglas's office complaining of throat pain, headaches, and a limp—the result of a fall he had taken the year before while gingerly traversing a patch of ice outside his home. Douglas, a handsome man with flowing gray hair and a fulsome beard, seated Grant on his examining table, adjusted his mirror, and peered into his throat. He saw that Grant's throat was inflamed but that it was not the source of Grant's pain. The real problem was at the base of Grant's tongue, where Douglas noticed a small, inflamed growth that looked scaly and infected. Douglas stood back and looked at Grant, the concern showing on his face. "Is it cancer?" Grant asked him. Grant had reason to be worried, but Douglas deflected his concern. "The question, having been asked," Douglas noted in his diary, "I could give no uncertain, hesitating reply. I gave him what I believed—qualified by hope. I realized that if he once found that I had deceived him, I could never reinstate myself in his good opinion." Douglas was blunt. "General," he said, "the disease is serious, epithelial in character, and sometimes capable of being cured."

In fact, Douglas had already concluded that Grant's inflammation was cancerous, malignant, and likely to kill him. The cancer was spreading. There were three small growths less than one-eighth inch in length in an irritated area at the back roof of Grant's mouth, and the gland on the right side of Grant's tongue was enlarged. This swollen gland was the primary source of the general's pain. At the base of Grant's tongue, Douglas observed what he believed to be the most serious problem: a tissue of membranous surface that was a carcinoma. This carcinoma, Douglas knew, would spread itself into Grant's neck, infecting and enlarging it and making it nearly impossible for him to eat and, later, to breathe. Douglas concluded that this cancer could not be treated and that eventually, in the midst of excruciating pain, Grant would die. The only thing to be done was to make the general as comfortable as possible and wait for the inevitable.

Douglas applied a muriate of cocaine to the swollen area at the base of Grant's tongue to ease his pain. There was immediate relief—the discomfort that Grant suffered seemed miraculously to disappear. Douglas knew that this would not last: The pain would return more frequently until it would be constant and excruciating. Douglas then told Grant that Iodoform, a derivative of chloroform that is a disinfectant, would help heal the ulcerated tonsil, which was also inflamed. Douglas told Grant that he should visit him twice each day to apply the medicine, as that would allow Grant to sleep and, for a time, to eat.

For the next week, Grant did as Douglas had instructed, keeping his malady and its seriousness a secret from his family. He wanted to spare Julia and his children, and he hoped that somehow his condition would improve. But by the end of October, both Julia and Fred were curious enough over Grant's frequent visits to Douglas to see him themselves. Douglas told them that Grant had cancer and that it was painful. He instructed Julia on how to apply the painkillers herself. At the end of their visit, Douglas told Julia and Fred that the disease would take a long course but that in the end, he said, Grant would die, most probably by choking to death.

Grant could not have been surprised by Douglas's pessimistic prognosis. Since June, when he had first noticed the pain in his throat, Grant had thrown himself into his writing. While in Long Branch, he had drafted, redrafted, and then rewritten one entire twenty-thousand-word article for the *Century* magazine and then begun a second. During that same period, he had talked on numerous occasions with his friend George Childs on what the prospective sale of his own memoirs might bring. Finally, in the moment immediately following Douglas's examination, Grant had asked him the one question Douglas might have expected—though from a patient far less prepared to hear the news than Grant: "Is it cancer?" That Douglas did not answer the question directly did not fool the general. While we do not know whether Grant, at the moment, knew for a certainty that he would die, his next destination certainly provides a clear hint that he did.

After Grant left Douglas's office, he took a streetcar to the office of Roswell Smith, president of the Century Company. Grant told Smith that he wanted to write his memoirs and hinted that more than one volume might be involved. He undoubtedly noted that, with one article completed for the *Century* and another on the way, it would be a relatively easy task to fill in the remaining battles and campaigns.

Smith was overjoyed. "General Grant has just been in," he noted, "spent some time and wants us to publish his book or books." Smith set about putting a draft of the agreement on paper. The Century Company would publish the book and hire agents to sell it across the country. The *Century* magazine, Smith believed, would provide a necessary advertising vehicle to promote the memoirs. There was no doubt in Smith's mind that the memoirs would be profitable both for his company and for Grant, but he was a conservative man by nature and not given to rewarding writers prior to the completion of their work. He told Grant that the Century Company would offer him a 10 percent royalty for his memoirs, with an expected sale of twenty-five thousand copies. When Grant did not object, Smith told him that a final agreement would be drafted for his review, but in the meantime Grant should continue to write his articles. Grant said that he was satisfied with the arrangement.

As ONE OF THE nation's most renowned throat specialists and a personal friend of the former general and ex-president, Dr. John Douglas realized that he faced a unique situation. He was treating America's greatest living ex-president and its greatest living general. Not only could he not afford to make mistakes, he wanted to give Grant the best medical care possible. Over a period of two weeks, from the time he first saw Grant until mid-November, Douglas consulted with Grant's personal physician, Fordyce Barker, and with two other specialists, Drs. Henry Sands and T. M. Markoe. Both were leaders in their field. All three, Barker, Sands, and Markoe, agreed with Douglas's diagnosis. Such agreement confirmed Douglas in his initial thinking about Grant's condition and the medical treatment he needed. But that was still not enough. During one examination, in early November, Douglas froze a part of Grant's ulcerated throat and excised it as a sample, which he sent to Dr. George Frederick Shrady, a stern-faced physician and a noted microbiologist. Not wanting to influence Shrady's opinion, he did not identify his patient, but he visited him in person to hear his opinion.

"This specimen comes from the throat and base of the tongue and is affected with cancer," Shrady told Douglas.

"Are you sure?" Douglas asked.

"Perfectly sure," Shrady answered with certainty. "This patient has a lingual epithelioma—cancer of the tongue."

"This patient is General Grant."

Shrady looked at Douglas for a moment before pronouncing his judgment. "Then General Grant is doomed," he said.

Shrady advised Douglas against operating on Grant, explaining that the cancerous tissue at the back of his tongue was already growing, had ruptured and spread cancer through the surrounding area. An operation would do the patient absolutely no good, Shrady said, and would only increase Grant's discomfort. In any event, it was too late. As Shrady later wrote: "The wisdom of such a decision was manifested in sparing [Grant] unnecessary mutilation and allowing him to pass the remainder of his days in comparative comfort. Relatively, however, it meant suffering for him until the end." Shrady believed that over the next months, Grant would go through periods of excruciating pain, relieved by short spells of exhaustion. The end would come soon, within a year at the most, perhaps much sooner. Douglas agreed with Shrady's diagnosis.

George Frederick Shrady was not simply well known in his profession, he was famous. He had been called on to provide medical treatment for President James A. Garfield after Garfield was shot by a spurned federal office seeker, and he had provided medical treatment to Frederick III of Germany. He was a clear and concise writer and an articulate and interesting speaker who was not given to subtlety or nuance. He was analytical to a fault and described the diseases he treated in a straightforward, blunt, even compassionless monotone. He was this way with Grant also, with the difference being that Grant, unlike many of Shrady's patients, appreciated such blunt demeanor. The two became good friends. For Shrady, the opportunity to treat Grant not only allowed him to study the course of the disease he had diagnosed, it provided him the opportunity to meet and assess the personality of a general who many Americans believed was much like Shrady—staid, upright, almost humorless. That Grant was personable and warm over the next months so influenced Douglas and Shrady that both left written accounts of their time with Grant, as did nearly everyone who befriended the ex-president.

Over the next months, Grant viewed Shrady as a kind of commander in chief presiding over an army—albeit one engaged in a losing campaign. Shrady always listened closely to Grant during such discussions, as it seemed that the former general was speaking about his own profession. During one discussion about the Civil War, for instance, Grant said that he viewed war as sometimes being necessary and added that he believed the more brutal the war, the more quickly it could be completed. "It was always the idea to do it with the least suffering," Grant said, "on the same principle as the performance of a severe and necessary surgical operation." Shrady immediately agreed, and though he did not say so at the time, that was precisely his philosophy in treating Grant. At key moments in the months ahead, Shrady would sometimes refuse to treat his patient, hoping that it would more quickly bring about his death, thereby putting an end to his suffering. Grant understood this perfectly well, and he accepted the discipline. Shrady also required Grant to give up cigars, which had doubtless contributed to the development of his cancer. If he must smoke, Shrady said, he must limit himself to three cigars each day. Grant agreed.

After his first meeting with Grant, Shrady wrote the following description of the ex-president: "It would hardly have been possible to recognize Grant from any striking resemblance to his well-known portraits," he said. "It was not until he bared his head and showed his broad, square forehead and the characteristic double-curved browlock that his actual presence could be realized. The difference in this respect between the lower and upper part of his face was to me most striking and distinctive. There was the broad and square lower jaw, the close-cropped full beard, the down-curved corners of the firmly closed mouth, the small straight nose with the gradual droop at its tip, the heavily browed and penetrating deep blue eyes and withal the head itself, which crowned the actual Grant with dignity and force."

At the end of November, with the pain in his throat now causing him visible discomfort, Grant visited Alden Goldsmith, a wealthy horse breeder, at Goshen, New York, where Goldsmith kept a stable. During the visit, Grant met with General George Meade's nephew. The two engaged in a lively conversation about Goldsmith's horses, and Grant, feeling relaxed, lit a cigar. "Gentlemen," Grant said, "this is the last cigar I will ever smoke." And it was. Soon thereafter, George Childs invited Grant to visit him in Philadelphia, but Grant declined. He wrote: "The doctor will not allow me to leave until the weather gets warmer. I am now quite well in every way, except a swelling in the tongue above the root, and the same thing in the tonsils just over it. It is very difficult for me to swallow enough to maintain my strength and nothing gives me so much pain as swallowing water. If you can imagine what molten lead would be going down your throat, that is what I feel when swallowing."

Knowing that he had less than a year to live, Grant began to plot out his last campaign. Bankrupt and now mortally ill, he viewed the publication of his memoirs not only as a fitting coda for his life, but as the sole means at his disposal to retrieve his reputation and leave his family financially secure. By the end of October 1884, Grant had nearly completed his second of four articles for the Century and was beginning to prepare a draft outline of his memoirs. He was assisted in this by his son Fred, who was his researcher and editor. Colonel Fred Grant was a devoted son with an eye for detail. He was quite unlike his father: He stood over six feet tall and could be irascible. In many ways he was more like Jesse Grant than his father. But unlike Jesse, Fred understood his father and, as an adult, had become his close friend. Over the final months of his father's life, Fred Grant would not only prove to be an indispensable researcher, an adept historian, and an accomplished editor, he would lead his father through the pain-racked days when writing seemed impossible. When Grant seemed at the edge of despair, when the pain of his illness threatened to undo his work, when visitors, family friends, and reporters pressed in on him, it was the ever patient Fred Grant who diverted their attention and allowed his father to work.

Grant also solicited the help of an old friend, Adam Badeau, who had been one of his closest aides during the war. A New Yorker by birth, Badeau first served during the war on General Sherman's staff but was transferred at Grant's request and joined him just prior to the Wilderness Campaign. Badeau continued to serve Grant during the first of his two terms as president and had accompanied him during his around-the-world tour. In many ways, people believed, Badeau was Grant's alter ego. Badeau knew, better than anyone, what Grant was thinking and what he would do; he prided himself on his ability to care for those routine duties that were beyond Grant's ken during his time as commander of the Union armies or as president. Badeau had spent seventeen years with Grant and was an adept student of his campaigns. When Grant retired from public life, Badeau wrote a three-volume account of Grant's wartime service, as well as a number of travel books and novels. Badeau's work makes for fascinating reading, and it is easy to see why he viewed himself as an important chronicler of his time.

While Badeau's work on Grant has faded with time, his book of sketches remains an important guide to his era, with its insightful portraits of Charlotte Brontë, Edwin Booth, and historian George Bancroft.

Badeau was not only an accomplished writer, he was a public figure; his views on Grant and on the war were solicited and admired, and his public talks on the war brought in huge crowds. In the immediate postwar period, it would have been difficult for any historian to write on Grant without referring to Badeau's definitive *Military Campaigns of Ulysses S. Grant*—a stolid but definitive account that added to Grant's stature. The chronicler and historian Henry Adams has left us a portrait of Badeau that recognized his unique gifts. "Badeau," Adams wrote, "was stout; his face was red and his habits regularly irregular, but he was very intelligent, a good newspaperman, and an excellent military historian." Adams was perhaps too kind to mention that Badeau was also a very difficult person: opinionated, ill-tempered, impatient, egotistical, and aggressively ambitious. He courted public notice and believed he deserved it.

Grant needed Badeau and his talents. He trusted Badeau's eye for detail and admired his writing ability. So it was only natural that after Roswell Smith and Robert Johnson visited Grant in Long Branch, Grant wrote to Badeau asking for his help with "the remaining articles for the Century." At the end of the summer, Badeau had come to Long Branch to discuss the memoirs with Grant and, while there, had edited large portions of the Vicksburg article and helped Grant outline his articles on the Chattanooga and Wilderness campaigns. But Badeau was hesitant to help Grant with his memoirs. He had his own work to do, he told Grant, and could not be diverted from it. The novel that he was working on, he said, needed his full attention. Grant was insistent—the memoirs promised to be a great success, he said, and they could not be completed without

Badeau's help. "The proposition was a great blow to me," Badeau later wrote, "for I had looked forward to going into history as his mouthpiece and spokesman, and, of course, if he wrote a new work himself my special authority would be superseded. But he was my chief and my friend and in trouble, and the work at least would distract him from his misery. We both considered his memoirs might yield from $30,000 to $50,000. I consented to aid him."

What he intended to do, Grant told Badeau, was write a full account of the Civil War "up to where the Wilderness Campaign begins, and then go back to the beginning." What Grant meant, of course, was that after finishing his work on the war, he wanted to go back to "the beginning" of his life. Sensing that in spite of his agreement in August Badeau might still reject his offer, Grant wrote to him that if he came to New York, he would put aside a room for him at his home on 66th Street. "There will be a room for you all the time you want to spend with us. There is also room for you to work on your own book. I have taken a room in the front—the small one at the head of the stairs for my own work and converted the boudoir into a bedroom . . . there is a table to write upon, and a large desk." Grant promised Badeau $5,000 out of the first $20,000 that the book earned and $5,000 out of the next $10,000. Grant knew that the offer was modest, but he told Badeau that he was bankrupt. He could not offer more.

The beginning of November found Grant, Badeau, and Fred at Grant's 66th Street home, researching and writing Grant's memoirs. Each day was consumed with the routine of outlining, researching, editing, writing, and rewriting. Badeau and Fred served as Grant's researchers, secretaries, fact checkers, critics, and readers. Grant's plan was to complete writing the four *Century* articles—on Shiloh, Vicksburg, Chattanooga, and the

Wilderness—and then string them together to get a complete picture of the Civil War. Only then, with the major part of the book completed, would Grant return to write about his early life. The midsummer suggestion of Robert Johnson that Grant focus on anecdotes and tell a story served him well. Yet for all of Johnson's suggestions and Badeau's experiences as a writer, Grant was still Grant, and his style was understated, almost skeletal. It was this understatement, this obsessive desire for absolute clarity, that had made Grant's written orders as a commander among the most precise of any American military officer; they remain models of clarity in a discipline that often rewards ambiguity. It was this same desire for precision in his orders that would now make him America's most successful memoirist.

In November, Grant discarded the initial plan for writing his book. He thought now that he could write the *Century* articles at the same time that he wrote his memoirs. Grant's writing habits were established through years of practice in composing military dispatches—a talent that, when used most effectively in the midst of battle, can make the difference between victory and defeat. He had mastered a precise, simple, clear, and understated style. But perhaps most important, he had learned to put events in their proper order. As he found it difficult to retrace his steps in life, so too now (when he was faced with the daunting task of writing what promised to be hundreds of pages of narrative) he found it difficult to write his book out of order. So he did what every good writer does. Despite the fact that he had already begun, and finished his article on Shiloh, he decided that the best place to start was at the beginning. So he started his account with a simple, spare, but powerful statement of fact: "My family is American, and has been for generations, in all its branches, direct and collateral."

HIS THROAT WRAPPED in a shawl, his head often covered from the early winter cold by a simple knit cap, Grant worked from the early morning each day to well into the evening in a small room at the head of the stairs on the second floor of his home on 66th Street. Two windows looked out onto 66th Street, which provided the light for his work. His bedroom was immediately available at the back of the library, and beyond it was Julia's room. George Childs sent flowers to Grant, sometimes two or three times each week, and Julia put them in water and set them nearby. Grant worked at a small desk that was filled with piles of notes compiled for him by the research of Badeau and Fred. Grant also made notes to himself and piled them, neatly, as reminders on small details and anecdotes from his life and his campaigns that occurred to him when he was not working—and which he feared he would forget. Nearby was a folding table on which Badeau and Fred had placed a series of maps, arranged in chronological order, that Grant could use when needed. In the beginning, before the spread of his disease became debilitating, Grant wrote out his memoirs in his own hand, returning to the pages he had written to edit or revise them after his son and Badeau had made their comments. Fred and Badeau worked in a nearby room, compiling research materials from books written on the Mexican war and the Civil War. Badeau used his own work as a reference, as well as *The Memoirs of General William T. Sherman*, which had appeared several years before.

"The small room at the head of the stairs was that in which he wrote the great part of his *Personal Memoirs*," Badeau later recounted. "The articles for *The Century* were remade there, and all the biographical part of the first volume, the story of the Mexican war, the beginning of his military career, indeed all of the work down to the Wilderness Campaign, and even the first draft of that—all were written and revised in that room, with me sitting by his side." At the end of each day, Grant reviewed the day's work and, with Badeau and his son, planned what needed to be done the next morning. His habits became those of a writer: He wrote, stopped, checked, and then plunged ahead, while Badeau and Fred checked names and dates and suggested revisions. Badeau and Fred discussed what Grant wrote as it became available, checked it against the records they had, made notes in the margins of the pages, and returned the material to Grant. He read their suggestions carefully and then revised what he had written or made deletions. It was exacting and physically exhausting work, but not without its rewards. Grant took pride in his writing and often called in Julia to reread a particularly well-written sentence or paragraph.

Harrison Tyrrell, an unappreciated and virtually unknown figure in Grant's life, did as much as anyone to ease Grant's suffering during the last months of his life and make it possible for him to write his memoirs. An African American servant, "the faithful Harrison"—as Grant and his wife affectionately called him—was Grant's valet, his messenger, and his confidant. Harrison was almost possessive in his care for Grant and would frown in disdain at the constant interruptions that Grant suffered. Badeau prided himself on his ability to read and react to Grant's moods, but it was Harrison who knew him best, and certainly as well as and perhaps even better than his own son Fred. His constant devotion was a source of wonder to Grant's doctors, who were forced to navigate past him to see the general. But they learned to use Tyrrell to gauge Grant's health and mood. Unfortunately, as an African American, Harrison Tyrrell has not been given proper recognition as one of Grant's closest friends in the last months of his life, and he has left us no written reflections on Grant's last days. But Tyrrell seemed always to be present when Grant needed him, and now, at the beginning of November, he staked out a place in the corner of Grant's study, watching him carefully as he wrote and providing papers for him when needed. As ever present as a trusted timepiece, he would rise occasionally to rearrange Grant's shawl when it slipped from his throat or fluff the pillow on his chair to make him more comfortable.

Harrison Tyrrell's role as Grant's valet was important for another reason: He had been with Grant during his visits to Douglas and Shrady and listened in rapt attention as Douglas outlined the course of medical treatment that Grant needed to undergo. Tyrrell understood that the disease was painful and fatal and that, as it progressed, Grant would become nearly debilitated. He also understood that Grant needed as much personal attention to his emotional state as to his physical condition—and that at times he would be near despair. It was vitally important that Grant maintain a good physical regimen, Douglas said. Before Douglas treated Grant in the privacy of the Grant home, Tyrrell accompanied the general during his twice daily visits to Douglas's office for treatment. They would leave Grant's 66th Street home and travel by streetcar the two miles to Douglas's office and then return in the afternoon for a second course of treatment. Douglas swabbed Grant's throat, a necessary and exhausting discomfort that eased Grant's pain and helped stem the early spread of the infection. When Douglas's treatment was impeded by a large molar at the back of Grant's mouth, Grant visited a dentist to have it extracted. Tyrrell was often required to swab the blood from the mouth of the nearly comatose Grant during his return to 66th Street—and he could be seen often, thereafter, providing support for the ailing ex-president.

By the second week of November, Grant was well into his

work on his memoirs, though he had not yet decided whether to sign the contract offered to him by Roswell Smith. He began his work by tracing his family history, his childhood in Ohio, his time at West Point, his service in the Mexican war, and the events leading up to the South's secession in 150 pages of sparse prose. Grant knew that this part of the book would be the easiest to compose, as it was dependent almost solely on his family history and his own memories. The more difficult work would come when he turned to his own campaigns, his four articles on Shiloh, Vicksburg, Chattanooga, and the Wilderness notwithstanding. His final task of compiling an index and appendixes and arranging for publication of battle maps would come later, when the major narrative of the work was finished. While Grant worked diligently and often for hours at a time, the effect of the cancer on his strength was apparent. His cough worsened, his throat seemed always aflame, and his voice began to fail. Harrison brought him milk on a tray twice each day and insisted that he drink it—as it was one of the few sources of nourishment he received. Within weeks of Douglas's diagnosis, Grant's health began to fail.

Grant's illness took an immediate toll on his family, despite his best efforts to protect Julia and his children from its ravages. But he could not hide his pain: The simple act of swallowing brought a searing discomfort, and he often had to leave the kitchen in the middle of a meal simply to keep his family from seeing his distress. His throat felt immediately better in the aftermath of being sprayed by a painkiller, a liquid mixture of cocaine and disinfectant, but the relief lasted only a short while and, after a time, only marginally eased his suffering. Any substantive meal was now stricken from his diet, and, always a hearty eater, he was imprisoned by a diet of soups and oatmeal. His throat began to constrict, and his breathing became more labored. Writing his memoirs helped to take his mind off his physical condition, even though, as time went on, the exhaustion that came from fighting the pain drove him to his bed. Seeing her husband in this condition was an emotional strain for Julia, who alternated between a hovering and suffocating concern and distant emotional rejection. One day she would be in despair, the next she was optimistic—and convinced that her regimen of prayer would save her husband. As Adam Badeau remembered:

> Mrs. Grant never could bring herself to believe she was about to lose him. A woman with many of those singular premonitions and presentiments that amount almost to a superstition but which yet affect some of the strongest minds, and from which General Grant himself was certainly not entirely free, she declared always, even at the moment which everyone else thought would prove his last, that she could not realize the imminence of the end. Her behavior was a mystery and a wonder to those who knew the depth of the tenderness and the abundance of the affection that she lavished on her great husband. Her calmness and self-control almost seemed coldness, only we knew that this was impossible.

Grant accepted Julia's advice on his disease, but he stubbornly refused her advice that he take a carriage during his daily visits to Dr. Douglas's office. It was only after Badeau angrily said that he would rather see Grant "stick a knife" in his throat than again use the streetcar that he agreed. That changed with the onset of winter, when Douglas and Shrady began to visit Grant in his home. The visits were formal, since neither doctor wanted to divert the general from his work. They stayed

only when he insisted. Both men found Grant nearly irresistible. When it was possible for him to speak without pain,
he shared his thoughts on the war. He liked to tell stories. Talking about the war became a way for him to refresh his memory
and to think through his own views. In the midst of this,
Shrady noted that Grant's physical fortitude was unique. He
could write for hours without a break, and he would sometimes go an entire day without a glass of water rather than suffer the pain that swallowing would induce. For Shrady, Grant
was an ideal patient: uncomplaining and willing to follow his
every instruction—no matter that, in the end, he could never
conquer his disease.

Shrady developed an unusual relationship with Grant and
was one of the few people capable of calming him during
Grant's most difficult periods. When Grant had difficulty sleeping and the pain of swallowing drove him to fits of coughing,
it was Shrady who often provided him with a means of finding rest. One evening, unable to sleep and gasping against the
pain that enveloped him, Grant called for Shrady. The doctor
appeared and noticed that Grant was in deep distress. He
calmed him after a time, but only after reassuring him that the
pain would pass and that he should lie down with his head on
a cold pillow. "Pretend you are a boy again," Shrady told the
ex-president. "Curl up your legs," he instructed soothingly, "lie
over on your side and bend your neck while I tuck the covers
around your shoulders." Grant turned over, as instructed.
"Now go to sleep like a good boy," Shrady said. Grant soon fell
asleep, and Shrady rose, noticing that Julia was standing in the
doorway. Attempting an apology, Shrady said that he hoped
Grant would not think that Shrady's exercise was demeaning,
he had wanted only to ease his pain. "There is not the slightest danger of that," Julia said. "He is the most simple-mannered
and reasonable person in the world, and he likes to have

persons whom he knows treat him without ceremony." With that she turned away and walked to her own room. Shrady was relieved—though he knew that now, for Grant, there would be many such nights.

∞∞∞

ON SEVERAL DAYS in October and for several more in November—as frequently as he was in New York and often simply to renew and deepen their friendship—Mark Twain would stop by to see Grant at his home on 66th Street. But if Twain noticed Grant's failing health, he did not mention it to his own family or friends or comment on it in his notebooks. Rather, he visited Grant because he found that he had a keen eye for detail and was always willing to talk about some odd or unique incident from the war. Grant, like Twain, was a storyteller and, like Twain, had a rich and unique body of experiences to recount. The difference between the two was that for Grant, the soul of a story resided in its elemental truth and its poignant humor, while for Twain, the soul of a story was in its rich detail—its mystery and nuance, its stunning and unpredicted outcome. While Grant loved to tell stories and told them well, Twain loved to tell tales, and the taller the tale the better. In his later years, one of the most compelling tales told by Twain was of how, in November 1884, he convinced the savior of the Union and the "greatest American since Washington" to allow him to publish his memoirs. It had all the hallmarks of a Twain story, and as Twain would have it, it also happened to be true. But as the story is recounted in his *Autobiography*, it was only *partly* true.

"One night in the first week of November, 1884 I had been lecturing in Chickering Hall and was walking homeward," Twain recalled in his *Autobiography*. "It was a rainy night and but few people were about. In the midst of a black gulf between lamps, two dim figures stepped out of a doorway and moved along in front of me. I heard one of them say, 'Do you know General Grant has actually determined to write his memoirs and publish them? He has said so today, in so many words.'"

The story is true—Twain *did* overhear two men talking about Grant's memoirs during a foggy November night in New York. But there is less mystery here than Twain implies. Twain knew quite well, and had known for many months, that Grant planned to write his memoirs. He also knew that the Century Company wanted to publish them. But Twain was coy for a purpose. He wanted the memoirs for his own publishing company, along with a book of those articles on the war that were being published in the *Century* magazine. Indeed, just as Roswell Smith and Robert Underwood Johnson were visiting Grant in Long Branch in September, Twain was urging his niece's husband, Charles Webster (his "nephew-in-law," as he called him), to maneuver their publishing firm into competition for some of the *Century*'s properties. "We want the Century's warbook," he wrote bluntly to Webster. "Keep on the best terms with those folks."

As told in his *Autobiography*, the dim figures disappear into the foggy night, never to be identified or referred to again. The mystery is never resolved by Twain in any of his writings—and the two men remain spectral figures whose late night conversation was overheard by Twain simply as a matter of great good fortune or, as he says, "an accident." In truth, Twain caught up to the two dim figures and introduced himself. A lively conversation resulted, with Grant's memoirs and their potential historical value, and profitability, at the center of the discussion. One of the men happened to be the *Century*'s Richard Watson Gilder, who invited Twain to his home on East 15th Street for dinner. Twain happily accepted. Over dinner, Gilder confirmed that the *Century* had been negotiating with Grant on the sale of his memoirs since late summer and that the negotiations were now nearly complete. Twain was apparently effusive and congratulated Gilder on the *Century*'s good fortune. While Twain later claimed that he heard the details of these negotiations from Grant, the truth was that Gilder was so confident of the *Century*'s offer that he was more than happy to tell Twain all about it. As far as Gilder was concerned, the only thing that remained was for Grant to sign the contract—which could happen at any moment.

"The thing which astounded me," Twain later wrote, "was that, admirable man as Gilder certainly is, and with a heart which is in the right place, it had never seemed to occur to him that to offer General Grant five hundred dollars for a magazine article was not only the monumental injustice of the nineteenth century, but of all centuries." In essence, Twain, forever calculating the profit to be made in any enterprise, was enthralled by the prospect of publishing Grant's book and was more than willing to outbid the Century Company for that privilege.

Early the next morning, in the wan hope of stopping Grant from signing any agreement with the Century Company, Twain hurried to his home. "I found him in his library with Col. Fred Grant, his son. The General said in substance this: 'Sit down and keep quiet until I sign a contract'—and added that it was for a book which he was going to write." Twain did as he was told and sat in a nearby chair, but he waited for just the right opportunity to state his views. "Fred Grant was apparently conducting a final reading and examination of the contract himself," Twain later recounted. "He found it satisfactory and said so and his father stepped to the table and took up the pen. It might have been better for me, possibly, if I had him alone, but I didn't. I said, 'Don't sign it. Let Col. Fred read it to me first.'"

Grant stopped for a moment, looked at Twain, and then agreed with his request. It would do no harm. Twain read the contract and shook his head in apparent disgust. The contract detailed how Grant would get a 10 percent royalty on the sale of his memoirs. "Of course this was nonsense—but the proposal had its source in ignorance, not dishonesty. The great Century Company knew all about magazine publishing. No one could teach them anything about that industry. But at that time they had had no experience of subscription publishing and they probably had nothing in their minds except trade publishing."

Twain stayed Grant's hand, argued against the Century Company's terms, and attempted to convince Grant to give the book to him instead. Grant was suspicious, but Twain pressed him: "Strike out the ten per cent and put twenty per cent in its place," he said, the tenor of his voice rising insistently. "Better still, put seventy-five per cent of the net returns in its place." Grant thought about this for only a moment, then shook his head. He said that the Century Company would never agree to pay those terms. Twain responded that what the Century Company wanted did not matter, since there was "not a reputable publisher in America who would not be very glad to pay" Grant the 20 percent or even the 75 percent that Twain had suggested.

Grant was surprised by this but again shook his head. He said that he wanted to sign the contract as presented to him, and he felt honor-bound to do so. Twain moved in, concentrating, marshaling his arguments: "I pointed out that the contract as it stood had an offensive detail in it which I had never heard of in the ten per cent contract of even the most obscure author—that this contract not only proposed a ten per cent royalty for such a colossus as General Grant, but it also had in it a requirement that out of the ten per cent must come some trivial tax for the book's share of clerk hire, house rent, sweeping out the offices, or some such nonsense as that. I said he ought to have three-fourths of the profits and let the publisher pay running expenses out of his remaining fourth." Grant eyed the contract again and looked up at Twain, conceding that the figures that he cited were correct. But he repeated that he thought he ought to sign the agreement, as he had been negotiating with Smith, Johnson, and Gilder for many months. He would feel bad about backing out of the agreement now and, he added, did not want to be thought of as dishonest or as a thief, a "robber of a publisher."

But Twain could see that Grant was wavering. What you are doing, Twain said, is not "robbery." In fact, Twain added, if Grant did not sign the contract, he would be "put in heaven with two halos." Twain's rhetoric was not swaying Grant, who continued to hold the wavering pen over the contract. As Twain later wrote: "The General was immovable and challenged me to name the publisher that would be willing to have this noble deed perpetrated upon him. I named the American Publishing Company of Hartford. He asked if I could prove my position. I said I could furnish the proof by telegraph in six hours. . . ."

Fred Grant, who knew that the American Publishing Company had successfully published many of Twain's books, was persuaded by this argument, but his father was not. To break the impasse, Fred suggested to his father that the contract "be laid on the table for twenty-four hours and that meantime the situation be examined and discussed." Fred added that "this thing" was not a matter of "sentiment," but rather "a matter of pure business and should be examined from that point of view alone." Twain agreed, but he knew that Fred's argument still might not sway Grant: "He was most loathe to desert these benefactors of his. To his military mind and training it seemed disloyalty." Finally, believing that it would do no harm to postpone signing the agreement for another day, Grant accepted Fred's advice. But, he added, he felt a certain loyalty to the Century Company because they had come to him first. Twain played his trump card. "In that case," he said, "I'm to be the publisher because I came to you first. I came to you in the company of William Dean Howells three years ago." Grant thought about this for a moment, remembered the incident, and was struck by what Twain said. "Well, that's true," he said. Twain concluded by saying that Grant should consider selling his book by subscription, and he laid out the arguments for doing so. Grant listened closely, but he did not respond. Instead, he agreed, he would give the matter some thought over the next twenty-four hours.

With that, the conversation ended, and Grant, Twain, and Fred rose and walked into the next room, where Julia and one of Grant's admirers, Lew Wallace, were waiting. Wallace was an old friend of Grant's and one of his former subordinates, having fought with him at Fort Henry, Fort Donelson, and Shiloh. But Wallace's military career was not viewed positively—he had had to defend himself from Grant's criticism that he had been late in reinforcing the Union army at Shiloh. Grant later graciously admitted that his criticism of Wallace was unfounded, and the two remained good friends, but the damage was done: After Shiloh, Wallace was never again given a major combat command, and at the end of the war he resigned his commission to follow a career as a politician and diplomat. He became the governor of New Mexico, minister to Turkey, and a well-known public figure in Washington. But Wallace is not remembered now for his career as either a politician or diplomat. Handsome and articulate (though often insufferably egotistical), Wallace gained immortality, and national fame, in

1880—when he published *Ben-Hur*. The book was admired by Grant and his wife, and Grant had stayed up all of one night reading it.

Awed by such an array of literary power, Julia greeted the three men with a smile. "There's many a woman in this land would like to be in my place and tell her children that she once stood elbow to elbow between two such great authors as Mark Twain and General Wallace," she said.

Wallace was flattered, but Twain thought the remark was amusing. "Don't look so cowed, General," he said to Grant wryly—his tongue firmly in his cheek. "You have written a book, too, and when it is published you can hold up your head and let on to be a person of consequence yourself." The four talked for a short time and then Twain left, but he returned the next morning to talk to Grant once again; this time, he was certain, he could marshal all the arguments to convince Grant that he, and not the Century Company, should publish his memoirs. Twain found Grant in an expansive mood and apparently willing to consider Twain's proposition. He talked about the memoirs written by General William T. Sherman and published several years earlier in a two-volume set.

"Sherman told me that his profits on that book were twenty-five thousand dollars. Do you believe I could get as much out of my book?" he asked Twain. Twain said that he thought Grant would make an even larger profit, because while Sherman's book had been published "in the trade," Grant's would be offered by subscription. A book sold by subscription, he said, would sell eight to ten times the amount of a book sold in bookstores by a publisher. Grant listened closely to this, but he was still skeptical. He told Twain that he doubted he was right, for he had told Roswell Smith that if Smith gave him $25,000, he would write his memoirs—but that Smith had turned him down.

Twain, though he might have been exasperated by having to restate his arguments, suddenly saw that all of the maneuvering had provided him with the opportunity he needed. Instead of referring Grant to the American Publishing Company, he told Grant he would sell the book himself. "Sell *me* the memoirs, General," he said. "I am a publisher. I will pay double the price. I have a checkbook in my pocket; take my check for fifty thousand dollars now and let's draw the contract."

Grant was stunned, but he rejected Twain's offer. He said that he and Twain were friends and that he would feel bad if Twain failed to make a profit out of his book. He would never allow a friend to run such a risk, he said. Twain was adamant: "Give me the book on the terms which I have already suggested that you make with the Century people—twenty per cent royalty or in lieu of that seventy-five per cent of the profits on the publication go to you, I to pay all running expenses such as salaries, etc., out of my fourth."

Grant laughed and asked just how Twain expected to make a profit out of such a deal. Twain answered that he would make $100,000 within six months. Grant thought about this for a moment, but he still refused to make a commitment. Instead, he said, he would refer the matter to an old friend, George Childs, who would review the Century Company's offer and Twain's and make his own recommendation.

This was only half a victory for Twain, but he knew that it was better than none at all. Just twenty-four hours before, Grant's pen had been poised in midair over the contract offered by Roswell Smith. Now, Twain believed, Grant not only was determined not to sign the Smith contract, he was seriously considering Twain's offer. If it came down to a matter of pure money, as Twain knew it would, then Grant's memoir would be his. The clinching argument, he believed, had come when Grant realized how much money he could make by offering his book through a subscription service. That was what Twain was about to do with his most recent book, *Adventures of Huckleberry Finn*, which was now being offered to the public. The prospect that *Huck Finn* would sell well were good. But writing it had not been easy. He had picked the manuscript up, written, laid it down, picked it up again, and then put it aside, apparently forgotten, until in a spurt of creative energy, he had finished. In all, it had taken Mark Twain nine years to write *Adventures of Huckleberry Finn*. It is unlikely that he could have finished it at all, were it not for Ulysses S. Grant.

Samuel Clemens in 1851.
Courtesy The Mark Twain House, Hartford, Connecticut

The Clemens home in Hannibal, Missouri.
Courtesy Library of Congress

The first Grant home, at Point Pleasant, Ohio.
Courtesy Library of Congress

The irascible and opinionated
Jesse Grant. *Courtesy Library of Congress*

Hannah Grant.
Courtesy Library of Congress

"Hardscrabble"—
the Ulysses S. Grant farm
in Missouri. *Courtesy
Library of Congress*

The Grant family, shortly after Grant's promotion to
commander of the Union armies. Grant and Julia and their
four children: Jesse Root Grant, Ulysses S. Grant Jr. ("Buck"),
Ellen Grant ("Nellie"), and Frederick Dent Grant (in his
West Point uniform). *Courtesy Library of Congress*

HARPER'S WEEKLY.

JOURNAL OF CIVILIZATION

NEW YORK, SATURDAY, JULY 16, 1864.

LIEUTENANT-GENERAL GRANT AT HIS HEAD-QUARTERS.—[Photographed by Brady.]

The classic pose of Grant as he appeared on the cover of *Harper's Weekly*—at his headquarters during the last campaign of the Army of the Potomac.
Courtesy Library of Congress

Robert E. Lee leaves the McLean House after surrendering to Grant in April 1865.
Courtesy Library of Congress

The definitive Mark Twain—complete with white suit and cigar. *Courtesy Library of Congress*

Livy Clemens with her children: Susy, Jean, and Clara. *Courtesy The Mark Twain House, Hartford, Connecticut*

Ulysses S. Grant,
president of the United States.
Courtesy Library of Congress

William Dean Howells.
Courtesy Library of Congress

Ulysses S. Grant in retirement.
Courtesy Library of Congress

Mark Twain's Connecticut home—which nearly
bankrupted him. *Courtesy Library of Congress*

Mark Twain at Quarry Farm, where he wrote most of
Adventures of Huckleberry Finn. Courtesy Library of Congress

"TURN HIM LOOSE!"

The views of *Huckleberry Finn* that we have come from the classroom: The raft in Twain's book, we are told, symbolizes Huck's and Jim's freedom. We are told that all of the bad things that happen to Huck and Jim take place when they are not on the "bucolic" river, but on land: There are feuds; people are tarred and feathered; there is a casual killing, an attempted lynching, and a fraudulent prince; Jim is nearly captured; and slave hunters, seen and unseen, gallop through the underbrush. We are also taught that Twain tried to tell us a number of other things: that the individual is good and society is bad; that it is possible for an innocent boy to be brought to manhood by a dignified slave; that the South was itself in bondage to its own romantic vision—that the steamboat *Sir Walter Scott* (named for a writer whom Twain loathed) is an icon of this vision. But through all of these great adventures and despite all the words written about Twain and Huck and Jim, there is a deep disquiet, what the critic Neil Schmitz calls "a large and suspicious reef," in Twain's manuscript. This reef shows itself at the end of chapter 16 and is vividly marked in tone and viewpoint. Even in the pages of

Twain's manuscript there is a decided shift, perceptible in the slight slant of Twain's penmanship—as if his writing had taken on a new intensity. Before chapter 16, *Huckleberry Finn* is what Twain had wanted it to be—"another boy's book"—but then, and quickly, it becomes deadly serious. "The first significant rift in the manuscript occurs here," says Schmitz. "Cairo is missed, the raft is destroyed, Huck and Jim plunge to the bottom of the Mississippi. Mark Twain stops work on the project."

That is true. At the end of chapter 16, writing in a rush of creativity, Twain had Huck and Jim poised on the raft above Cairo in southern Illinois—on the lookout for the Ohio River. And freedom. The rush of the writing is almost palpable as Twain sketches the steamboat bearing down on Huck and Jim in the dark. When the steamboat strikes their raft, Huck goes overboard.

> I dived—and I aimed for the bottom, too, for a thirty-foot wheel had got to go over me, and I wanted it to have plenty of room. I could always stay under water a minute; this time I reckon I staid under water a minute and a half. Then I bounced for the top in a hurry, for I was nearly busting. I popped out to my arm-pits and blowed the water out of my nose, and puffed a bit. Of course there was a booming current; and of course that boat started her engines again ten seconds after she stopped them, for they never cared much for raftsmen; so now she was churning along up the river, out of sight in the thick weather, though I could hear her.

And then, right there, Twain stops. He hits his "reef." Through the rest of that summer of 1876, Twain struggled with his book. But he could not continue, and at the end of the summer he put the book away. It was not to be revived for another seven years. The "reef" that caught Twain was more than a simple sandbar disguised by clear but shallow water. It was one of those famous "snags" that nearly caught Twain as a riverboat captain—and it consisted in a single question that plagued Twain until 1883: Why would a slave seek freedom by going *south*? We do not know precisely how Twain resolved this problem (for he never gave any explanation of his own), but what we do know is that in 1883, after fits and starts of writing that included composing a chapter on a southern feud between the Shepherdsons and the Grangerfords (which was published in the *Century* magazine in December 1884), he returned to *Huckleberry Finn* and finished it in a flurry. It may be that Twain simply decided the problem could not be resolved and so continued on by ignoring it. Or it could be that he decided that one way to write past the "reef" was by hoping no one would notice; he would send Huck and Jim south because that is what he was determined to do. Or it could be that a resolution to Twain's problem suggested itself to him during a journey he made on the Mississippi in the late spring of 1882. Twain's trip down the Mississippi, the first he had made since being a riverboat captain, was undertaken not simply to fulfill a promise he had made to his publisher to write a book about his steamboat years, or to retrace his youth, or to discover a way to revive Huck's great river adventure, but to visit those cities and battlefields that his friend Ulysses S. Grant had made famous during the Civil War.

———— ⚙ ————

TWAIN COULD ILL AFFORD his Mississippi journey. While he was a successful and even lionized writer, his lifelong search for personal wealth was still a dream. Happily married and the father of three young girls—Susy, Clara, and Jean (born in 1880)—Twain was spending as much in one month on household expenses as most people of his era earned in a single year. He was a great believer in a sound education (he provided tutors for his daughters) and good health (at one point he employed seven nurses to look after his children), rarely denied himself any culinary delight (and hired a cook to prepare them), and loved to play the host. Grant's friend William Tecumseh Sherman visited Twain's home in Hartford, as did the actor Edwin Booth and the British poet and essayist Matthew Arnold. Twain regaled all his callers with tall tales and stories from his youth, pacing up and down his living room and stabbing the air with his cigar. He was loud, ribald, scathingly small-minded, and intemperate, and then, eyeing his wife, he became self-effacing and apologetic. His guests loved the entertainment, and Twain loved to entertain. But it was expensive. To offset these habits, Twain dabbled with inventions and schemes. But not one of them, including a complex history game he invented to entertain and educate his children, ever made him wealthy, and most of them were decided failures. Part of the problem was with his writing, for while Twain was prolific, none of what he wrote netted him the profits he had enjoyed in his earlier years.

After setting aside *Huckleberry Finn*, Twain wrote and published *1601*, a tale of Elizabethan England. But instead of continuing to write, he took his family on an expensive and extended seventeen-month tour of Europe. When the tour ended, the Clemenses returned to Hartford, where Twain installed a telephone—one of the first private phones in New England (it made him mad, he said, "just to hear the damn thing ring"). Then he was off to Chicago, where he introduced Grant at a reunion of the Army of the Tennessee (and gave his famous "To the babies" toast) before returning home to face his bills. But he was revived by his travels, thrilled by the public acclaim that greeted his introduction of Grant, and rearmed with an avalanche of new book ideas sparked by his European tour.

Over the next eighteen months, Twain wrote and published *A Tramp Abroad* and completed and published *The Prince
and the Pauper* (which he had begun two years previously,
before his European tour). His daughter Susy, who was to
become his lifelong friend (and who knew him better than
anyone, perhaps even better than Livy), recognized the genius
in the book, even though she was still an adolescent. "It is unquestionably the best book he has ever written," she said. "It
troubles me to have so few people know, I mean *really* know
him. They think of Mark Twain as a humorist *joking* at everything. That is the way people picture papa. I wanted papa to
write a book that would reveal something of his kind sympa-
thetic nature. The book is full of lovely charming ideas and oh,
the language, it is perfect!"

Not everyone thought so. In New York, the journalist
Whitelaw Reid—a veteran Civil War correspondent and the
most accomplished and publicly lionized voice of Horace Gree-
ley's *New York Tribune*—was not only unimpressed by Twain's efforts, he was increasingly irritated by what he viewed as a
minor Twain boomlet among their mutual friends. Reid seemed
a little taken aback, even envious, of Twain's growing public
stature and was not intent to add to it. But he knew how
vengeful Twain could be when he felt cornered or betrayed,
having felt his wrath when Reid's paper gave *Roughing It* a
decidedly mixed review, which was followed by a less-than-
enthusiastic notice on *The Gilded Age.* Twain sensed his lack of
enthusiasm. "He is a contemptible cur, and I want nothing more
to do with him," he wrote to Charles Dudley Warner at the
time. "I don't want the *Tribune* to have the book at all." That
suited Reid, who viewed Twain as the worst sort of hypocrite—
writing send-ups of the rich and famous, all the while wishing
he had their money. He said as much now, when it was suggested to him that Twain's good friend William Dean Howells

review *The Prince and the Pauper*. Reid smelled a setup, for How-ells admired Twain, and Reid knew he loved Twain's new book. "It isn't good journalism," Reid wrote to his personal friend, the diplomat John Hay, "to let a warm personal friend and in some matter literary partner, write a critical review of him in a paper which has good reason to think little of his deli-cacy and highly of his greed." This was not nearly enough: "As you remember, we agreed, years ago, a new book by Twain is not a literary event of such importance that it makes much difference whether we have our dear friend Howells write the review, or whether indeed we have any review."

While Reid eventually relented and Howells was commis-sioned to write a review of *The Prince and the Pauper* for Reid's paper, Twain was enraged by Reid's insults, which had now en-tered the New York and Hartford literary grapevine. He began to plot his revenge, telling Charley Webster to look through every edition of the *New York Tribune* for the past months to see whether Reid had written anything about him that he might have missed. Twain was convinced that Reid was on a "cru-sade" to ruin his reputation—a campaign that, Twain believed, could be trumped only by one of his own. He dropped every-thing, hastily putting aside his plans to publicize *The Prince and the Pauper* as well as his preparations for his journey down the Mississippi, to focus on Reid. With his Mississippi book now all but forgotten, he began to plan a "dynamitic" biography of Reid that would destroy his reputation. He hired a stenogra-pher to take down his background views on Reid for inclusion in the biography and hired researchers to trace Reid's career. He filled his notebooks with his ravings: Reid was a "skunk," a "eunuch," the "missing link," and he noted with pride that his friend Ulysses S. Grant (who suspected reporters in general, but especially those who trailed after national armies) had once referred to Reid as "Outlaw Reid." It was only when Livy in-

tervened that Twain regained his balance. She pointed out that
Webster had found little evidence of a Reid vendetta, a position
confirmed by his friend, the reporter John Russell Young.
Twain was humbled, but he attempted to deflect the public
mutterings his ranting had sparked. It was not his fault: "What
the devil could those friends of mine have been thinking
about?" he asked himself ruefully.

The Reid episode was an interlude, but it reinforced in
Twain his belief that he must focus on his work, not his feuds.
Still, he found it hard to believe anyone (even the "idiot"
Whitelaw Reid) could underestimate the power of *The Prince
and the Pauper.* It was not only a unique book and unlike anything he had ever written, it was proof that, at the age of forty-
six (and now a father, husband, successful writer, and public
figure), he was at the height of his powers. The only thing missing, and the only thing left that he truly wanted, was money. If
it had not been clear to him before, it was clear to him now—
the only way he could become wealthy was to write. For Twain
that meant finishing his unfinished and promised manuscript
on his apprenticeship as a Mississippi steamboat captain and
then return to his boy's book in an attempt to finish it. Traveling again on the Mississippi was not something Twain had originally wanted to do, for he had dropped the subject of the
Mississippi after a series of sketches, *Old Times on the Mississippi,*
had appeared in the *Atlantic Monthly* in 1875. But by early 1882
the subject had rekindled his interest, primarily because the
journey would give him a chance to revisit his boyhood home
of Hannibal. His plan was to take a steamboat from St. Louis
south to New Orleans, before heading back north, all the way
to Minnesota. Now that he had fixed his mind on the project,
the trip on the Mississippi looked like the perfect way to refill
his "dry well" and fulfill a promise he had made to his wife
many years before. "When I come to write the Mississippi book,

then look out!" he had written to Livy. "I will spend 2 months on the river & take notes, & I bet you I will make a standard work."

Twain prepared for the trip by making extensive notes of what he remembered from the river, including anecdotes from his time as a pilot. He then hired a stenographer in Hartford by the name of Roswell Phelps and gave him careful instructions on how to write out what he said—and which of his outbursts he could ignore. Twain invited William Dean Howells to accompany him, but Howells's responsibility as an editor made this impossible. When Twain instead decided to invite his publisher, James Osgood, on the trip, Howells kidded him on his selection "I am sorry Osgood is with you on this Mississippi trip," he wrote, "I see it will be a contemptible half-success instead of the illustrious and colossal failure we could have made it."

The three, Twain, Phelps, and Osgood, left New York for St. Louis on April 17, 1882. They arrived in St. Louis on April 19 and immediately booked passage on the *Gold Dust*. On the evening of April 20, the steamboat departed St. Louis and headed south. Twain talked, Osgood listened, and Phelps took notes. The author was in rare form, meeting people on the river who remembered him, who knew of his friends, and who could trade stories about who had died when and from what, and these observations fill the pages of Twain's journals. "Mike Gavin is dead. Strother Wiley is alive. All the Cables are dead," he wrote at one point, but that was by no means the end of it—pages later there are another half dozen names.

Twain was irrepressible, talking to pilots, traders, gamblers, river men, clerks, war veterans, and engineers and meticulously following his own progress on navigation charts. He was joined on the river by his old mentor and friend Horace Bixby, the riverboat pilot ("Sam was ever making notes in his memorandum book, just as he always did," Bixby remembered). In what surely must have been an uncanny and chilling recollection of what he had left off with in chapter 16 of *Huckleberry Finn,* the *Gold Dust* nearly destroyed a river raft—and nearly at the same point in the river where Huck and Jim "dived" and "aimed to find the bottom, too." The incident (as with Huck and Jim) took place on a pitch-black night just south of Cairo, Illinois, where the cold, clear water of the Ohio River joins with the muddy, sluggish Mississippi. Twain was clearly thrilled by the near accident and brimful of the vigor of his youth: "To-night when some idiot approaching Cairo didn't answer our whistle but rounded to across our bows and came near getting himself split in two I felt an old-time hunger to be at the wheel and cut him in two,—knowing I had fulfilled the law and it would be his fault. By shipping up and backing we saved him, to my considerable regret—for it would have made good practical literature if we had got him." One day later, Twain's appetite for piloting was finally satisfied by Lem Gray, the *Gold Dust*'s captain. "When we got down below Cairo, and there was a big, full river—for it was high-water season and there was no danger of the boat hitting anything so long as she kept in the river—I had her most of the time on his watch. He would lie down and sleep, and leave me there to dream that the years had not slipped away; that there had been no war, no mining days, no literary adventures; that I was still a pilot, happy and care-free as I had been twenty years before."

Twain passed Columbus, Kentucky, near where Grant had once fought, and stopped at New Madrid, near a series of bends and backwashes in the Mississippi River that form the shifting western boundaries of Kentucky and Tennessee. Twain was not so much looking forward to seeing New Madrid as he was to hearing once again the story of a famous southern family fight—and one that he would put on paper in chapter 17 of *Huckleberry Finn* as the Grangerford-Shepherdson feud. The real-life feud, however, was the vindictive and murderous family quarrel between the Darnells and the Watsons, who vied over a spot of land near the ironically named Compromise Landing, in Kentucky. When Twain was a riverboat pilot, the head of the Darnell family was General Henry M. Darnell (who was no more a general than Ulysses S. Grant's father-in-law, "Colonel" Dent, was a colonel). Darnell became the model for Saul Grangerford, the unforgettably harsh and amoral "gentle-man" of Twain's *Huckleberry Finn*. Dan Watson was the model for the head of the Shepherdson clan. In his journal of his Mississippi journey, Twain comments at length on the Darnell-Watson feud and remembers the time when, as a pilot, he was nearly caught up in it and witnessed the shooting of a nineteen-year-old boy, apparently one of Dan Watson's sons: "He dodged among the wood piles & answered their shots. Presently he jumped into the river & they followed on after & peppered him & he had to make for the shore. By that time he was about dead—did shortly die." Twain compared notes on the feud with the *Gold Dust*'s pilot. "Well, nearly all of those old parties were killed off," he said. "They used to attend church on the line (part of the church in Tenn. Part in Ky.). Both Dar-nell & Watson went to that church armed with short guns, & neither party would allow the other to cross the line in that church."

While Twain was intent on finishing his sketches on the Mississippi River, and had embarked on his journey for just that purpose, finding a way to finish *Huckleberry Finn* remained his greatest puzzle. He thought of the puzzle throughout the trip, constantly adding ideas for the novel in his notebook in the form of scribbled and often curious anecdotes. Passing Co-lumbus, he jotted down a reminder to himself to write "some rhymes about the little child whose mother boxed its ears for inattention & presently when it did not notice the heavy slamming of a door, perceived it was deaf." This anecdote was later written into *Huckleberry Finn* during an episode where Jim anguishes about his own daughter and remembers the time when he disciplined her for not listening to him, only to find that "she was plain deef en dumb, Huck, plumb deef en dumb—en I'd ben atreatin her so!" This—that black parents could love their children as much as or more than whites loved theirs (undermining a vicious belief of slaveholders used to salve their consciences for breaking up and selling families)—was a common theme in Twain. He had touched on it in an 1874 story written for the *Atlantic Monthly* ("A True Story"), after hearing his sister-in-law's cook talk about her children at Quarry Farm: "Well, sah, my ole man—dat's my husband—he was lovin' an' kind to me jist as kind as you is to yo' own wife. An we had chil'en—seven chil'en. Dey was black, but de Lord can't make no chil'en so black but what dey mother love 'em an' would give 'em up, no, not for anything dat's in this whole world." Howells saw that the story was a landmark. "The rugged truth of the sketch leaves all other stories of slave life infinitely far behind," he wrote.

Twain then visited Memphis and Helena, Arkansas. He barely commented on either city, except to note the increased use of profanity, the loose sidewalk boards, and the poverty. But he wrote at length about Napoleon, Arkansas, a town on the Mississippi just south of Helena. "The town (2000 inhab.) used to be where the river now is," Twain wrote. "Washed entirely away by a cut-off and not a vestige of it remains—except one little house and the chimney of another which were out in the suburbs once." But Twain was not finished with the Darnells and Watsons—and committed himself to telling his story of their feud in the pages of his book on the Mississippi and again in *Huck Finn*. The spite and ugliness in men such as

Grangerford worked on Twain, and it all came out in his most cutting and damning commentary on the South's genteel civilization: "Col. Grangerford was a gentleman, you see. He was a gentleman all over; and so was his family. He was well born, as the saying is, and that's worth as much in a man as it is in a horse, so the Widow Douglass said, and nobody ever denied that she was the first aristocracy in our town; and pap he always said it, too, though he warn't no more quality than a mud-cat himself."

This was a kind of obsession with Twain, for he saw in their murderous hatred the seeds that had led to the war and changed his life forever. At the root of it all, Twain felt, was the southern tradition of fake gentility, the terrible fraud of propriety that men like "General Darnell" took pride in and which led to their murderous hatreds. Behind it all was the "maudlin Middle-Age romanticism" of Sir Walter Scott, whose books adorned the shelves of southern homes and who "made every gentleman in the South a Major or a Colonel or a General or a Judge, before the war; and it was he, also, that made these gentlemen value these bogus decorations. For it was he that created rank and caste down there, and also reverence for rank and caste, and pride and pleasure in them." This was Twain on his journey south, as he sharpened his criticism of his native land and began to envision how he might allow his readers to see that land through the eyes of a young boy. It is hard to miss the plot that Twain was now weaving so effortlessly—for the only way to tell the southern story and the only way to free Jim and Huck was to send them south. It was a conclusion that Ulysses S. Grant had come to during his own journey down the Mississippi almost exactly nineteen years before: The only way to free the slaves, to end the war, to go home, he had said then, was to go south.

TWAIN GOT HIS first glimpse of Vicksburg on April 26. Once a booming river town and a major southern trading crossroads, Vicksburg was "now a country town." Other things had changed: "Instead of coming in above the town as we used to do, boats come through a cut-off now which is clear below the town. In low water boats can get up only to [the] lower verge of town, where they land." That same day Twain wrote, in an apparent pun, of Grant's strategy to "cut-off" the rebel garrison in Vicksburg by using a "cut off" in the Mississippi River and moving south of the town. Grant's maneuver, as Twain noted, did not immediately work. In response to this failure, Grant did not retreat, did not retrace his steps or start again, but moved farther south in a strategy that so confused his enemy that before they could respond, Grant's army moved inland and captured Mississippi's capital, Jackson, before turning back west for the assault on Vicksburg. The city fell on July 4, 1863, one day after Lee was defeated at Gettysburg. More than any of his other laurels, the campaign to capture Vicksburg would be cited as evidence of Grant's military brilliance. "Rode to National Cemetery," Twain wrote, and then parenthetically noted the number of the graves of the dead—"16,600"—and quoted the motto over the gateway: "Here rest in peace 16,600 who died for their country in the years 1861 to 1865." It was a solemn day for Twain, and one that he wanted to put behind him. He looked forward to arriving in New Orleans, which was just two days south on the river.

Twain arrived in New Orleans on April 28 and visited the St. Louis Hotel, where he had once stayed. It reminded him, he said, of "one vast privy." He met with the writers George Washington Cable and Joel Chandler Harris, and they had dinner

with Edward Burke, editor of the *New Orleans Times-Democrat.*
The wine flowed liberally, and Cable's "thin but melodious
tenor" mingled "sweetly" with the music. On Sunday morning,
Twain and Harris went to a cockfight (which both found vicious) and that evening attended services at a black church,
where, Harris observed, the sermon was "bold, logical and
powerful." Twain thought otherwise: "Clergyman then lined a
hymn. Offer prayer very well,—better than some white minister because it was short." Twain toured the city and was feted
by its mayor, who offered him the use of a tugboat to tour the
city's shipyard. "I did the steering myself," he wrote tri-
umphantly to Livy. "There was a fine breeze blowing, the sun
was bright & orange groves and other trees about the plantation dwellings in full & sumptuous leaf. Splendid trip." Twain
was pleased that at least one part of New Orleans had not
changed: "The big bar of the St. Charles Hotel with its saw
dust floor and groups of mint-julep suckers is as it was 25 years
ago," he wrote, "and they seem to be the same juleps and the
same suckers; no change noticeable. The cool porch overlooking the street just the same, with its big columns."

Twain's notebooks reflect his joy at returning to the river,
even though it had changed to such a degree that he had difficulty remembering what had happened where. "The river is so
thoroughly changed that I can't bring it back to mind even
when the changes have been pointed out to me," he wrote. "It
is like a man [who] points out to me a place in the sky where
a cloud has been. I can't reproduce the cloud. Yet as unfamiliar
as all the aspects have been to-day I have felt as much at home
and as much in my proper place in the pilot house as if I had
never been out of the pilot house. I have felt as if I might be
informed any moment it was my watch to take a trick at the
wheel." The river also brought back sometimes bitter and painful memories. Riverboats were no longer the kings of industry—

the engine of trade was now the railroad, whose boxcars and marshaling yards dotted the shoreline. Nor was the river the boundary of the frontier, as it had been on the eve of the Civil War. People were now moving farther west, using other rivers as their highways. Twain also noticed that the once prosperous villages along the river were now mired in poverty, a fact he attributed to the backwardness of the South and a remnant of slavery's stain. He commented endlessly on the South's impoverishment, on its people's lack of industry; both were ugly reminders of its defeat. On his way back north, Twain looked longingly and quietly at the spot in the river where the *Pennsylvania* had caught on fire and where his brother was fatally burned. He visited with old friends, stopped at plantations, and commented in awe at the lush green of the lower Mississippi Valley. But always, and no matter where he stopped, talk of the river ceased and talk of the war began. The war was still the South's obsession.

"What a splendid moon," Twain said, looking out over the Mississippi one evening.

"Laws bless you, honey," came the rejoinder, "you ought to see dat moon befo' de waw."

People talked about the war as if it had just ended, though it was now fully seventeen years in the past. In nearly every conversation, the Civil War and the South's loss in the war was a constant subject. "People talk only about the war," Twain wrote. "Other subjects are started, but they soon pale & die & the war is taken up." The obsession surprised Twain, but at key moments in his journey south it reinforced in him the importance of Grant. Clearing the Mississippi of rebels and Grant's capture of Vicksburg had been a key to the Union victory. It occurred to Twain that the Mississippi had served as much as a highway of freedom for Union troops as it had for the young Samuel Clemens. As the river was the nation's greatest economic artery, so too its conquest spelled the end of the southern cause and the end of slavery. That Grant looked at the Mississippi in the same way Huck did—and that Sam Clemens and Jim did— is so true as to be clichéd, but there are a number of remarkable similarities between Grant's descent of the Mississippi to capture Vicksburg and Huck's descent of the river to free Jim.

It is surely a coincidence that Grant made eight attempts to capture Vicksburg (and, except for the last, failed at each) and that Huck and Jim came ashore eight times on their journey south before Jim was finally freed. It is undoubtedly a coincidence that both Grant and Huck came south, in part, to flee their fathers. It is probably a coincidence that Cairo, the last free city in the North, is the starting point for both journeys. And it is certainly a coincidence that victory was no more assured for Grant when he left Cairo at the head of his army than freedom was for Jim when he headed south on the raft with Huck. All of these may simply be and surely are accidents of history and literature. But they are remarkable nevertheless. So if we now see, in Huck, a bit of Sam Grant—heading south because it was the only way home—it is because Mark Twain put him there.

Always there is Jim: For while the Mississippi River transformed Sam Clemens into Mark Twain (from a Missouri boy into an adult writer), and while the Mississippi transformed Captain Sam Grant into General Ulysses S. Grant (the greatest military commander in American history), the transformation it worked on Jim and on African Americans was even more profound. Jim was freed because of his journey on the river; and because of Grant's victory on the river, men and women held in bondage were emancipated. Grant's journey was intended to free the slaves, Huck's to free *a* slave. We do not know, and cannot know, how Twain shaped his ideas of Huck or whether he purposely, or perhaps unconsciously, melded the personalities of a young boy and the son of a tanner. We must believe Twain when he says that Huck was patterned on his boyhood friend Tom Blankenship. But such knowledge does not detract from Twain's special attraction to what Grant meant and symbolized: For in descending the Mississippi in the summer of 1863, and in a series of brilliant maneuvers surrounding, besieging, and then capturing Vicksburg, Grant had transformed the "war for the Union" into a "war to free the slaves"—the political conflict became a social revolution. So, too, after chapter 16, *Adventures of Huckleberry Finn* becomes less of "another boy's book" and more of a symbolic journey. In the final and most remarkable coincidence, we note that just as an army of one, a scruffy young white boy named Huck, had the fate of one African American in his hands, so too an army of thousands of white boys clad in blue carried with them the fate of hundreds of thousands of Jims. Great writers and great teachers teach us about Huck Finn, but the last great words of the book, and the most profound written by Twain, are spoken not by Finn but by Tom Sawyer—who understood what this journey that Twain and Grant and Huck and Jim were on was all about.

"They hain't no right to shut him up! Shove!—and don't you lose a minute. Turn him loose! He ain't no slave; he's as free as any cretur that walks this earth!"

───❧───

ON MAY 14, Twain arrived in Hannibal. He was greeted by the town's most eminent citizens and registered in the Park Hotel. Twain was treated as a conquering hero by Hannibal, though he remarked in a fit of regret mixed with nostalgia that the town's boys paid more attention now to the railroad than they did to steamboats. It almost seemed as if time had passed him by. "The romance of boating is gone now," he wrote. "In Hannibal the steamboat man is no longer a god. The youth don't talk river slang any more. Their pride is apparently railways—which they take a peculiar vanity in reducing to initials ('C B & Q')—an affectation which prevails all over the west. They roll these initials as a sweet morsel under the tongue." Not surprisingly, it was not just Hannibal's boys who had changed, but the city itself. "Alas! Everything was changed in Hannibal," Twain wrote, "but when I reached third or fourth sts the tears burst forth, for I recognized the mud. It, at least, was the same—the same old mud—the mud that Annie McDonnold got stuck in."

Twain left Hannibal three days later aboard the *Minneapolis* and headed north. His goal was to traverse the Mississippi in its entirety, and he was keenly interested in seeing the upper part of the river. But after leaving Hannibal, he was anxious to return to Hartford. The trip was all but over—Osgood had departed in St. Louis, and Twain was uncomfortable with the cold weather. He remembered his youth and Hannibal as always basking in the summer sun and the Mississippi as a river of summer currents. Minneapolis was cold, and for Twain it hardly seemed a river town. "Arrived per Minneapolis at St Paul & put up at the Metropolitan," he wrote on May 21. "Cold as the very devil." He did not stay long. Three days later, after an uneventful train ride through the Midwest, he was in Philadelphia, commenting again on the ignorance of the human race. "Entering Philada, May 24, cut an Italian laborer's foot off. The train stopped, & crowds gathered to gaze. Our tracks ought to be fenced—on the principle that the majority of human beings being fools, the laws ought to be made in the interest of the majority."

Now anxious to begin writing again, Twain returned to Hartford to gather together his family. He stayed only several days in the city and then, as was their habit, he, Livy, and their three daughters retreated to Elmira and Quarry Farm for the summer. Twain's Mississippi trip had been exhausting but exhilarating, and that summer—the summer of 1882—Twain quickly finished up his reminiscences of his time as a riverboat pilot on the Mississippi (this book was published as *Life on the Mississippi* in May 1883) and gave it to his companion on the trip, James Osgood, to publish. Twain was pleased to be finished with the book, but he was far from satisfied with Osgood's efforts to sell it. Twain and Osgood spent months debating the book's sales potential until finally, frustrated with the debate, he instructed his nephew-in-law to help Osgood as much as he could; he then washed his hands of the effort. "Charley, if there are any instructions to be given [to Osgood], you may give them," he wrote to him. "I will not interest myself in anything connected with this wretched God-damned book."

Twain wrestled with Osgood throughout the early months of 1883, deriding his skepticism that *Life on the Mississippi* would not have good advance sales. Once again, as had been the case with his former publisher, the American Publishing Company, Osgood seemed suspiciously disinterested in the value of Twain's work. Twain pushed Osgood to rely on subscription sales instead of sales from bookstores. The sales from a book "in trade" (when a subscription campaign is complete), Twain wrote to Osgood, "don't amount to a damn," and he added, "Just write that up amongst your moral maxims, for it is truer than nearly anything in the Bible."

Life on the Mississippi appeared to mixed reviews. The *New Orleans Times-Democrat* praised the work as "the most solid book that Mark Twain has written," while the *Athenaeum*, a leading literary journal, labeled it a "disappointment" and "vulgar." At the end of 1883, it was clear to Twain that the sales of the book would never match his expectations. Like *The Prince and the*

Pauper, Twain wrote to Osgood, the sales of *Life on the Mississippi* were a disappointment. "*The Prince and Pauper* and the *Mississippi* are the only books of mine which have ever failed. The first failure was not unbearable—but this second one is so nearly so that it is not a calming subject for me to talk upon," he said. "I have never for a moment doubted that you did the very best you knew how, but there were things about the publishing of my books which you did not understand. You understand them now, but it is I who have paid the price of the apprenticeship."

Putting aside his disappointment, Twain plunged once again into a series of disastrous business ventures. As always, money was a constant concern. In early 1883, Twain and William Dean Howells collaborated on a number of plays, hoping to make a fortune on the stage. Together they wrote *Colonel Sellers as a Scientist* and then interviewed prospective producers, directors, and actors. But their ardor soon cooled when it became apparent that the play would not yield a significant profit, and certainly not enough to offset the organizational headaches that writing and producing the play would cause. Twain lost interest and felt guilty that he might have let down his best friend, but Howells was dismissive. "Never mind about the play," he eventually wrote, "we had fun writing it anyway."

Twain revived his interest in marketing his inventions. He designed a new typesetting machine (which would, years later, bankrupt him), spent hours thinking about marketing a "perpetual calendar," once again tried to interest the public in the history game that he had designed for his daughters, and invented and attempted to market an improved "bed clamp" (designed to keep a mattress from sliding off its anchor). He strung together a series of letters to Charley Webster, imploring him to investigate other business opportunities, and invested (and lost) thousands of dollars in stock transactions. Finally, having exhausted all of his opportunities except one—and now, in the summer of 1883 once again at Quarry Farm after a season of entertaining in Hartford—he retrieved the manuscript of *Huckleberry Finn* and began to write. This time the well did not run dry.

"I haven't piled up MS so in years as I have done since we came here, three weeks ago," he wrote to Howells. "Why, it's like old times to step straight into the study, damp from the breakfast table, & sail right in & sail right on, the whole day long, without thought of running short of stuff or words." Twain worked, diligently and without interruption, throughout the summer. "I wrote 4000 words today & I touch 3000 & upwards pretty often, & don't fall below 2600 on any work day," he continued in his note to Howells. "And when I get fagged out, I lie abed a couple of days & read & smoke, and then go at it again for 6 or 7 days . . . am away along in a big one that I half-finished two or three years ago. I expect to complete it in a month or six weeks or two months more. And *I* shall like it, whether anybody else does or not."

He was even more effusive with his family. "I haven't had such booming working-days for many years," he wrote to his mother in July. "I am piling up manuscript in a really astonishing way. I believe I shall complete, in two months, a book which I have been rolling over for 7 years. This summer it is no more trouble to me to write than it is to lie." At the end of August, he again wrote to Howells: "I'm done work for this season. I've done two seasons work in one, & haven't anything left to do, now, but revise. I've written eight or nine hundred MS pages in such a brief space of time that I mustn't name the number of days." It had, indeed, been an astonishingly productive summer. While he had completed parts of chapter 17—the Grangerford-Shepherdson feud—over the previous seven years, from June 1883 to the middle of September of that same year,

Twain had written the end of the feud and taken Huck and Jim down the river and then, after Jim was freed, back north. He was satisfied with the finished book, though there is no evidence that he believed it would be forever remembered as his best.

Just after finishing the manuscript, Twain gave it to his wife to read, as was his habit. Livy was his best and at times harshest critic. She was especially impatient with some of his more vulgar phrases, which she would pencil through, often without suggesting any alternative words or phrases. At other times she would simply, silently, turn down the page on an offending phrase, knowing that her husband knew very well what offensive words he was using. Her daughters were a part of this process; they often sat and watched as she read their father's work simply to delight in the looks on her face. As his daughter Susy later recounted: "Ever since papa and mama were married papa has written his books. . . . And she has expergated [sic] them. Papa read Huckleberry Finn to us in manuscript and then he would leave parts of it to mama to expergate [sic], while he went off to the study to work, and sometimes Clara and I would be sitting with mama while she was looking the manuscript over, and I remember so well . . . one part perticularly [sic] which was perfectly fascinating it was to [sic] terrible, that Clara and I used to delight in and ho, with what despair we saw mama turn down the leaf on which it was written, we thought the book would almost be ruined without it. But we generally come to think as mama did."

Twain, ever the prankster, played on his wife's prudity. "For my own amusement and to enjoy the protests of the children I often abused my editor's innocent confidence," he wrote in his *Autobiography*. "I often interlarded remarks of a studied and felicitously atrocious character purposely to achieve the children's brief delight, and then see the remorseless pencil do its fatal work. I often joined my supplications to the children's for mercy . . . and pretended to be in earnest. They were deceived and so was their mother. . . . But it was very delightful, and I could not resist the temptation. . . . Then I privately struck the passage out myself."

Disappointed with Osgood and embittered with his experience with the American Publishing Company, Twain vowed that *Huckleberry Finn* would be published by his nephew-in-law—who seemed to understand the exotic details of selling a book by subscription. Being published by Charley Webster would also allow Twain to oversee every part of his book's production. Twain gave Webster the manuscript in mid-1884, with strict instructions that the book could be issued only after a large number of copies had actually been sold. At first, Twain and Webster agreed that *Huckleberry Finn* would be published as a companion book to *Tom Sawyer* in time for Christmas 1884. Doing this, Twain believed, would enhance his new book's sales and spur those who had not read *Tom Sawyer* to purchase it. Selling forty thousand copies of this combined set would provide Twain with the financial bonanza he needed to meet his mounting bills. But Twain abandoned the idea just weeks after it was proposed: Christmas was a full six months away, and he realized that it would take at least that long to hire the subscription agents, correct the constant mistakes made in the galleys, hire a good illustrator, and make certain the final typesetting was up to his standards. Doing so for two books meant postponing the publication of *Huckleberry Finn* by six months, which was something Twain was simply unwilling to do. By the end of the summer of 1884, Twain was deep into reading the proof sheets for the books and here and there, dabbling with the manuscript itself. There was still much to do, with the publication date just four months away. Nor had Twain yet decided on an appropriate dedication.

"My book is draining me day by day, and will continue the drain several months yet," he protested to Howells. "My days are given up to cursings—both loud and deep—for I am reading the Huckleberry Finn proofs. They don't make a very great many mistakes, but those that do occur are of a nature to make a man curse his teeth loose."

It was well worth the effort: Slowly but certainly, Twain realized that *Huck Finn* might be the one book for which he would always be remembered. The revelation was slow but certain and aided by the months that Twain (and Webster) took from the book's completion to its final publication. Twain always tinkered with his writing. But somehow *Huckleberry Finn* was different. He found he needed to make few corrections, and while he would change a word here and there, the more he read the manuscript, the more he understood its depth. Twain felt as many writers do upon completing a book—it was as if someone else had written it. As he reread *Huckleberry Finn*, that feeling became more overwhelming.

He read and reread the manuscript, making it perfect; by August he was satisfied with the final product. All the while, he continued to monitor Webster's sales efforts and to insist that the book not be published until it was certain to make a profit. "There is no date for the book," he had written to Webster in April. "It can issue the 1st of December if 40,000 have been sold. It must wait till they are sold, if it [be] seven years." To help promote the book, Twain met with the *Century* magazine's Richard Watson Gilder in the early summer of 1884 and offered him three chapters of *Huckleberry Finn* for serialization— "An Account of the Famous Grangerford-Shepherdson Feud," "Jim's Investments, and King Sollermun," and "Royalty on the Mississippi." Originally, Gilder had pressed Twain to provide him with four chapters—one each for the first months of 1885— but Twain wanted to sell excerpts of the book to as many publishers as possible and as soon as possible. Gilder settled for three excerpts, the first one scheduled to appear in December 1884.

Canvassing for the book was begun by Webster in November, at about the same time that Twain was talking to Gilder about Grant's memoirs. In December, the *Century* magazine published "The Grangerford-Shepherdson Feud." It was deemed by many critics to be among Twain's best writing and the one chapter in *Huckleberry Finn* that his readers could identify as a comment on southern culture. Twain was pleased by Webster's efforts: By December, the canvassing effort was well under way, and the book's agents were reporting that sales continued to be strong. For the first time in many years, and perhaps for the first time since the publication of *Tom Sawyer*, Twain was optimistic, even ebullient. For Twain, the prospective success of *Huckleberry Finn*, fifty thousand copies of which would actually be in the canvassers' hands in February 1885, brought an end to three years of crisis that had been fueled by rising expenses and only moderate success. The future looked bright; *Huckleberry Finn* gave every indication of being a popular success, and Twain and Grant were on the verge of an unprecedented publishing venture. When Twain left Grant's home on November 20, he was convinced that the general would give Charles L. Webster & Co. the rights to publish his memoirs. "We have the book," Twain told Webster at the end of November; all that needed to be done now was for Webster to draw up a contract for Grant to sign. Of course, it was not that simple.

———— ❦ ————

WHILE GRANT WANTED Twain to publish his book, by the end of November he had realized that his memoirs provided him and his family their last chance to escape penury. Given the failure of Grant & Ward, the still rankling betrayal by his business associates, and the public embarrassment at having to borrow money to feed his family, the former president was not about to leap into a new business venture, at least not until he was certain that it would be successful. Moreover, in a stark departure from his previous habits, Grant decided that this time he would make his decision after consulting with someone he trusted, a person who had proven business acumen and nothing to gain by giving him the best advice possible. After Twain left Grant's home on November 20, Grant talked about Twain's offer with Fred, Julia, and Adam Badeau and then wrote to George Childs, asking him to come to New York to review the book offers and handle the negotiations. Childs arrived in New York in early December with his lawyer in tow and spent several days reviewing the bids. For once, Grant had chosen the right friend: Childs was not only honest, his friendship was unquestioned. He had been responsible for raising the money that had allowed Grant to purchase his home on East 66th Street—a campaign conducted by Childs when he learned that Grant, who had resigned his army commission to run for president, was no longer eligible to receive a military pension.

Childs was well established and well respected, and he lived modestly. He was also an amateur historian and sophisticated writer. He understood business and was friends with some of the nation's most successful businessmen, including those who had provided funds for Grant's New York home: J. Pierpont Morgan, Anthony Drexel, Thomas Scott, and Hamilton Fish, who had served as Grant's secretary of state. Perhaps most important of all, Childs never used his friendship with Grant to promote his own career or business interests, and he deliberately and carefully made certain to see Grant only when he was not engaged in any official or personal business. In sum, Childs had nothing in common with the likes of Ferdinand Ward or the fast-buck artists who provided the gilding for his age, and he was cautious and conservative in both his investments and his advice. Childs looked at the various contracts that Grant had received and gave them to his lawyer for perusal.

It did not take long for Childs to decide what Grant should do. By early December, Childs was convinced that Twain had made the better offer. But he was not yet ready to make his verdict official. That did not bother Grant; with his condition now stable, he was able to continue his writing and was nearing completion of a full draft of the first part of his memoirs. In many respects, retracing his childhood, his years at West Point, and his service in the war with Mexico were the most difficult parts of his memoir to write, as they required that he revisit some painful episodes. The section of his memoirs on the war with Mexico posed a particular challenge, for while it had provided Grant with a much needed apprenticeship on war (and revealed the first glimmerings of his genius), he felt he needed to be honest with his readers on his own feelings, no matter how controversial they might be.

He wrote bluntly and plainly about the fighting, his role in the fighting, and his own political misgivings on America's policy toward Mexico. He called the conflict a political war carried out by a particular political party for its own profit. He stated, again plainly and bluntly, that the United States sent its troops to the border of Mexico to provoke a fight, and while he made it clear that he opposed the war, it was also clear why he would never have made his opposition public—Grant was a soldier, required to obey orders, and he would not court oblivion. "Experience provides that the man who obstructs a war in which his nation is engaged, no matter whether right or wrong, occupies no enviable place in life or history," he wrote. "Better for him, individually, to advocate 'war, pestilence, and famine,' than to act as obstructionist to a war already begun." Grant's writing is emotional but reasoned, and he relies on principle and common sense. But there is no doubt, and Grant left no doubt, of where he stood. In private, his views on the war with Mexico were more outspoken and more controversial. As he once told a friend: "I do not think there was ever a more wicked war than that waged by the United States on Mexico. I thought so at the time, when I was a youngster, only I had not moral courage enough to resign: I had taken an oath to serve eight years, unless sooner discharged, and I considered my supreme duty was to my flag. I had a horror of the Mexican War, and I always believed it was on our part most unjust."

He spent weeks working and reworking his chapters on the war with Mexico, and the effort left him exhausted, but he plunged on, into early December, slowing his pace only once winter had set in and the pain in his throat worsened. Childs and his lawyer talked with Charles Webster about the contract for the memoirs, and Webster told Childs that he would give Grant a choice: He could accept a 20 percent gross royalty on sales or 70 percent of the net profits. Grant found this excessive, writing to Twain that he (Twain) might be bankrupted by such terms. He then asked which would be better, and Twain responded that Grant should accept 20 percent of gross royalty on the sales of the book. Grant was satisfied, and soon thereafter, Childs gave Grant his decision. "Give the book to Twain," he said. Grant looked at his son, who nodded his agreement. Twain celebrated in a note to Charley Webster. "If these chickens should really hatch according to my account," he wrote, "General Grant's royalties will amount to $420,000, and will make the largest single check ever paid an author in the world's history. Up to the present time the largest one ever paid was to Macaulay on his History of England, 20,000 [pounds]. If I pay the General in silver coin at $12 per pound it will weigh seventeen tons."

When Grant read the contract given to his lawyer by

Charley Webster, he was surprised by its liberal terms. Twain seemed to have remembered everything. Not only did he stipulate that Grant would be entitled to a 20 percent royalty payment, Twain had put aside $10,000 as an advance—a highly unusual practice at the time—for Grant's use in the belief that while Grant was writing his book, he and his family would need money to live on. Twain also stipulated that in the case of Grant's death, the rights to the book would be assigned to Julia, who could then transfer the book to Charles Webster for the sum of $1,000—a detail that Twain had had Webster insert in order to keep Grant's creditors from seizing the book's profits. While Grant said that he was complimented by Twain's thoughtfulness, he would not be needing the $10,000 advance and would not apply for it. Grant's lawyer, Clarence Seward, took this in but said that Grant would sign the contract, as written, and immediately transfer title of the book to Webster for the sum of $1,000. He told Webster that while Grant considered it a point of personal pride to forgo the $10,000 advance, the family was in desperate straits and could use the $1,000 (in place of the advance) as soon as it could be released. When Webster related this story to Twain, the author shook his head. "It was a shameful thing," he later recounted, "that a man who had saved his country and its government from destruction should still be in a position where so small a sum—$1000—could be looked upon as a godsend."

If the *Century*'s Roswell Smith, Robert Underwood Johnson, or Richard Watson Gilder were embittered by Twain's maneuverings or angered by Grant's apparent change of heart, they did not say so. The three acted honorably. Only Robert Johnson betrayed any sense of bitterness. "The General, who knew nothing of the customs or etiquette of the publishing business, had been won over by a humorist," he said. "It was not time for a contest, nor was it a book to be contended for in the customary fashion, and Mr. Roswell Smith, pocketing his disappointment, wrote a polite and generous letter to the General conveying our regrets that we were not to be associated with so distinguished an enterprise and our cordial wishes for its success." It was best, Smith, Johnson, and Gilder knew, to bow to Grant's wishes gracefully. In the end, and in spite of all their fine words about the "customs" and "etiquette" of American publishing, it was neither customs nor etiquette that dictated Grant's decision. This was a business decision—it was all about what publishing in America has always been about. Money.

"THEY HAVE EXPELLED HUCK"

New York celebrated the winter season of 1884 with renewed vigor: The nation was at peace, and a recently elected Democratic president was just weeks away from taking office. But for Ulysses S. Grant, the onset of winter brought new worries. By mid-December, the pain that had been throbbing in his throat had worsened and his sleep was interrupted by constant nightmares. He cried out in the night as his son Fred stood listening at his door. "The cannon did it," he shouted one night. "I am detailed from four to six," he shouted on another. He told Douglas about his dreams. "It seemed to me as though I had been traveling in a foreign country. I had only a single satchel and I was only partially clad. I found to my surprise that I was without any money and separated from my friends. While I was traveling I came to a fence. There was a stepping stile but it led up to only one side. I climbed over, however, and then found I had left my satchel on the other side. Then I thought I would go back home and borrow the money from Mrs. Grant. I asked her for it, but she said she had only seventeen dollars and that was not enough; at which I woke."

This was vintage Grant and a reflection of his three greatest worries: having to retrace his steps, having to ask for money, and being unable to care for Julia. Because of the dreams and the difficulty he had sleeping, he now had to be coaxed to bed; his greatest fear was that he would choke to death, his second greatest that he would somehow find it impossible to finish his memoirs. If he died now, he knew, he would leave his family, his reputation, his medals, and little else. By Christmas he was depressed, moody, and unable to work. He sat in his chair each day, looking out the front window onto 66th Street, barely moving, never smiling, and rarely talking. At regular intervals Julia looked in on him and rearranged his pillow, while Badeau and Fred sat in the next room, waiting vainly for him to retrieve enough of his strength to continue his writing. On some days he coughed so hard that he could barely breathe. As the sun set on New York's cold and dark winter nights, his coughing and wheezing would worsen until, exhausted, he slept.

Julia wrote to Grant's old friend and fellow commander William Tecumseh Sherman, worried that her suffering husband had now retreated into sullen silence. Sherman, who still did not know all the details of Grant's illness, was philosophical and almost nonchalant in his answer, reassuring Julia that Grant would soon emerge from his funk. This was typical of Grant, Sherman wrote. He had seen it before. Grant was the kind of man who was always silent, especially in a time of crisis. He remembered, he said, how often generals would argue about strategies in Grant's presence, particularly in the midst of battle, but that Grant would always sit quietly, waiting for the argument to end before issuing his orders. He was a calm man, particularly so when things seemed the worst, Sherman said, so she should not worry about him. Julia appreciated the advice, but she kept her own counsel, for Grant was not simply in the midst of a crisis, he was fighting for his life. Grant knew this better than anyone. At the beginning of January, with his strength slowly fading, Grant wrote to an old friend, Edward P. Beale, hinting at his illness and saying that he was weak and could not sleep. Swallowing was now an unrelenting agony, and he began to lose weight. "My tears blind me," Julia wrote to a friend, "General Grant is very ill. I cannot write how ill."

Julia Grant had been steeled by John Douglas to expect the worst, and she was ever mindful that her husband's sullen suffering was simply one aspect of his illness. Douglas had told her that Grant would sometimes feel like giving up, that he would refuse to eat, be unable to sleep, reject his work, and become fatalistic. This was all of life's work, he had told her, and the normal mental preparation necessary for a person who was terminally ill. Eventually, Douglas knew, Grant would come to accept his illness and work through the pain that seared his throat. Where Badeau, Fred, and Julia were horrified by Grant's deteriorating condition, and shocked to see him nearly defeated by the prospect of his certain death (for he had never looked defeated, even in the midst of the bloodiest war in American history), Douglas watched the slow but certain evolution of Grant from a man who rejected the fact of his illness and fought it to one who came to accept his own mortality. It could be, Douglas believed, that Grant's descent into depression would lead to his quick death, but it was more likely that within weeks, perhaps days, Grant would revive and discover new ways to continue living.

That Grant was able to keep his disease a secret from even his closest friends for such a long period of time is a testament to his commitment to maintaining his privacy. As a public figure, Grant had learned how to separate his personal life from his public responsibilities. But his secret would not last forever, and in early January, within days of the letter he had sent to Edward Beale hinting at his illness, a Philadelphia newspaper reported that Grant was sick. The paper stated that it did not know the cause of Grant's illness but supposed it was the result of his financial troubles. The New York papers made similar reports, and a number of enterprising reporters sought out Grant's doctors for their views. Both of them repeated the same story, apparently at Grant's insistence, that while it was true that Grant was sick, he was expected to make a quick recovery. "The General is cheerful and comfortable," they said, "and spends a great part of his time at home writing the history of his military life, which is to be published by a prominent house as soon as it is completed." Fordyce Barker stated publicly that he and Douglas had prevailed on Grant to give up cigars, which he had done. "The improvement in his condition since then is marvelous," he said.

Reporters kept on the trail, believing that neither Barker nor Douglas was being completely honest. They sensed in their patented answers a slight hesitancy and a well-rehearsed optimism. A report circulated in January that Grant had cancer of the tongue, a rumor that became so persistent that Douglas was required to reject it. "Gen. Grant has not cancer of the tongue," he said. "The difficulty is in his mouth, and it is of an epithelial character. The irritation has now been greatly relieved, and that is all I feel at liberty to say."

It was clear now to Grant's friends that something was terribly wrong, in spite of a number of newspaper stories that testified to Grant's good health. Certainly those who visited him just after the New Year noticed a remarkable difference in his appearance from what it had been just weeks before. Grant was not yet gaunt, but he had lost the girth that marked his time as a public figure. His voice was strained, he winced when he swallowed, and he made an effort to keep from laughing, which aggravated his throat and caused him pain.

Because of his increasingly serious physical deterioration, and obviously fearful that his closest friends would gather around him in pity, Grant carefully pleaded that he was too busy with his book to see anyone. He deliberately shunned invitations to attend reunions or meetings. Such a step was unusual for Grant, for while he had always been a private person, and certainly not given to boisterous or rousing oratory, he enjoyed meeting veterans and looked forward to visiting with his old comrades. One of the few exceptions that Grant made to this rule came when he learned that his old friend William T. Sherman was in New York. Sherman stopped by to see Grant at 66th Street just before Christmas 1884, and the two talked for several hours. Grant told Sherman that he was writing his memoirs and hoped that he could count on his support. Sherman was surprised. He knew Grant well and understood how difficult it would be for him to retrace and recount his campaigns. But he said that he would of course help Grant in any way he could.

If Sherman noticed any deterioration in Grant's health, he either ignored it or was satisfied with Grant's explanation—that he was ill but recovering and was under the care of doctors. What stunned Sherman was not Grant's physical appearance, but the unmistakable signs of his material distress. Sherman left his meeting with Grant convinced that his old friend and commander was near penury, with little hope for financial recovery. The bankruptcy of Grant & Ward, he decided, had had a far greater impact on Grant than Grant would ever admit and certainly was far more devastating than Sherman had thought when he had first heard of it back in Ohio. He told a reporter that he was so disturbed by Grant's condition that he would give him half his pension—if he thought that Grant would take it. Of course, as Sherman well knew, Grant would never accept such a gift, even from a good friend like Sherman. So on December 28, Sherman arranged for a meeting with a number of financiers in the hopes that they would begin a subscription for Grant's relief. The group, which included George Childs, Cyrus Field, and Anthony Drexel (as well as others who had provided the funding that allowed Grant to purchase his 66th Street home), agreed that they would raise $150,000 for Grant.

Sherman saw Grant again on New Year's Day, but he did not mention the December 28 meeting: He must have known that Grant would reject such an offer. Instead, the two talked about the war and about Grant's memoirs. Sherman repeated his offer to help Grant and was complimented when he was told that his old commander was using his own book as a research guide in recounting those campaigns in which the two had served. While Sherman did not express his concern about Grant's financial situation, he knew it was only a matter of time before Grant found out that he, Childs, and others were attempting to raise money for his relief.

But it took far less time than even Sherman would have predicted. Just one week after Sherman's visit, Grant wrote a carefully worded letter to his friend George Childs. Much to Grant's chagrin, the letter found its way into the New York Tribune, where it appeared on January 8: "Through the press and otherwise I learn that you, with a few other friends of mine, are engaged in raising a subscription for my benefit. I appreciate both the motive and the friendship which have dictated this course on your part but, on mature reflection, I regard it as due myself and my family to decline this preferred generosity. I regret I did not make this known earlier." Grant's message was firm and unmistakable: While he might be penniless, he would keep his pride, he would not accept gifts, and he would not be an object of pity. Of all his friends, Sherman should have known this best.

———❧———

WILLIAM TECUMSEH SHERMAN is one of the few military commanders in American history whose caricature fits his character. "War is hell," he said, and then he set out to prove it. He was a strange but imposing man: ramrod straight, disciplined, tough-minded, direct, forceful, and remote. His face was pockmarked, and if there is a photograph of him smiling, no one has ever found it. He was known for his volcanic temper. For all of that, Sherman was often uncertain. He was plagued by self-doubt and given to bouts of depression. He suffered a nervous collapse early in the war, though this was more a loss of confidence than a loss of nerve. Grant retrieved him from this despair. Like Grant, Sherman was born and raised in Ohio, but he suffered from tragedy early in his life, when his father died, leaving eleven children. Sherman was taken in by the family of Thomas Ewing, a U.S. senator. After attending West Point and serving in the Mexican war, Sherman went west but resigned from the army to pursue a career as a lawyer and businessman. He was marginally more successful in his private life than Grant, and while he managed to go bankrupt during the California Gold Rush, he came east and deftly managed the accounts of a major St. Louis banking firm. For a time he served as superintendent of the Louisiana State Military Academy.

When war broke out, Sherman became a colonel of volunteers, served in Kentucky, and then was a commander at Bull Run, where his actions were called into question. He suffered from the criticism and was plagued by a sense of failure. Newspaper reports said he was "crazy." He recovered his balance in time to participate in the taking of Fort Donelson, where he willingly provided Grant with the reinforcements he so desperately needed. On the second day of the Battle of Shiloh, he led the attack that recovered Grant's position. Grant and

Sherman became the best of friends just months after Shiloh, when, out of frustration with the actions of his superiors—who vetoed most of his ideas for prosecuting the war—Grant considered resigning from the army. Remembering what Grant had done for him after his own bout of depression, Sherman talked him out of it and pledged his continued loyalty. The friendship between the two was solidified by these crises. When Grant was named commander of all the Union armies, he promoted Sherman and placed him in command of all the armies in the West. Grant was never given to open affection, so his praise for Sherman was so out of character as to be remarkable: "How far your advice and suggestions have been of assistance, you know. How far your execution of whatever has been given you to do entitles you to the reward I am receiving, you cannot know as well as I do. I feel all the gratitude this letter would express," he wrote to Sherman after being named commander of all the Union armies. Sherman felt the same way about Grant, though he typically used fewer words to express it. He told a friend that he had as much faith in Grant as "a Christian has in his savior."

The two remained friends after the war, though Sherman counseled Grant to stay out of politics. He worried when Grant was elected president. Earlier in their relationship, Sherman had warned Grant about politicians, telling him that while Lincoln might have appointed him to command all of the Union armies, he should stay in the West, with Sherman. For Sherman, the "East" was "the impoverished East," while the Mississippi Valley was "the seat of the coming empire"—the one being a home for the effete and out of touch, the other the home of hardy pioneers. For Sherman, this kind of thinking was not evidence of any prejudice, merely a statement of fact. In our country, he had once said, "one class of men makes war and leaves another to fight it out." The phrase was not meant to offend, and Sherman would never have called Lincoln, whom he admired, a coward; but for Sherman, politicians were talkers and military men were doers. That Grant had not succeeded as president, that he was not able to command the respect in Washington that he had in the field, did not surprise Sherman; he was simply saddened that Grant had failed to understand the fundamental dishonesty of politics.

History has treated Sherman poorly. While one of our greatest generals, he is not fixed in our minds. We do not see his face always before us; we retain no sense of his depth. In our history he is most like George Patton: profane, unforgiving of failure, seemingly unaffected by death. As with Patton, we admire Sherman even as we are embarrassed by him. Asked on the eve of his last campaign about his plan for victory, Grant said that he would "hold the cat" while Sherman would "skin it." People laughed at Grant's quaint ability to turn a phrase, but Sherman knew what he meant, and after he captured Atlanta he set off with his army of sixty thousand for Savannah and the Atlantic. "I can make that march and make Georgia howl," he crowed. His army was followed by a ragtag mob of criminals, looters, and freed slaves, called "bummers." He approved of the phrase, and for a time, at least, it was a unique part of our lexicon. We judge him harshly for this, and his reputation is that of a man who willingly made war on the innocent. But for Sherman, the purpose of war was to kill. The sooner that was done, he thought, the sooner the war would end. Sherman was Grant's "bad boy," the man the South loves to hate, and America's own Macbeth, who believed that when a war " 'tis done" it would be better " 'twere done quickly." During the war, Sherman was confronted by a southern woman, who was outraged by the looting of his troops. "Madam," he said, "my soldiers have to subsist themselves even if the whole country must be ruined to maintain them. There are two armies here.

One is in rebellion against the Union; the other is fighting for the Union. If either must starve to death, I propose it shall not be the army that is loyal." Seeing her horror, he lowered his voice: "War is cruelty. There is no use trying to reform it. The crueler it is, the sooner it will be over." Second only to Grant, Sherman embodies the character of the American army of the twenty-first century.

Sherman owed Grant his career, his meteoric rise as a Civil War commander—and his livelihood. That was as true after the war as it was during it. In 1868, when Grant was elected president, he decided that he would resign his rank as commander of the Union armies in order to allow Sherman and Phil Sheridan, his cavalry commander during the Civil War, to succeed him in the army hierarchy. In so doing, Grant was following the tradition that he had himself established: Each time he was promoted during the war, Sherman was promoted to fill his vacated rank, from division to corps commander, from corps commander to commander of an army, from army commander to overall command. The only place Grant had gone that Sherman wouldn't was commander in chief. "I will not accept if nominated and will not serve if elected," he told James G. Blaine when his name was mentioned for the vice presidency. Ironically, it was Blaine who recommended to Grant that he simply take a "leave of absence" from the army when he became president and thereby ensure that he receive his Civil War pension. Grant refused, saying it would mean that other generals would not be promoted. He was thinking mostly of Sherman. When Grant was elected president, Sherman took his spot as commander of all the nation's armies.

Sherman remembered all of this in January 1885 and vowed that just as Grant had once helped him, so now he would help Grant. While his former commander might not accept a subscription, Sherman knew that he would welcome being reinstated to his former rank. So after Grant had politely but firmly rejected Sherman's offer of a subscription raised in his name, Sherman solicited the help of Drexel, Childs, A. T. Stewart, and ex–secretary of state Hamilton Fish to help lobby Congress for Grant's reinstatement on the regular army retired list. Grant's reinstatement on the list, Sherman argued, would allow him to collect a lieutenant general's salary, but without endangering the promotion of any other officer. Reinstatement would also ease Grant's concern about the financial health of his family; upon his death Julia would receive $5,000 each year. At Sherman's urging, George Edmunds of Vermont quickly brought the bill before the Senate, but it did not find much support. Some senators argued that Grant had enough money without the pension (this in spite of their knowledge of the scandal surrounding the bankruptcy of Grant & Ward), while others said that such pensions should be reserved for those wounded and still suffering from their wartime injuries. Edmunds argued eloquently against this, and the Senate eventually passed the bill. But getting the bill through the House of Representatives proved much more difficult.

Grant approved of Sherman's lobbying and was hopeful that southern representatives in the House would pass the legislation. He had good reason for optimism: He had spent considerable time with southern representatives during his two terms as president, and many of the northern representatives remained his strong supporters. Sherman, on the other hand, concluded that the fight to restore Grant's rank would be difficult. A similar bill had failed to pass Congress in 1880, and in 1884, then president Chester A. Arthur had vetoed a bill that would have placed Grant and Union general Fitz-John Porter (who was charged with failing to obey orders at the Battle of Antietam but was later exonerated) back on the active list. Arthur vetoed the bill on a technicality, arguing that it was his right as president, and not Congress's, to determine who should or should not be on the military's list of active officers. Sherman and his team of influential lobbyists, therefore, worked nearly every day during the first two weeks of January to line up votes for their position. But in mid-January the House refused to consider the bill and the matter was tabled indefinitely. Grant was profoundly disappointed, and by the end of January his depression had increased. His doctors, seeing his condition deteriorate, decided to release a public declaration pleading for his reinstatement—though carefully omitting the fact that Grant was terminally ill. "The action of Congress in refusing to pass the bill restoring him to his honors has been very depressing," they wrote. In a final act of desperation, Senator William Mitchell of New York proposed that Congress pass a pension for Grant of $3,000 per year, to take effect retroactively as of the date of Grant's retirement. If passed, the bill would have provided Grant with an immediate cash award of $27,000. When Grant heard of the proposal, he wrote to Mitchell that while he appreciated his efforts on his behalf, he could not support such a bill.

Impatient with Grant because of his denial of Mitchell's initiative, Sherman went back into action. At the end of January he met once again with his wealthy New York friends, convincing them that all they had to do was return to the House and persuade them to reconsider their January bill. George Childs wrote an editorial in his Philadelphia newspaper on the subject, telling his readers that it was customary to reward a national hero. Sherman, with the help of his wealthy friends, even convinced the New York State Assembly to instruct its congressional delegation to vote affirmatively on the Grant initiative. In the hopes of convincing former confederates to vote for the pension, James Speed of Kentucky made public a letter describing how Grant had preserved the paroles of the soldiers of the Army of Northern Virginia in order to make certain that they were safe from arrest or harassment. Speed added that Grant had personally defended many of the South's most senior commanders, including Robert E. Lee and James Longstreet, from prosecution after the war.

None of this helped. While Sherman's lobbying effort gained some important adherents and a great deal of public attention, on February 16, 1885, by a vote of 158 to 103 (sixteen fewer than the two-thirds needed), the House of Representatives refused to suspend the rules to consider placing a bill on the retired list of the U.S. Army. "Thus," *The New York Times* editorialized, "four Confederate brigadiers, eleven colonels, one lieutenant colonel, one major, five captains, two lieutenants, and twelve enlisted men did to Grant in Congress what they couldn't do in the field." Disappointed, Sherman returned to his own New York brownstone, but not before pledging to Grant that when the time came, he would try again.

Grant was also disappointed, though it was clear that the crisis of the pension bill did not weigh on him as much as the crisis in his health. Yet by the end of January his mood had improved. The perceptible slide in Grant's health and mental outlook that was so obvious at the end of December was beginning inexplicably to vanish. He seemed suddenly buoyed by the prospect of finishing his life story. He now rose early each morning, wrapped himself in his shawl, and focused on writing his memoirs. He received family and visitors and even took a carriage to see his doctors. He joined the family each evening for dinner and, no matter how bad the pain, remained uncomplaining and cooperative. After dinner he sat with Julia, who read aloud from books written on the war, from diaries, letters, and memoirs, while her husband sat nearby, nodding in agreement or, at times, shaking his head in denial at some mistake of fact or memory. He rarely talked during these sessions but listened closely, using the time to restore his strength for the work he would do the next day. His spirit seemed suddenly revived, as if he were setting out to meet a new challenge. Perhaps it was the persistent rumors of his ill health and early demise that spurred Grant to new efforts, or perhaps it was the growing realization that now that the pension bill had been defeated, he had little choice but to finish his memoirs. Whatever the reason, Dr. John Douglas was not surprised by Grant's newfound strength. The former president, he decided, had simply reached an understanding of what he faced and decided he would fight it out.

MARK TWAIN MISSED all of this. Through most of November and December and all of January, he was on a reading tour with George Washington Cable—marketed by the two of them as the "Twins of Genius" tour. It was an exacting and exasperating time: During the tour Twain worried about the subscription sales of *Huckleberry Finn*, threatened to sue a company for printing pirated copies of his book (they are "thieves and swindlers," he wrote to Charley), debated with Richard Watson Gilder about edits to the chapters that would appear in the *Century*, and argued incessantly with Cable, whom he described to Livy as "the pitifulest human louse I have ever known." Twain complained about the long train rides, the weather, the people, the hotels, and Cable's piety. During the first night of their tour, as Twain was relaxing in his hotel room with a book, Cable came to see him, Bible in hand, and read a chapter from the Old Testament. Twain listened politely, puffed on his cigar, and nodded seriously. Guileless, Cable waited for a note of thanks, but Twain was having none of it. "See here, Cable," he said, "we'll have to cut this part of the program out. You can read the Bible as much as you please so long as you don't read it to me." With that, Twain went back to his reading. The problem may well have been that during the tour Cable was greeted as warmly as Twain, and often had more success. *The New York Times* thought so, eviscerating Twain's performance with words that Twain would not soon forget:

The management, in its newspaper advertisements, spoke of the entertainment as a "combination of genius and versatility," but neglected to say which of the gentlemen had the genius and which the versatility. Some of those who were present last evening may have felt justified in coming to the conclusion that Mr. Cable represented both these elements, while Mr. Clemens was simply [a] man, after the fashion of that famous hunting animal one-half of which was pure Irish setter and the other half "just plain dog." Mr. Cable was humorous, pathetic, weird, grotesque, tender, and melodramatic by turns, while Mr. Clemens confined his efforts to the ridicule of such ridiculous matters as aged colored gentlemen, the German language, and himself.

This rankled. "With his platform talent he was able to fatigue a corpse," Twain wrote of Cable. By the end of December Twain, like Huck, was in a "sweat"—which was one of the words that Gilder wanted to excise from the chapters that Twain had given him. Just after the New Year, after a much needed break with Livy and the children in Hartford, Twain was on the road again. The first part of the tour had taken him and Cable to New England, New York, and as far west as Cleveland, but the last part of the tour would take the two into the Midwest and back to Twain's Hannibal, before finishing in Philadelphia, Baltimore, and Washington. Twain and Cable were overwhelmed by the publicity they received. The two were greeted by packed houses, and in some cities over one thousand people turned out to hear them read. By the end of his tour, during the last week of February, Twain was exhausted. The lectures had been a success, for he and Cable had done readings in over seventy cities in nearly two dozen states before rapt and often raucous audiences.

The readings made more demands on Twain that he might have imagined. Unlike his humorous "lectures" (which were the staple of his public appearances for two decades), the "Twins of Genius" tour demanded that he memorize entire swaths from his own work and then recite them, dramatically, while sprinkling these presentations with witty aphorisms and anecdotes. Early in the tour, when Cable and Twain were practicing among smaller audiences in the mill towns in New England, Twain reverted to form, spicing his presentations of "King Sollermun" with the comic touches that marked his previous tours as a humorist. The audiences were welcoming, but Cable seemed to elicit a more respectful applause. Twain decided that he could be serious, too, and attempted to give meaning to controversial subjects in public, like slavery and racism, that he rarely talked about even in private. He admired this in Cable, for while Twain had wanted to read from his works before audiences in the South, Cable couldn't: The publication of a number of Cable's essays on the treatment of African Americans by white southerners had made him a pariah anywhere south of Louisville.

Twain learned from Cable, giving his own writing the respect that he thought it deserved—and that Cable gave to his. With this seriousness as a new weapon in his repertoire, Twain began to mesmerize audiences, and by the time he and Cable returned to their tour after their Christmas break, Twain was dominating the stage, while Cable was merely lecturing. Twain, always keenly competitive, noticed the difference and gloried in it. "He keeps his programs strung out to one hour, in spite of all I can do," he wrote to Livy. "I am thinking of cutting another of his pieces." But despite these complaints, Twain secretly enjoyed Cable's company and admired his writing and intellect. After reading together in Rochester, they visited a local bookstore, where Cable pointed to a copy of *Le Morte d'Arthur* on a front table. He predicted that Twain would "never lay it down until you have read it cover to cover." Twain bought the book and read it in nearly one sitting. This was the genesis of *A Connecticut Yankee in King Arthur's Court*, written in the months following the publication of *Huckleberry Finn*. It was one of Twain's great successes, and he gave Cable the credit he was due, calling him the "godfather" of the book.

In Albany the two visited President-elect Grover Cleveland, and the next night in Buffalo, Twain began his reading by looking out over the audience and pronouncing: "I miss a good many faces. They have gone—gone to the tomb, to the gallows, or to the White House. All of us are entitled to at least one of these distinctions, and it behooves us to be wise and prepare for all." Impatient, imperious, quick to anger, incessantly worried, and often self-centered, Cable endured Twain as much as Twain endured him. At one point in the tour, Cable joined Twain in the passenger seat of a railroad passenger car. "Cable, why do you sit in here?" Twain asked him after a moment. "You don't smoke, and you know I always smoke, and sometimes swear." Cable thought for a moment: "I know, Mark, I don't do these things, but I can't help admiring the way you do them." Twain wrote to his wife in February: "Cable is a great man." A few days later, their tour completed, they parted.

<hr />

TWAIN RETURNED TO New York on February 21 and immediately made his way to Grant's home. Grant was upstairs in his study, working on his memoirs and being examined by Dr. John Douglas, when Twain arrived. Grant greeted him affably, and they chatted for a short time about Twain's tour. But Grant soon turned to the issue of his memoirs and confirmed to Twain that he, his son, and George Childs had been busily negotiating the details of a contract for the memoirs with Charley Webster. "I mean you shall have the book—I have made up my mind about that," Grant said.

This was not surprising, but Twain beamed and nodded his approval. They talked for a time about Grant's writing, about the progress he had made over the last three months, and about what yet needed to be done. While Twain had been regularly informed on the negotiations for Grant's books by Charley, hearing that he would be the publisher was the culmination of months of work. While he tried not to show this and covered his pleasure by listening intently to Grant's summary of his writing, he was overjoyed.

But Twain was disturbed by Grant's wan appearance. The general looked exhausted and spoke with difficulty and barely above a whisper. Twain had noticed this before but decided that Grant was simply sick and suffering from no more than a nagging cold. This time Grant seemed different; he was noticeably thinner and weaker, and he spoke only with great effort. At times, Twain noticed, the general clutched at his throat. He was clearly in pain. The presence of John Douglas was also suspicious, for he seemed particularly attentive to Grant, as if ministering to a patient who was at the end of an illness and not in its midst. Twain had heard rumors that Grant was seriously ill and had closely followed reports on his health that had appeared in New York papers, but he could not bring himself to believe that Grant was dying. Like many others, he was comforted by a report that had appeared the day before his visit in the *New York World*, which said that Grant was suffering not from cancer (as had been rumored), but rather from "a case of chronic superficial inflammation of the tongue" that had been brought on by "excessive smoking." With an eye toward ferreting out the truth, Twain mentioned the article and commented that he was happy to hear the general would recover.

"I took for granted the report," Twain wrote soon after, "and said I had been glad to see that news. He smiled and said, 'Yes—if it had only been true.'"

Dr. Douglas, standing nearby, heard the conversation and turned to face Twain. The general's condition was serious, he said somberly, and then added that it would worsen. But he said no more. Twain left then, sobered by Douglas's words but still hopeful that the reports were exaggerated. Grant had enormous reservoirs of strength, Twain believed, and could conquer his illness as certainly as he had conquered Lee's army. Fred Grant was waiting for Twain outside his father's study, and the two men walked down the front stairway together, talking about the memoirs and the details that had yet to be cleared up in the publishing contract. At the bottom of the stairs, Fred turned to Twain for a final word. He spoke quietly but calmly. His father was ill, he said, and he was not expected to recover. His doctors believed that he might have only a few weeks to live.

Twain was shocked. He had had no idea that the general's ailment was so serious or that a man he had known as robust and outgoing could be stricken so quickly. Fred attempted to calm him. Twain should not be concerned about his father's illness, he said, or worry about how it might effect his work. The work was proceeding as planned, and his father was working diligently each day. The first volume of the memoirs was finished, he told Grant, and work on the second volume was well under way. Twain nodded, still clearly shocked by this report, and left for his office.

In fact, Twain was not the least bit concerned with Grant's ability to finish his work. He had known the general for nearly two decades, and over the last eighteen months, their easygoing but distant relationship had deepened. Twain now considered Ulysses S. Grant not simply a great soldier and former president, but a good friend. Some of the most relaxing days he spent in New York away from his work had been with Grant. Twain was "a Grant-intoxicated man," to be sure, but he was now also much more: He was a close confidant and admirer, a moral support, and a man whom Grant himself admired. It must have been an odd situation for the son of a Missouri judge. Twain was of a different generation, from a different part of the country, and he was as far from being a student of military history as Grant was from being a novelist. Yet the two had created a strong bond and shared important obsessions: Both were consumed by America, its people, and its past—and had lived with and seen its most ugly manifestation. That in their time they had seen others bought, sold, and chained was a source of constant reflection for both of them. The issue had become an enduring passion.

Twain was so certain that Grant would finish his memoirs and that they would stand as a lasting monument to his triumphant life that he never once wavered in this confidence. Over the next months, as Grant faded, recovered, nearly slipped away, and then finally rallied, Twain never lost faith that his friend would win his last battle. It was with this unshakable faith in Grant in mind that Twain immediately reported to the offices of Charles L. Webster & Co., where he instructed his nephew-in-law to put the finishing touches on the Grant contract and deliver it to his home. As an afterthought, Twain agreed with Grant that he should hire a stenographer to help him with the manuscript. Grant entered into talks with Noble E. Dawson, who had accompanied the general during a trip to Mexico. Dawson's job was to set down in plain prose what Grant dictated to him, then read it back to the general for his corrections. Some days Dawson arrived at the Grant residence early and stayed for dinner, primarily to educate himself on the Civil War and the personality of his client. Dawson maintained close contact with Twain and Webster, whose offices were now a flurry of activity.

Within twenty-four hours of announcing that Charles L. Webster & Co. would publish Grant's memoirs, Webster and Twain were besieged by reporters. Most of them arrived to find Twain being Twain: He barked orders at Webster, made notes on what needed to be done, modestly reviewed his own friendship with Grant, and sent Webster's assistants scurrying out the door with instructions on whom to see on what topic. He moved quickly. He instructed Webster to put together the best subscription department possible, complete with a public relations machine that would capitalize on Grant's notoriety. That he was short of funds to underwrite his venture did not faze him. He immediately borrowed $200,000 to underwrite the printing and publishing of the Grant book, and he provided increasing sales incentives to his team of canvassers. Twain was everywhere at once, insisting that he oversee every part of the operation, from reading the galleys to ordering the paper to ensuring that the book was properly printed, marketed, advertised, and sold. "Clemens was boiling over with plans for distribution," Twain's biographer Albert Bigelow Paine later wrote. "Webster was half wild with the tumult of the great campaign." He stopped only once, reflectively, to make certain that Charley understood they would now have to change their company's stationery. Twain designed it himself: "Charles L. Webster and Company," and just below that, "Mark Twain's Books and the forthcoming Personal Memoirs of General Grant." Twain was specific. The last five words were to appear, as he said to Webster, in "just a shade larger type, and in RED INK."

Twain might well have thought that publishing Grant's memoirs could prove to be his financial salvation. But for Grant the rewards were even greater. It was no longer simply the case that Grant wanted his memoirs to provide an income for his family after the bankruptcy of Grant & Ward. It was now obvious to him that the success of his memoirs was essential to provide for his family after his now certain death. But they provided much more. Over the months ahead, Grant's battle with cancer would be fought at the same moment he was fighting to retrace his campaigns. This was now more than just a task, it was a great challenge—and it fortified him in ways that he could not have imagined. His memoirs would become his reason for living, the means by which he tapped into the enormous reservoirs of strength that, at the most important moments of his life, he had always believed were there. Grant was aware of how his writing was strengthening him, giving him a new resolve. He spoke of this, bluntly, in a letter to his daughter, Nellie. "It would be very hard for me to be confined to the house if it was not that I have become interested in the work which I have undertake[n]," he wrote. "It will take several months yet to complete the writing of my campaigns. The indications now are that the book will be in two volumes of about four hundred and fifty pages each. I give a condensed biography of my life leading up to the breaking out of the rebellion. If you ever take the time to read it you will find out what a boy and man I was before you knew me. I do not know whether my book will be interesting to other people or not, but all the publishers want to get it, and I have had larger offers than have ever been made for a book before. Fred helps me greatly in my work. He does all the copying, and looks up references for me."

In his offices just two miles from Grant's home, Twain was also wrestling with his own book. For on the day that he visited Grant and learned of his illness, Twain and Webster were anxiously awaiting reviews of *Huckleberry Finn*, which had been released, finally, just three days before.

"THE BOOK IS to be issued when a big edition has been sold—and not before," Twain had written sternly to Charley in mid-1884. He meant it: While he hoped that his book would be published in time for the holidays, Webster was not able to notify him until early February 1885 that the forty thousand threshold he had stipulated for its release was met. The delay was frustrating, but Twain was adamant that, unlike most of his previous books (and most particularly the deeply disappointing *The Prince and the Pauper*), *Huck Finn* would bring a handsome profit. But Twain was not optimistic. For a time it seemed as if *Huckleberry Finn* was beset by a streak of bad luck: Not only were other publishers attempting to sell pirated copies of the book, an engraving error (purposely brought about by the apparent sabotage of an illustration by a mischievous engraver) nearly led to the publication of a lewd illustration showing old Silas Phelps with a penis. Webster quickly fixed the engraving and destroyed all evidence of the miscast illustration. The sabotage caused yet another postponement, though for only a few weeks. "Had the first edition been run off," Webster told a reporter, "our loss would have been $250,000," and he added, unnecessarily, "Had the mistake not been discovered, Mr. Clemens' credit for decency and morality would have been destroyed."

The book was finally ready for release in mid-February,

with a publication date of February 18. Twain was hardly relieved. "I am not able to see anything that can save Huck Finn from being another defeat," he wrote to Webster on February 10. Webster disagreed and attempted to calm Twain's frayed nerves. "Huck is a *good* book," Webster wrote on February 14, "and I am working intelligently and *hard* and if it don't sell it won't be your fault or mine but the extreme hard times. It *shall* sell however." Twain began to evidence some calm only when the publication date was reached and passed. He knew that *Huck Finn* was a good book, and he remained its most ardent champion. But for a time, at least, he was alone. Few reviews of the book were issued, even after it reached the hands of Twain's closest friends. Twain had to do with mere palliatives, though some were soothing. "The announcement that Mark Twain is going to write a book is sufficient," the *San Francisco Morning Call* editorialized. "The report spreads like an epidemic disease, and from that moment everybody is waiting for it." Twain hoped this was true, but in the meantime he waited in vain for the reviews to be issued. Some of the delay, he realized, was his own fault. "Heavens and earth," Twain exclaimed to Webster, "the book ought to have been reviewed in the March Century and Atlantic!—how have we been dull enough to go and overlook that? It is an irreparable blunder. It should have been attended to, weeks ago, when we named the day of publication."

Finally, on March 9, the *San Francisco Examiner* weighed in, but the review was negative. *Huck Finn*, the reviewer said, was nothing special and "is very much the same character as many of the author's Pacific Coast sketches, in the utter absence of truth and being unlike anything that ever existed in the earth, above the earth, in the waters under the earth." The *Sunday Chronicle* pointedly disagreed. "Anyone who has ever lived in the Southwest, or who has visited that section, will recognize the truth of all these sketches and the art with which they are brought into this story." Meanwhile, the *Hartford Courant,* Twain's hometown newspaper, nearly gushed in praise. "Everybody will want to see Huckleberry Finn," its reviewer wrote. "As to stirring incidents, the story is full of them. It will hugely please the boys, and also interest people of more mature years." One week later the *Courant* published a second review, as rare then as it is now, calling Twain's work irresistible and predicting that readers would not be able to put the book down. The *New York Sun* was nearly as laudatory. "Who on earth except Mark Twain would ever cotton to a youth like Huckleberry Finn for the hero of what is neither a boy's book nor a grown-up novel?" All of this was positive, and Twain was overjoyed. But he knew that the bad reviews would come sooner or later, as they did to every author. A taste of the type of controversy that would surround the book, then and even into the next century, came when the *New York World* attacked *Huckleberry Finn* as "cheap and pernicious stuff." The *World* took exception, in particular, to Twain's recounting of "two or three unusually atrocious murders in cold blood, thrown in by way of incidental diversion." Twain, who was unusually thin-skinned to begin with, was enraged and kept a running tabulation of all the burglaries, rapes, murders, and attacks mentioned in the *World*'s pages, hoping to throw them back at the paper's editors at an appropriate time.

Because Twain sold the book by subscription, he did not have to depend on the reviews for the sale of the book "in the trade." But he knew that good reviews meant that Webster could send his subscription agents back into the field, and that given good luck and good notices, *Huck Finn* would be an enormous success. The best way Twain could be assured of that success would be through controversy stoked by reviews that focused on Twain's coarse narrative and by public debate over the book's value. Twain had a taste of the growing controversy over his book in January, when the *Boston Herald* labeled the excerpt from *Huckleberry Finn* published by the *Century* "vulgar and abhorrent." Twain blanched but let the comment pass. He had always had trouble in Boston, ever since he had lampooned Ralph Waldo Emerson, Henry Wadsworth Longfellow, and Oliver Wendell Holmes during a speech given at a dinner honoring the seventieth birthday of John Greenleaf Whittier. In one of the few times he completely misjudged his audience, Twain told of a meeting among the three in a cabin in California. Twain described Emerson as "a seedy little bit of a chap," while Holmes was "fat as a balloon" and Longfellow built like a prizefighter. "They had been drinking—I could see that. And what queer talk they used!" It was vintage Twain, but it was a disaster, or, as William Dean Howells later said, Twain (filled with the scene he was sketching) failed to notice the stunned silence of his audience and went on and on with "the amazing mistake, the bewildering blunder, the cruel catastrophe."

Twain wrote letters of apology to Emerson, Holmes, and Longfellow, but the damage was done, and Twain felt the literary lights of Boston (whose publishing houses did not deign to publish books by subscription) had lain in wait ever since. On March 5, the scions of literary Boston finally struck when the *Evening Traveler* told its readers that they should not bother with Twain's new book, which was "singularly flat, stale, and unprofitable." One week later the *Advertiser* told its Boston readers that *Huckleberry Finn* was "wearisome and labored." One week after that the (Boston) *Transcript* repeated the charge: *Huckleberry Finn*, it said, was "so flat, as well as coarse, that nobody wants to read it after [a taste of it in the] *Century*." The *Boston Evening Traveler* then returned to the subject, telling its readers that no one would ever buy the book, except at the point of a bayonet. The attacks then rolled in, with the next seemingly worse than the last. Twain took it all, believing that *Huckleberry Finn* would find its readers, though he was disturbed by the vehemence of the responses. Finally, in what its members supposed might be the death knell for Twain's literary career, the Committee of the Concord Free Library banned the book. "While I do not wish to state it as my opinion that the book is absolutely immoral in its tone," stated one of its unnamed members, "still it seems to me that it contains but very little humor; and that little is of a very coarse type. If it were not for the author's reputation the book would undoubtedly meet with severe criticism. I regard it as the veriest trash."

Twain watched curiously as word of the Concord action reached into the nation's newspapers, which now gave him a blessed second round of reviews. Now, he knew, everyone would want to see just what all the fuss was about. "It is time," the *Springfield Republican* editorialized, "that this influential pseudonym should cease to carry into homes and libraries unworthy productions. Mr. Clemens is a genuine and powerful humorist, with a bitter vein of satire on the weakness of humanity which is sometimes wholesome, sometimes only grotesque, but in certain of his works degenerates into a gross trifling with every fine feeling. The trouble with Mr. Clemens is that he has no reliable sense of propriety."

Propriety? For Twain this was almost too good to be true. Within weeks, papers across the nation chose sides—the *Cleveland Leader and Herald* agreed that *Huckleberry Finn* "cannot be said to have a very high moral tone," while *Life* magazine said that Twain's writing was filled with "blood-curdling humor" and should be "banished into limbo." Even the estimable Boston author Louisa May Alcott decided that Twain's work should not be read, let alone be given to children. Considering her popularity and influence (for she had penned *Little Women*, the very model of propriety for millions of American girls), she decided to keep her criticism short, in the hopes that it would thereby be more effective. "If Mr. Clemens cannot think of something better to tell our pure-minded lads and lasses," she said as if scolding a wayward child, "he had best stop writing for them."

By the end of March, however, more reasonable reviewers were astutely noting that the actions of the Concord committee were undoubtedly having the opposite effect than the one intended. "If the Concord people are not in league with Mark Twain to advertise the book, they should have kept their proceedings profoundly secret," noted the *Sacramento Daily Record-Union*. Twain agreed. "Dear Charley," he wrote to Webster in the midst of the controversy, "The Committee of the Public Library of Concord, Mass., has given us a rattling tip-top puff which will go into every paper in the country. They have expelled Huck from their library as 'trash and suitable only for the slums.' That will sell 25,000 copies for us sure."

"HE WAS JUST A MAN"

On March 1, *The New York Times*—then, as now, the most prestigious paper in New York City and, in many ways, the newspaper of record for the nation—sprayed a black-bordered headline across its front page: GRANT IS DYING. New York's other newspapers followed suit: SINKING INTO THE GRAVE, GEN. GRANT'S FRIENDS GIVE UP HOPE, DYING SLOWLY FROM CANCER. By the evening of March 2, the *Tribune*, *Times*, *World*, *Sun*, *Post*, *Journal*, *Daily News*, and *Brooklyn Eagle* all had reporters standing on 66th Street, peering into Grant's second-floor study window. Within days they were joined by reporters from Philadelphia, Boston, Baltimore, and Washington. Within another week reporters from half a dozen news services and journalists from Los Angeles, San Francisco, Chicago, and St. Louis had come to New York to join what the reporters were already calling "the death watch." On any single day, the reporters who camped across the street from Grant's home were inevitably joined by a crowd of curious onlookers.

The Grant family struggled to manage the news. Harrison Tyrrell took the lead, telling reporters each day, both before and after running errands for the Grant family, that "the general is fine, thank you" or "he's better today, thank you" or even the more ambiguous (and untrue) "I think he grows better every day." But Tyrrell only rarely said more than this, and he was very careful to say nothing of substance. While appreciative of Tyrrell's loyalty and optimism, Grant's doctors soon realized that his explanations would never do. After consulting with the general and Julia, the doctors determined that they would be honest and forthright about the general's illness, but without causing increased public attention, which might interrupt the general's routine and seriously undermine their efforts to ease his pain. Their purpose was not to keep the public informed, but to keep Grant calm. Everything, they agreed, must be done to ensure not only that the general maintained his privacy and got his rest, but that he would thereby be able to keep to a regular schedule so that he could finish his book. Grant's interest in his book, John Douglas concluded, was the one thing that could lengthen his life.

There was some disagreement on this last point. Julia Grant was convinced that the harder her husband worked, the weaker he became. His work on his memoirs, she said in early March, should be dropped—or at least severely curtailed. She was adamant. John Douglas disagreed, as did Fred and Adam Badeau. Grant's focus on his book, Douglas argued, might be tiring him, but it was a diversion from his pain and worsening illness. There was a direct correlation, he claimed, between Grant's ability to work and his desire to live. If you remove the one, he implied, you would almost certainly remove the other. Julia listened carefully to this argument but remained unconvinced. Her husband's condition, she said, was getting worse each day. What he needed was rest, not work. The debate did not divide the family or cause a falling-out between Grant's wife and Grant's doctors—but only because, in the end, it was

Grant himself who decided that he would continue his work, no matter what his condition.

Within days of *The New York Times* report, Grant's doctors were issuing twice daily bulletins on their patient's health. But more often than not, the bulletins contained little news. They were carefully crafted to give little actual detail to the progress of Grant's illness and were written so as not to be either overly optimistic or too pessimistic: The last thing the doctors wanted was for Grant, an avid reader, to read about his illness every day in the newspapers. While the newspapers received and commented on the twice daily medical bulletins, most reporters relied on Grant's friends for news, receiving the most important information on the general's health from those who stopped at 66th Street to pay their respects. When those ruses did not work and there was no other news to print, the New York newspapers ran memorials of Grant's life, reviewed his campaigns, or sought out and interviewed his childhood friends. Each of the papers provided special supplements on Grant's military and political career as a paean to his accomplishments, and each of the newspapers kept their readers informed, at least minimally, with daily front-page updates of his health—even when there was nothing to report.

At the end of the first week of March, New York police chief Adam Gunner visited the Grant home and told Julia that he was posting police on 66th Street to control the reporters and the growing crowd of well-wishers. Julia was relieved, as it was getting nearly impossible for the Grant family to lead a normal life. Each morning, she noticed perhaps half a dozen carriages parked on 66th Street; some people would stroll ostentatiously, back and forth, in front of the Grant home, hoping to be a part of the story. Such people frightened Julia, and she was pleased that Gunner was taking steps to control them.

Additionally, most of the reporters covering Grant's illness decided that the interminable death watch they were mounting might actually do more harm than good and that there might be a public backlash against their ghoulish obsession. A small group of them decided to establish a command post on Madison Avenue, just down the block from the Grant residence. The move was made as much out of necessity as courtesy: Renting space nearby allowed reporters to string telegraph wire to their downtown headquarters.

Grant's illness attracted the usual set of frauds, phonies, religious zealots, and thrill seekers: One man came to pray and did so so fervently (on the sidewalk outside the Grant residence) that others joined him. Soon dozens of people were praying in front of Grant's home. The sight upset Julia but only puzzled Grant, who looked out his window one day, spotted the prayer vigil, nodded his head—and went on with his writing. Another well-wisher made it past the police barricade and rushed the front porch of the Grant home, shouting that if only the general abstained from coffee, he would be miraculously cured—a piece of advice studiously ignored by Douglas and Shrady. Another citizen threw a home remedy he had concocted over the back fence into Grant's yard, with a note attached. Every day a mass of packages arrived at the Grant home containing vials and pills guaranteed to cure the ailing general. Added to this were the more modest special gifts given by veterans groups, former commanders, and women's auxiliary organizations, each of which claimed to have a special relationship with their dying commander. One day a one-armed veteran passed by the Grant home—marching as if passing in review before his former commanding general. "He's my former commander and I love him," the man told a reporter. "When the Battle of the Wilderness was over and the Rebs had taken to their heels, I was a-lying in a shady spot I had a-crawled to, when the General rode by. My arm and my leg was a-hanging by a thread and as he passed me I shouted, 'Hooray!' and the General's face lit up with a smile of joy and sadness. That was my last battle and I never saw him again."

Old friends, former commanders, and simple soldiers whom Grant knew came in pairs or singly to his home throughout March and April to pay their respects. The more dependable and courteous among these sent prior notice of their arrival and were accorded time with Grant, though each appointment depended on his writing schedule and health. In the end, very few of Grant's old friends were turned away. John Frémont ("the Pathfinder" and founder of the Republican Party) came to visit, as did Comfort V. Lane, an old friend of Grant's from St. Louis. Thomas L. Crittenden, a Union corps commander, visited with Grant for a short time, as did the sons of Generals Robert E. Lee and Albert Sidney Johnston (who commanded the Confederate forces at Shiloh and was killed there). Roscoe Conkling and Benjamin Bristow, two of New York State's most powerful political bosses, spent an afternoon with Grant, which occasioned endless commentary in New York's newspapers. Each public official was given a short time with Grant, though Julia and Douglas hovered nearby, waiting for an appropriate time to shoo each of them away. Grant rarely objected to these visits. He seemed to enjoy the attention: A once active man, he now rarely left his home. There was one exception. In early March, Grant took the family carriage to meet his beloved daughter, Ellen—"Nellie"—who was returning to New York to see her father from her home in England. Nellie had always been special to Grant and may well have been closer to him even than his sons. Grant was proud that Nellie, the first daughter of a president married in the White House, had grown into a respectable and respected woman. That she was married to Algernon Charles Francis Sartoris, a notorious womanizer and spendthrift (who left her in favor of his dissipations), did not matter to her father; he loved his Nellie.

Nellie aside, nothing could equal Grant's happiness when he was visited by his wartime commanders or those who served with him. He seemed revived, his family noticed, after each of these visits. General John A. "Blackjack" Logan visited, and the two discussed the Vicksburg Campaign in detail. Logan, a political general during the Civil War (appointed to be a Union commander by Lincoln, who needed Democratic votes in Illinois), was a special visitor. Grant had initially suspected Logan's loyalty to the Union cause: He was not only a state representative for Illinois's southernmost "Little Egypt" section (at Cairo, where the Mississippi and the Ohio join), he had been an ardent defender of slavery and the fugitive slave act. But when Grant heard him extolling a crowd to defend the Union during a recruiting rally in 1862, he left his doubts behind. He remembered the speech when Logan joined the army as one of Grant's commanders. Despite his political background, Logan proved to be one of the Union's bravest and most competent warriors and took over command of the Army of the Tennessee after the death of James B. McPherson during the Battle of Atlanta. Logan went on to spend twenty years in the House of Representatives and was James G. Blaine's running mate in 1884—after Sherman gave his "Shermanesque" response to Blaine's inquiry of whether *he* would serve as his vice president. Logan was no Sherman: He never saw a political office he did not want. Logan loved politics, though a certain odor accompanied his campaigns. He was a ruthless and, it was widely reported, a corrupt vote buyer.

None of that mattered to Grant. He respected Logan, and they spent a long afternoon together as Grant read from the Vicksburg section of his memoirs. As Grant was just then finishing his article on the campaign for the *Century*, he asked

Logan if he would read and comment on it prior to its submission. Logan agreed, though he immediately saw that this would be a chore: The article ran some eighteen thousand to twenty thousand words in length. Logan was deeply impressed by Grant's dedication. "His physical suffering seems to have nerved his mind for its best efforts," he later told a reporter.

Grant gave certain sections of his memoirs to close friends who had served with him. He not only gave Logan the Vicksburg sections, he passed on his section on the Mexican war to Zealous B. Tower, who had served with him in 1848. He did the same with Horace Porter, shuffling some of his papers into a neat pile and pushing them toward his former aide for a quick review. Porter had been one of Grant's closest comrades. A graduate of West Point, he had helped to save the Union forces during the Battle of Chickamauga, before going on to be one of Grant's most trusted military aides-de-camp. He served Grant as a personal secretary after the war and wrote a book that was complimentary to his old commander. He then served as ambassador to France, where he spent a considerable amount of his own money to locate the grave of John Paul Jones. He worked to have his remains reburied, with honors, at the U.S. Naval Academy at Annapolis. But unlike Logan, Porter was shocked to witness the effects of Grant's illness. "To see him wasting and sinking in this way is more touching and excites deeper sympathy among his friends than if he had made some sign of his suffering, as ordinary men do, by grumbling and complaining," Porter told the press after his visit.

❦

"In the history of the United States," Mark Twain wrote in *My Autobiography*, "there had been one officer bearing that supreme and stately and simple one-word title, 'General.' Possibly there had been two. As to that I do not remember. In the long stretch of years lying between the American Revolution and our civil war, that title had had no existence. It was an office which was special in its nature. It did not belong among our military ranks. It was only conferrable by Act of Congress and upon a person specially named in the Act. No one could inherit it. No one could succeed to it by promotion."

That was true, of course, but only partly so. After his stunning victory at Vicksburg in July 1863, Grant had moved his headquarters to Chattanooga, then besieged by the Confederate army. In a series of brilliant moves, he lifted the siege, scattered the surrounding rebel host, and chased them into Georgia. Coming in the wake of Union general George Meade's victory at Gettysburg and his own at Vicksburg, Grant's Chattanooga triumph seemed, at last, to assure the ultimate success of Union arms. The Congress was so grateful that it struck a medal in Grant's honor and revived the rank of lieutenant general, which had been held only once before—by George Washington. The rank was well deserved. Grant had won seventeen battles, imprisoned over 150,000 rebel soldiers, opened up the Mississippi River, and cleared Tennessee. "He has organized victory from the beginning," Wisconsin senator James Doolittle proclaimed at the time, "and I want him in a position where he can organize *final* victory and bring it to our armies and put an end to this rebellion."

But, as Sherman knew, Grant's resignation of his rank (instead of a simple retirement) produced an unintended effect: It barred him from receiving a pension when he was most in need of one. That reality had motivated Sherman from December to mid-February, when the House of Representatives had refused to take up the case for Grant's reinstatement. But in the short period of time between the House's refusal to act and the certain knowledge that Grant was dying, a bare two weeks, Sherman had continued his lobbying efforts. The beginning of

March saw him in Washington (a city he disliked, primarily because it was filled with politicians) nearly as much as it saw him in New York. His efforts, he reported to Grant's friends, were beginning to yield results. With the eyes of the nation on them, the Congress was busily reconsidering its actions. Samuel J. Randall, the Democratic Speaker of the House, told both Sherman and Childs that he would reintroduce the bill reinstating Grant—S. 2530.

But time was short. The Congress was required to recess prior to the inauguration of a new president, and Grover Cleveland was scheduled to take his oath of office at noon on March 4. In addition, as Sherman and Childs knew, no matter how important the Grant bill might seem, the House (in particular) had business that it considered even more important: It had to vote appropriations to establish the Brooklyn Navy Yard, approve monies for an Indian reservation in Montana, and resolve a disputed congressional election in Iowa. When the House adjourned on the evening of March 3 without the Grant bill having even been discussed, Sherman and Childs concluded that they were once again defeated. But Randall reassured them that the Grant bill would somehow pass in the next twenty-four hours and that he would maneuver the House into passing it. Grant was morose but realistic, telling Childs that while he trusted Randall, he doubted that his maneuverings would work: "Mr. Childs, you know during the last day of a session everything is in turmoil. Such a thing cannot possibly be passed. If anyone in the world could pass such a bill, I think Mr. Randall could. But I don't think it is at all likely, and I have given up [the] expectation."

On the morning of March 4, Samuel J. Randall reconvened the House and ordered the clerk to date all business as having been transacted on the day before—on March 3. He then quickly moved the House through its parliamentary paces, wielding the

power he had to garner votes to pass agenda items that had
not been brought up on March 3. With that done, at precisely
eleven A.M., he surrendered the chair and asked his replacement
for a suspension of the rules to consider the Grant reinstatement bill. The new chair, however, overruled him, arguing that
the House had not yet considered the matter of the disputed
Iowa election. The dispute, between George Frederick (who
had been certified by the Iowa Board of Elections) and James
Wilson (the incumbent Republican, who was not certified by
the board), was a contentious partisan issue. Wilson had claimed
that the Iowa board had wrongly certified his challenger and
that he, and not Frederick, was the rightful holder of Iowa's
congressional seat. The debate, it seemed, would drag on forever, as Democrats and Republicans began to muster their votes.
But at the last minute, Wilson rose from his chair and announced that he would withdraw his objection to the Iowa
election results if the House would immediately move to consider the Grant bill. The announcement was met with a stunned
silence and then cascading applause; Wilson had given up his
seat so that Grant could receive his pension. Within minutes
the Grant bill was passed.

Randall, stunned by the sudden turn of events but overjoyed with his unexpected victory, rushed from the House
and crossed through the Capitol rotunda, where senators were
beginning to congregate for Cleveland's inauguration. Randall
spread the word among them: They must return to their chamber and vote on the House bill reinstating Grant. The senators
walked quickly to their chambers and scrambled into their
seats. Nearby, in one of the Senate offices, outgoing president
Chester A. Arthur waited impatiently and, he was convinced,
vainly for the House to act so that he could convene the Senate in one last session. A Grant partisan, and a heroic combat
veteran of a number of Civil War battles, Arthur had made

Grant's successful reinstatement one of his administration's primary goals. At the front of the Senate chamber, a clerk scaled a ladder and turned back the clock (it had just run past noon, when by law the Congress was required to adjourn) so that the Senate could legally consider the Grant bill. This was duly done. But Arthur was not satisfied. As his last act as president of the United States, Arthur directed the president pro tem of the Senate to send Grant a telegram telling him of his reinstatement. With that, Chester A. Arthur and Samuel J. Randall finally joined the procession escorting Grover Cleveland, the new president of the United States, to his inauguration. Behind them, the Senate clock tolled noon. It was twenty minutes slow.

Unaware of this victory, a fearful and untrusting Sherman watched as the time slipped slowly toward noon. Twain and Grant, in Grant's study on 66th Street, were chatting with Julia, Fred, and Adam Badeau. Grant said nothing as the clock on his mantel slipped toward midday. In the early afternoon, the telegram from the Senate arrived. Grant read it and turned to Childs. "I am grateful the thing has passed," he said simply. Julia was overjoyed. "Hurrah, our old commander is back," she said, emerging from the library. Twain beamed. "Every face there betrayed strong excitement and emotion—except one—General Grant's," he later wrote. "He read the telegram, but not a shade or suggestion of a change exhibited itself in his iron countenance. The volume of his emotion was greater than all the other emotions there present combined, but he was able to suppress all expression of it and make no sign."

The next morning the new president, Grover Cleveland, made the reinstatement official by signing Grant's commission. The papers were presented to him by Robert Lincoln, the martyred president's son and the outgoing secretary of war. Cleveland signed the papers and suggested that Lincoln also affix his signature—after all, Cleveland said, Lincoln's father was the man who had promoted Grant; it would be only fitting if Lincoln's son would reconfirm that rank. But Lincoln demurred, saying that that duty was best left in the hands of the new secretary of war. Cleveland agreed, but reluctantly.

As a retired lieutenant general, Ulysses S. Grant earned a salary of $13,500 each year, and his wife, Julia, was assured of a retirement of $5,000 each year. The salary did not wipe out all of Grant's debts, but for the first time since the collapse of Grant & Ward, he began to worry less about his financial condition and more about finishing his memoirs. He told Childs that it was vitally important that he (Grant) immediately write a letter to Cleveland accepting the reinstatement. "The law," he told him, "is to date the commission from the time one accepts. In the early part of the war I saw in the newspapers I was appointed to a higher rank and I wrote at once and accepted on the strength of the newspaper report. In about two months' time, through red tape, I got my appointment, but I got my pay from the time I wrote."

Grant impatiently awaited his check, which was due to arrive on March 31. His doctors and family were concerned that he believed he might die before its arrival. But when the check arrived, Grant deposited it immediately and hastily wrote a check of his own: to Union veteran Charles Wood of Lansingburgh, New York, who had loaned Grant $1,000 "on account of my share for services ending April, 1865." Wood received Grant's payment and immediately gave the money to charity—in Grant's name.

WHILE THE STREET OUTSIDE the Grant home bustled with reporters and the merely curious, the Grant home itself was usually very quiet. The general worked nearly every day on his book, taking a day off only when the pain in his throat became excruciating or after a night of fitful sleep. There were a handful of regular visitors: Mathias Romero, Mexican ambassador to the United States, Senator Jerome Chaffee, and Mark Twain. Grant's doctors—John Douglas, Fordyce Barker, and George Shrady—were also regularly present, though their visits were purely professional. All were solicitous and careful of the general's feelings; none discussed his illness but sought only to ease the pain he was suffering. Grant's memoirs were a constant source of conversation, and Grant's room, facing the street, was beginning to resemble a good-size Civil War library. The general's desk was piled high with notes, orders, memos, maps, and books—as well as the list Grant made each late afternoon of which parts of the book should be completed the next morning. Grant sat in a large chair near the desk in his by now regular attire of loose-fitting shirt, scarf, and knit cap. Nearby was Dawson, writing what the general dictated, then waiting during pauses while Grant either rested his throat, retrieved a map, memo, or paper, or called to Badeau or Fred to clear up some point, add a date, check a spelling, or offer advice on a certain topographical feature. Dawson would often help Grant by reading back what he had dictated, and Grant would correct and shape his words depending on what he had heard. Often he would think for long moments, trying to remember a particular event, a face, or just how a battle had proceeded. At the end of each day he collected what Dawson had written and edited it before reading it to Julia. Only then would the stack of papers be given to Badeau and Fred for their suggestions. Twain participated in this process after Grant had read the final product of his labors (after Fred and Badeau had seen it) and made more corrections. Dawson was essential to this process.

The General had a good army library and knew where to find things. In the evening he would have more reading, often done by his daughter-in-law, Ida, and when the family was away, he would sit and think and make more notes. He never dictated at night, as he was much too weak, but several of us would look through books to verify dates and little bits of fact. Sometimes Colonel Fred Grant and I would do this together.

General Grant dictated very freely and easily. He made very few changes and never hemmed and hawed. Mr. Mark Twain was shown the manuscript of the first volume during one of my dictation sessions with the General. Mr. Twain was astonished when he looked at it and said there was not one literary man in one hundred who furnished as clear a copy as Grant. The General's sentences rarely had to be revised in any way. . . .

March 1885 was a good month to write—the New York late winter turned suddenly rainy and dark, and after the initial shock of publicity following the announcement of Grant's illness, a distinct and measurable calm descended on the Grant household. It was as if Grant, Julia, Fred, the doctors, and all of his regular visitors had now steeled themselves for Grant's last campaign. This was true also of Twain, who came from Hartford nearly every day to visit the offices of Charles L. Webster & Co. before stopping at 66th Street to check on Grant's condition and his progress on the memoirs. Twain and Grant fit well with each other, though their age, outlooks, and pasts were markedly different. While their visits often resulted in animated conversations on one or another aspect of the war, with Grant using Twain as a kind of sounding board for his own views and memories, they just as often spent their time together in silence, with Twain gingerly reading parts of chapters that Grant had written or talking with Badeau, Fred, or others of the household. It was Grant's strength, however, that most impressed Twain. "General Grant was a sick man," he later wrote in his *Autobiography*, "but he wrought upon his memoirs like a well one and made steady and sure progress."

During the last week of March, Grant concluded his article on the Vicksburg Campaign. It had taken him months to do so, months that were also spent writing the concluding chapters of the first volume of his memoirs, which covered the same campaign, though in much more detail. During the last two weeks of March, Grant had been particularly prolific, writing upward of ten thousand words on some days, while spending others editing and correcting what had already been written. Twain, who saw Grant nearly every day during this period, was stunned by Grant's abilities. "It kills me these days to write half of that," he commented. Twain was particularly interested in Grant's article on the Vicksburg Campaign written for the *Century*. One day he noticed the article on Grant's desk, leafed through it, and concluded that the general's article was four times the length called for in his agreement with Roswell Smith. When he told Grant this, the general was indifferent. "Then I have fulfilled my contract to them," he said, and he went on working. Twain was not so easily deflected.

While Grant's "modesty in money matters was indestructible," as Twain later commented, Twain's certainly was not. He vowed to bring the matter of Grant's measly payment to the attention of Roswell Smith, and he did—in a meeting he had with him at his offices. Twain marched into Smith's office trailed by Grant's lawyer, Clarence Seward, and Charley Webster. They appeared mainly as reinforcements, for it was Twain who led the charge, saying that the *Century* was clearly profiting by their relationship with Grant. He found it surprising, he said, that they paid him so little for so handsomely increasing their subscriptions. Twain may well have wanted to pick a fight with Smith, but the publisher was not rising to the bait. He agreed with Twain: Grant had done a great deal to help his magazine's Civil War series, he said, and he should be rewarded. Smith said he would double Grant's payment, from $2,000 per article to $4,000. This was a generous offer, but the idea had not been Twain's: Smith had already agreed to increase Grant's payments during a conversation he had had with the general several months previously.

Indeed, that Twain should be so outraged by Smith's modest payments to Grant comes as something of a surprise: The Century Company had always treated Grant fairly and had allowed him remarkable latitude in writing his articles. Their lack of interference was in their best interests, of course, but it is difficult to find evidence that they purposely exploited his fame for their own profit. Two thousand dollars for an article was certainly a modest payment for a man of Grant's reputation, but it was hardly a modest payment for a writer working in the mid–nineteenth century. It may well be that the real reason for Twain's visit to the *Century*'s office was occasioned by his sudden realization that Grant was using the pieces he was writing for them as the foundation for his work on his memoirs. This was a simple matter of who actually owned the pieces—if the *Century* owned them, Twain realized, then Grant would have to rewrite each of the pieces in a different way for his memoirs and might well be barred from using parts of the articles for his book. With Grant's health clearly failing, the question of rights became all the more important. For if the general had to rewrite even part of his sections on the campaigns at Shiloh, Vicksburg, Chattanooga, and the Wilderness, he might never finish his book.

For Twain, this was the most difficult and uncomfortable part of his meeting with Smith. So before even mentioning a word about Grant's payment, he nonchalantly noted that Grant should own title to all he had written. Smith understood immediately what Twain was saying and agreed that all rights to Grant's work would revert to the general—but only after the *Century* had published them. Irritated by Twain's presentation, Smith ostentatiously showed him the receipt that Grant had signed giving the *Century* full rights to print his articles. "It was easily demonstrable they were buying ten-dollar gold pieces from General Grant at twenty-five cents a piece, and I think it was as easily demonstrable that they did not know there was anything unfair about it," Twain later wrote. But Twain was being disingenuous. In fact, he was relieved: Grant would not have to produce differing accounts of Shiloh, Vicksburg, Chattanooga, or the Wilderness, and the accounts written by Grant of the four campaigns in *Battles and Leaders* are virtually extracts of what he had written for his memoirs. With the question of rights now resolved, Twain rushed the first volume of Grant's memoirs (a period covering Grant's life from his birth and childhood through the Mexican war and thence up to the surrender of Vicksburg) to the printers.

A SLIGHT RELAPSE in Grant's condition slowed his writing pace in mid-March, but this was neither a medical nor a physical crisis of the kind that had plagued him in December and at the beginning of February. Grant was exhausted; the pace that he had set for himself in finishing the first volume of his memoirs was sparked by his own concern for his failing health. He could feel himself getting weaker. He knew time was running out. Through the end of March, up until the very last day of the month, he had plotted out what he would do next, beginning volume two of his book with his relief of Chattanooga and then carrying the war to its conclusion. Still, with all of that completed, he still would not be finished. Grant wanted to add a special appendix of his letters, choose the maps that would most appropriately accompany the most important campaigns and battles, and decide on what other illustrations, if any, should be included in the book. In other words, finishing volume two of his memoirs would demand all of Grant's remaining strength; and even then the book would not be finished. Evidence of the work that remained became crushingly clear during the third week of March, when Twain appeared with the proofs for volume one, which he wanted Grant to approve. Days later, in the midst of this, Twain appeared once again, this time with Karl Gerhardt, an amateur sculptor from Hartford. Twain wanted Gerhardt to make a small portrait bust of Grant for use in the memoirs.

Gerhardt was one of Twain's innumerable human hobbies. A self-educated machinist at the Pratt & Whitney Machine Tool Company of Hartford, Gerhardt painted and sculpted on the side. It was an obsession that consumed almost every moment of his nonworking life. His wife, Hattie, believed he was a brilliant artist who lacked only a patron to help him claim his fortune. Hattie arrived at Twain's doorstep at Nook Farm early one morning, pleading with the writer to accompany her to her home in Hartford to view her husband's work. Twain was amused, but he demurred, though he was intrigued enough to visit the Gerhardts' modest apartment in Hartford several days later. The apartment was scattered with Gerhardt's work—an assortment of paintings, sketches, busts, and full sculptures of his wife, Hattie, including his most recent work of her naked from the waist up. Twain was impressed by the sculpture, but not only because the winsome Mrs. Gerhardt was apparently quite well endowed. "Well, sir, it was perfectly charming," Twain wrote to Howells, "this girl's innocence & purity—exhibiting her naked self, as it were, to a stranger & alone, & never once dreaming there was the slightest indelicacy about the matter. And there wasn't; but it will be many a long day before I run across another woman who can do the like & show no trace of self-consciousness."

Intrigued by the sculptures that he saw and taken with the mysterious Gerhardt, who remained silent during their first meeting while his wife did the talking ("There was too much thought behind his cavernous eyes for glib speech," Twain decided), Twain recommended that the machinist meet with his friends, the sculptors James Wells Champney and John Quincy Adams Ward. Gerhardt did as Twain suggested, and several weeks later both Champney and Ward told Twain that they believed Gerhardt had considerable talent. They recommended that he study art at the famous École des Beaux-Arts in Paris. Twain agreed to provide for Gerhardt during his education and gave him $3,000 to underwrite his studies for five years. Prior to his departure, and again on Twain's recommendation, Gerhardt visited Augustus St. Gaudens in New York. While St. Gaudens was less enthusiastic in his judgment of Gerhardt than either Champney or Ward, Twain was not deterred, and Gerhardt's transfer to Europe went forward. When Gerhardt arrived in Paris, he immediately looked up St. Gaudens's teacher, François Jouffroy. After a few months of study, during which he consistently ranked among Jouffroy's top students, Gerhardt requested further funding from Twain so that he could hire live models for his work. Twain agreed.

Twain considered Gerhardt a good student and a wise investment, but even Twain's funding had a limit, and after three years he suggested that Gerhardt return to America to pursue a number of commissions so that he could repay Twain for his generosity. Twain's plan was not the result of his impatience with Gerhardt, nor did he intend any insult: He knew that the couple had lived sparingly in Paris while Gerhardt pursued his education. Twain had this on good authority. When William Dean Howells told Twain that he was planning to tour Europe, Twain prevailed on him to meet the Gerhardts in Paris. Howells was impressed, writing Twain that both were hard at work on their art (Hattie had signed up for drawing lessons) and they were living as modestly as Twain had hoped. The Gerhardts were perfectly charming people, Howells said, and lived a primitive and simple life. Their art was the sole focus of their attention. The Gerhardts were not unmindful or ungrateful, Howells said. They knew that their good fortune had been due to the good heart of Mark Twain. "You are those poor little people's god—I don't know but they'd like me to write you with the large G," he wrote.

When Gerhardt returned to America, Twain promoted him to the Hartford town fathers, who were looking for a sculptor for a statue of Nathan Hale. The competition was keen, and for a time it appeared that Gerhardt might not win the commission—a possibility that sent him into a deep depression. He refused to meet with or speak to the governor, who was on the committee assigned to choose the appropriate statue. Hartford's town fathers eventually decided on the Gerhardt statue, but not without noting Gerhardt's rude sulk. "You have behaved miserably but your statue is admirable," the governor wrote.

The Hartford incident did not sour Twain on Gerhardt but rather seemed to confirm in him Gerhardt's greatness. Gerhardt, for his part, now began to act the role of the sensitive, misunderstood, put-upon sculptor—a Paris-educated man of genius who, in keeping with his aerie tradition, could often be seen staring into the near distance, as if contemplating his next great work. On the afternoon of March 20, Gerhardt accompanied Twain to the home of Ulysses S. Grant. He was overwhelmed by the opportunity given him by Twain, who had suggested several days previously that he provide a life-size bust of Grant to be used in the frontispiece of Grant's memoirs. Gerhardt was duly armed: He carried with him a clay bust of the general that he had completed from a photo of Grant given to him by Twain just days before.

We can only now imagine the effect Gerhardt had on Julia, Adam Badeau, and Fred, who exclaimed proudly over Gerhardt's bust, saying it was the very likeness of the general. It was Julia who insisted that Gerhardt enter Grant's study to see the subject in person. Grant, ever patient, greeted Gerhardt affably, then sat unmoving as his wife posed him for Gerhardt's study—prevailing on him to "stop moving" and "move your head just this way Ulyss" and "now just a bit more." Grant submitted silently to all of this, but then, when his wife and Gerhardt had finished their examination, he wordlessly returned to his writing. "One marked feature of General Grant's character is his exceeding gentleness, goodness, sweetness," Twain recorded that night in his notebook. "I wonder it has not been more spoken of."

Convinced that he could do little to deter Julia's newfound interest, Grant told Gerhardt to bring his clay into the study and work while he was writing. Gerhardt dutifully went to work at a small table set up for him, with Twain (who had picked up a book) seated nearby. Grant, seeing that everyone was settled, soon fell fast asleep in his recliner. After an hour or so, Adam Badeau came in with some sheets of manuscript in his hand, interrupting the general's nap. "I've been reading what you wrote this morning, General," Badeau said, "and it is of the utmost value; it solves a riddle that has puzzled men's brains all these years and makes the thing clear and rational."

Grant, and Twain, looked over the manuscript pages for a moment. Gerhardt, meanwhile, was magically transforming a lump of clay into a bust of Grant, an image that, it would later be said, was the "most nearly correct likeness of the general."

Finally finished, and with the day nearly at an end, Twain and Gerhardt departed, but not before Gerhardt had determined that this was not the last he would see of Grant. Meeting Grant was a transforming experience for Gerhardt; he found in Grant, he believed, a reflection of his own genius—as well as a means of achieving the public acclaim he believed was his due.

Twain, meanwhile, was ecstatic: His sacrifice in supporting Gerhardt had been confirmed by Gerhardt's visit to Grant on March 20. More important, after appearing exhausted and unable to write through much of the first two weeks of the month, Grant was now working steadily on the first part of volume two of his memoirs. Twain remained optimistic. Though Grant was being weakened by the progression of his disease, his mental outlook remained positive and the routine that he had set for his writing throughout February was beginning to return. With any luck, Twain believed, Grant would finish his memoirs long before his condition deteriorated to the point where he would no longer be able to work. This optimism was confirmed in the days that followed—as Grant not only met but even exceeded his previous output. But on March 25 Grant suffered a choking fit of such violence that he was immediately sedated with a cocktail of cocaine and morphine. He awakened the next morning to continue his work, but another choking fit followed that evening, and every evening thereafter, until the evening of March 30—when it appeared that Grant's condition had deteriorated to such a degree that his doctors believed he could not last through the night. "The truth is the disease has gotten away from the doctors," Mathias Romero told the press on the night of March 30. "It is possible he may die tonight and at the very best he cannot live ten days. As soon as the disease reaches the vital point, it will create a hemorrhage. As he is too weak, he cannot expectorate the blood and will choke to death." The doctors huddled to determine whether they should remove Grant's tongue in an effort to make certain that he would not choke on his own blood. But they decided against such radical surgery, believing that it would only postpone the inevitable. "It is doubtful if the General's health could stand another choking attack," Dr. George Shrady announced to the press. "We have decided he could not survive a tracheotomy for very long."

Telegrams poured into the Grant household from friends and well-wishers, and tributes to him began to appear in the nation's newspapers, many of them now appearing in the past tense, as if it were a foregone conclusion that Grant would die. "He was a far greater man than people thought him to be," Phil Sheridan, Grant's old cavalry commander, telegraphed to the family. "He was always able, no matter how situated, to do more than was expected of him." General Pierre Gustave Toutant Beauregard, who had ordered the firing on Fort Sumter (and was not only an unreconstructed Confederate, but was very busy just then overseeing the fraud-ridden Louisiana lottery), was almost forgiving: "Let him die in peace. May God have mercy on his soul." In St. Louis, meanwhile, William Tecumseh Sherman was his old irritable self as he turned on a reporter who asked him why President Cleveland had not sent the Grant family his condolences. "When General Grant dies, President Cleveland will have something to say," Sherman snapped. "After that, the rest will have our say. Until that time comes, I will have nothing to say."

March 31 passed uneventfully, but as the sun set on New York, dozens of newspaper reporters manned their posts across the street from the Grant household. Grant was not expected to live through the night. In Hartford, on the morning of April 1, Mark Twain wrote in his notebook: "Many a person between the two oceans lay hours awake listening for the booming of the firebells that should speak to the nation simultaneously and tell its calamity. The bells' strokes are to be 30 seconds apart and there will be sixty-two, the General's age. They will be striking in every town of the United States at the same moment." Twain fully expected Grant to die—as did the nation. On 66th Street, Julia Grant entered her husband's bedroom and sat beside him, waiting for his last breath and weeping.

But Grant did not die. At five A.M. on the morning of April 1, the lights came on in the Grant home. Dr. Douglas appeared in his carriage and quickly mounted the steps without talking to reporters. He was followed soon after by George Shrady. Grant struggled through that afternoon, hovering between life and death, but by the evening of April 1 his labored breathing steadied and he slept soundly. The next afternoon he hobbled from his room on the arm of his son. He slept soundly again that night, and the next morning he arose and continued his work. Dr. Douglas and Dr. Shrady were pleased with his stamina and praised his return to work. On April 4, the anniversary of Grant's occupation of Richmond, Dr. Douglas turned to him with a smile: "General, we propose to keep to this line if it takes all summer"—a play on Grant's official dispatches during his campaign against Lee. Douglas's comment was met with a smile and laughter from Grant, though this caused him increased pain. On 66th Street, meanwhile, the community of reporters was dispersed. On April 9, the anniversary of Lee's surrender at Appomattox, Grant plaintively asked if he might celebrate by taking "one or two puffs" on a cigar. George Shrady saw no harm in this and gave his permission. Grant settled in his chair and puffed away, contented.

❊

AFTER THE CRISIS of March 31, Grant recovered the vigor that had marked his most productive and satisfying days. He resumed dictating for three to four hours each afternoon and listened attentively as Julia read to him each evening. While the pain in his throat was worsening and he sometimes coughed uncontrollably, the crisis of his near death seemed part of a forgettable past. Some days were even pain free, and he took advantage of the respite in his illness to attack his work with increasing strength. When Julia complained that he was not getting enough rest, he waved her off. He did not have to explain himself: As time went on, there would be fewer and fewer pain-free days. He had to work while he could. On those days when his strength gave him a renewed vigor, he would dictate succinctly from his notes. He rarely made a false start, and the corrections he made to what he dictated took less and less time. On some days Dawson took down enough material to fill twenty-five printed pages. Grant was now well into volume two, moving easily through that part of the war that followed his great victory at Vicksburg but that predated his appointment as commander of all the Union armies. While Grant attempted to dictate the story of his battles and campaigns in a strict chronological order, the sheer volume of the material and the details that he was required to master often forced him to dictate certain events out of order. This piecemeal attention to events required greater discipline in editing and arranging the story in its proper sequence—a job that was given to Adam Badeau and Fred each evening.

Early April found Twain checking and rechecking the proofs of the first volume and making notes on proposed changes. But all these recommendations and emendations were minor. "My marks will not be seriously important," Twain told Webster, "since they will concern grammar and punctuation only." For Twain, the printing of the first volume was not only a triumph, it was evidence that the wager he had made over the last months, that Grant would win his race with death and that he would finish the account of his life, was paying off. There was still a worry that Grant's health would collapse and that he would die within weeks, or even days (as some of his doctors thought distinctly possible), but Twain believed that enough material had been gathered for the second volume that Fred or Badeau, or both, could complete Grant's work. While Twain always believed the worst when it came to the publishing of his own work (accusing his publishers of poor marketing, slipshod salesmanship, and conspiring to undo his well-laid plans), he nearly bubbled over with enthusiasm for Grant's memoirs. He believed that Grant's personal resources and deep internal strength would see him through to the end. While Grant was sometimes confined to his bed, or even went one or two days without writing, Twain noticed that he always found some inner resource, some strength, to continue. More important, Grant had proven that he was capable of writing well, even brilliantly. The pages that Grant gave Twain were evidence that, unlike his other commanders (Sherman stands out as a rare exception to this rule), the simplicity of Grant's writing gave it a power that few others had mastered.

It never occurred to Twain to actually edit Grant's work or to even suggest additions or deletions. "Whenever galley proofs or revises went to General Grant a set came also to me," Twain later wrote. "General Grant was aware of this. Sometimes I referred to the proofs casually but entered into no particulars concerning them." Grant noticed this, and it bothered him. Perhaps one of the reasons that Twain remained silent on his work, Grant believed, was that his writing was not that good. In early April, Fred confided his father's fears to Twain, saying that his father was puzzled as to why he had never offered any opinion on his writing. Twain was surprised by the comment. It had never occurred to him that someone as seemingly stolid and self-confident as Grant (for that was how Twain, and the nation, viewed him) could remain so uncertain about a task that was nothing as compared to routing Lee's army or running for president. Fred suggested that it might be good for Grant to hear Twain's opinion on the matter, and that doing so could serve as a reinforcement for his work. A comment from Twain, Fred suggested, would boost his father's confidence, and it would steel him for the difficult weeks ahead, when his entire focus would be on fighting his illness and finishing volume two.

"I was as much surprised as Columbus's cook would have been to learn that Columbus wanted his opinion as to how Columbus was doing his navigating," Twain later recounted. "It could not have occurred to me that General Grant could have any use for anybody's assistance or encouragement in any work which he might undertake to do. He was the most modest of men and this was another instance of it. He was venturing upon a new trade, an uncharted sea, and stood in need of the encouraging word, most like any creature of common clay. It was a great compliment that he should care for my opinion and should desire it and I took the earliest opportunity to diplomatically turn the conversation in that direction and furnish it without seeming to lug it by the ears."

The appropriate opportunity presented itself several days later, when Twain visited Grant at 66th Street. After reading through some of the pages of volume two, he turned to Grant with his own judgment of his writing. "By chance I had been comparing the memoirs with Caesar's 'Commentaries' and was qualified to deliver judgment," Twain recounted in his *Autobiography*. "I was able to say in all sincerity that the same high merits distinguished both books—clarity of statement, directness, simplicity, unpretentiousness, manifest truthfulness, fairness and justice toward friend and foe alike, soldierly candor and frankness and soldierly avoidance of flowery speech. I placed the same two books side by side upon the same high level and I still think that they belonged there."

It is not known how Grant reacted, for he never wrote of the incident—and Grant's son, wife, and Adam Badeau never recounted Grant's response to Twain's lavish praise. Twain, for his part, was unusually modest, even self-effacing, in recounting the episode: "I learned afterward that General Grant was pleased with this verdict. It shows that he was just a man, just a human being, just an author. An author values a compliment even when it come from a source of doubtful competency."

On Easter Sunday, Ulysses S. Grant stood in the window of his study and waved to the crowd of well-wishers that had gathered below. Later in the afternoon, he appeared on the front stoop, smiling but weak from his disease, to listen to hymns sung by the Excelsior chapter of the Columbia Masonic Council, whose thirty-three-member choir had come to pay their respects. Later that afternoon, Grant's doctors issued a medical statement that was accompanied by a message from Grant: "I am very much touched and grateful for the prayerful sympathy and interest manifested in me by my friends," the statement read, "and by those who have not hitherto been regarded as my friends. I desire the goodwill of all, whether hitherto friends or not." Later that evening, exhausted by his afternoon appearance, Grant fell asleep in his chair.

SEVEN

"THE COMPOSITION
IS ENTIRELY MY OWN"

In the epic story of Grant's illness and slow physical deterioration—for that is what it would be, an epic tale recounted and passed down to succeeding generations by those closest to him—a number of impressive historical figures stand out. Among them was Grant's wife, Julia, Grant's son Fred, Adam Badeau, George Childs, Mark Twain, and the irrepressible William T. Sherman. But others deserve mention—bit players, to be sure, but also characters of uncertain repute who, through sheer good fortune, would be remembered solely for their ability to place themselves in the warmth of his reflected glow. The sculptor Karl Gerhardt, a man of some talent and all-too-human flaws, was one of these figures. Another was the Reverend John Philip Newman, a respected and well-known Methodist minister who was born and came of age during America's Second Great Awakening, the name given the religious revival that swept through Newman's upstate New York region in the 1840s, when he was first entering his career as a clergyman. Newman was himself a symbol of New York's famed "burned-over district," a description of the region of upstate New York from Troy, on the east, to Buffalo, on the west, that was transformed by the fires of religious transformation that burned there during the first four decades of the nineteenth century. Newman preached in the burned-over district and gained his reputation as a fiery orator before seeking his fortune among the rich and famous.

Newman found himself first in New Orleans in 1862, soon after that city's capture by Union troops. He called southerners to redemption with such fervor that his orations drew vast crowds, an accomplishment of some merit in the then northern-hating crescent city. Newman was properly modest about this success, attributing his new stature to the power of God. All *he* had come to do, he said, was to "blow the Federal and the Gospel trumpets." He was next called to Washington, D.C.'s Metropolitan Church, where he ministered to members of Grant's cabinet as well as to Chief Justice Salmon Chase and Senator John A. Logan, both of whom were regular church-goers. Newman was appointed chaplain of the Senate in 1869, a position he held until 1874. But while Newman rubbed shoulders with official Washington, his most ardent fan and strongest supporter was Julia Grant, who admired his sermons and came to value his friendship. Julia's husband rewarded Newman for this friendship, appointing him inspector of United States consulates. Newman toured the world at government expense and reported his findings to Grant, but mostly to Julia. Julia related Newman's findings to her husband, who listened closely, nodded his agreement—and changed the subject. There is no evidence that Grant ever held Newman in disdain, but it cannot be said that he held him in any great esteem, either. For Grant, Newman was simply one of those ministers it was better not to ignore. A hint of this was given by Grant himself in a meeting with a group of ministers during his campaign for a second term as president. After thanking them for their endorsement of his candidacy, Grant indelicately explained that it seemed to him there were three political parties in America—the Republicans, the Democrats, and the Methodists.

While Grant studiously ignored Newman, Newman viewed Grant as a particularly unique challenge. Grant, he believed, was a gentle man of God who had not yet received the blessings of a "religious experience" and who remained blithely unaware of the dark stains visited on his soul. During his presidency, for instance, Grant insisted on working on Sundays when it was plain for all to see (it was right there in the Bible) that the Sabbath was a day of rest. Newman counseled Grant to cease his Sabbath labors and was assisted in this crusade by no less than the financier Jay Cooke, who warned Grant that such Sabbath work was not only bad for the soul, but bad for America. "God will not reward us," Cooke said, "unless our rulers are righteous." Grant took all of this in and paid the proper obeisance to the power of religion by studiously attending those huge religious rallies where his constituents took note of his attendance. But he kept right on working, even if it meant that on some Sundays he would not accompany his wife to church. In this respect, Grant was much like Lincoln, who was so often accused of not being pious that he was forced to admit that he had never denied the possibility of the existence of a supreme deity. Of course, Grant (and Twain, for that matter) would have noted that not doubting the possibility of an all-powerful deity was not the same as saying there *was* one. That was Grant's position: He certainly believed in God, but he mistrusted the opulent displays of religious fervor that were then becoming a major industry in the nation.

Newman was in California when he learned of Grant's illness, and he immediately traveled to New York to be at Grant's side. "A great sufferer is passing away," he confided to his diary. He added that he hoped his presence at Grant's side would help persuade him "to help redeem the world by leaving behind some immortal saying of his return to Christ." Grant would have been surprised to learn from Newman that he had actually ever "left" Christ, but he let this go, probably because he knew that one of his wife's greatest disappointments was that he had never been baptized.

Newman arrived in New York in mid-March, presented himself at the family home, and joined their evening gatherings to ensure that he was present when they prayed. Newman soon led these prayers, though for Grant they seemed interminable: At one point Grant was so relieved Newman had finished with his devotions that he proclaimed an overly loud "Amen." Newman interpreted this expression of relief as convincing evidence that Grant was finally ready for redemption and, as Newman explained, showing "more dependence upon God in prayer than I have ever known him to do." Newman was present two weeks later when Grant seemed near death, and he hovered over Julia's shoulder as, it seemed to him, Grant was about to breathe his last. Julia begged him to baptize her husband, but Newman could not do it, saying that Grant must be fully conscious in order to receive this sacrament. Grant awakened then and looked at Julia and the minister.

"As I began to pray," Newman later recalled, "the General opened his eyes and looked steadily at me. As the physicians believed he could not live five minutes longer, I prayed that God would receive his departing soul. I then observed, 'General, I am going to baptize you,' and he replied, 'I am much obliged to you, Doctor. I intend to take that step myself.' I then baptized him in the Name of the Father, of the Son and of the Holy Ghost. He was conscious and wiped the water from his face. It was a solemn scene. Mrs. Grant knelt by his side and called for prayer and I offered the Lord's prayer."

Dr. Douglas and Dr. Shrady were nearby, and now, seeing that Grant was conscious, they administered a syringe of brandy, hoping that Grant would thereby gain strength and remain conscious. "If you doctors know how long a man can live under water, you can judge how long it will take me to choke when the time comes," Grant said as they administered the potion. When Grant began to choke a second time, Shrady and Douglas administered a second injection. Grant's coughing fit worsened as Julia and Newman stood aside, horrified at the agony of what both were convinced were his last minutes. But Grant suddenly expectorated a clot of blood and began to breathe more easily. Newman looked on, praying, joined by a distraught Julia. As the night progressed and Grant slept soundly, the doctors concluded that the crisis had passed.

The next morning, exhilarated by his good fortune at having baptized Grant, Newman crossed from the Grant home to the knot of reporters who stood at their posts on the Grant death watch. Prayers had saved Grant's life, he said, and he described the scene in the Grant home of the evening before. The general had been baptized, he said. His soul had been saved. The reporters took it all in, scribbling the details of this near death experience into stories that headlined the New York newspapers on the morning of April 2. Newman's account caused a sensation. Religious officials were exhilarated by this deathbed baptism, temperance officials were horrified that brandy was being administered to the nation's greatest hero, doctors scoffed at the power of prayer, and Newman became a national hero.

Just two weeks later, Newman was again posted on the sidewalk across from the Grant residence, declaiming that the nation's Easter prayers had been answered. Grant's slow but certain recovery from the crisis of early April, he said, was evidence that Providence had a special mission reserved for the former president. Shrady, who had walked from the Grant home with Newman, listened skeptically to this report but could not bring himself to disagree. "They mourned his death two weeks ago," he told a reporter. "Let them now rejoice in his resurrection." Senator Jerome Chaffee, now nearing the end of his public career and apparently immune from public disdain through the power of incumbency, had no compunction about calling Newman what he thought him to be: a fraud. "There's been a good deal of nonsense in the papers about Dr. Newman's visits," he told one reporter. "General Grant does not believe that Dr. Newman's prayers will save him. He allows the doctor to pray simply because he does not want to hurt his feelings."

That seemed about right, particularly when it came to Newman's much ballyhooed claim that in the midst of his struggle with death, Grant had pressed Newman's hand in his and declaimed: "Thrice have I been in the valley of death, and thrice have I come out again." Thrice? Grant would no more say "thrice" than Huck Finn would say the Lord's Prayer. As for pressing Newman's hand, it seemed unlikely that Grant would do so with his beloved wife, Julia, nearby. For Twain, who watched some of this in person, Newman's public displays seemed evidence that Lucifer, not God, was being loosed on the world. Twain never passed up the opportunity to heap disdain on ministers like Newman, who in his opinion more resembled the notorious swindlers from his novels (like the "Dauphin" from *Huckleberry Finn*, who exclaimed, "Preachin's my line, too; and workin' camp meetin's; and missionaryin' around") than they did the run-of-the-mill corner clergymen who dotted the American landscape. For Twain, Newman's words of Grant's journey to the valley of death were like red meat to a ravenous dog, and he devoured it. "Ten cents to a thousand dollars he never used that form of words," Twain confided to his notebook. "This piece of reporting comports with Newman, gush, rot, impossible." Badeau had the same reaction, telling reporters that what Grant had actually said was more a plea for a quick ending than for redemption: "The doctors are responsible three times for my being alive, and—unless they can cure me—I don't thank them."

But Newman continued to press his point, to Twain, to Badeau, to Grant's doctors, to Grant and Julia, to the public—to anyone who would listen, and, of course, to himself. "Oh, how grieved I was for God's cause," he wrote in his diary. "But I wrestled with God in prayer to vindicate His own cause and not let the General die until he had borne glorious testimony to Christ." Having saved Grant from death (or, rather, having borne testimony that God had saved Grant from death), Newman was now intent to show that God could wholly heal his disease. "I believe you will be raised up, restored to health, to be a great spiritual person in the land," he told Grant in mid-April. "You are a man of Providence; God made you His instrument to save a great nation; and now He will use you for a great spiritual mission in a skeptical age."

When he heard this, Grant blinked and turned to look blankly at Newman. "Can he cure cancer?" he asked.

Unwavering, certain, Newman had a ready answer. "Why not? You must hold on to him by prayer and faith."

Grant took this as it was given, nodded in agreement, but was clearly disbelieving. He did not think that he had a special mission to save America (he had, after all, already done that) but tolerated Newman only for the sake of his wife, a fact testified to by his children many years later. "I do not care how much praying goes on if it makes your mother feel better," he told Fred. He even refused Newman's offer to give him communion, saying he was "unworthy." Newman certainly sensed Grant's reticence, his barely concealed disdain, for his diary was filled with questions and doubts about his mission to convert Grant, to find in him the redemption he believed America so desperately needed. In the end, it was Grant's great courage that trumped Newman's religion—though for many years after, the minister would be remembered as "Grant's pastor" during the general's final pain-racked days, even as Fred, Badeau, Twain, and Shrady consigned him to his proper place, at the back of the room, ministering to Julia.

∞

THERE IS ALWAYS HOPE, perhaps most particularly in the midst of darkness. Grant's near death on April 1 plunged his family and friends into a deep depression from which it was almost impossible to recover. His death had not come, but it now seemed certain. The recovery from the near loss had been particularly painful, and the family was once again required to prepare for the worst. So too his almost miraculous recovery sent hopes soaring: Was it possible for a man who was so sick to recover so completely? Could it be that the miraculous recovery of early April portended an even more miraculous cure? It must have seemed that way, even to those who had heard again and again the prognosis of Grant's doctors. "The diagnosis of the doctors might be wrong," Senator Jerome Chaffee, Buck Grant's father-in-law, told the press on April 17. "Grant in my opinion has not been suffering from cancer but from an ulcerated sore throat. I have no doubt the General will pull through." The reporters scrambled for their telegraphs to report this news, and the next morning the *New York World,* sensing an exclusive, focused on the Chaffee report: NOT CANCER AFTER ALL, read the headline of their newspaper. Grant was amused by this, but his family was upset. The report, they felt, not only gave the public false hope, it was likely to revive public suspicions about the treatment Grant was receiving. "The people rejoice that their great soldier Grant whose death a syndicate of doctors led them to expect at any moment for the past weeks is now apparently on the road to recovery," stated the *World*'s report. Not wanting to be left out of the story, the *Tribune* focused on the quality of Grant's care; the paper based its reporting on suspicious or nonexistent sources. "It appears the doctors have been mistaken," the *Tribune* concluded.

Questioning doctors had become a journalistic pastime in the late nineteenth century, but not without reason. When James A. Garfield was grievously wounded by Charles J. Guiteau, an unstable office seeker, in Washington, D.C., on July 2, 1881, his doctors (including Surgeon General Joseph K. Barnes, who had attended Lincoln after he was shot at Ford's Theatre, and D. W. Bliss, a leading and noted Washington surgeon) had insisted on releasing optimistic reports of his condition and imminent recovery. For a time the public believed that Garfield was able to fulfill the duties of his office. In fact, however, Garfield never left his bed—and died in it (at Long Branch, New Jersey) eighty days after he was shot. Garfield's death stunned the nation, not least because his doctors' reports implied that he might appear in public, fully healed, at any moment. When confronted with the public's anger, the doctors implied that they had released the overly optimistic medical bulletins for purely political reasons; there was no acknowledged legal procedure for replacing an incapacitated president, and it was simply easier, they reasoned, to let the public believe that Garfield was fulfilling his duties.

Reports that Garfield's doctors had purposely lied stained the reputation of the medical profession. Another scandal erupted soon after, when it was found that Garfield's doctors had misdiagnosed his condition. An independent autopsy showed that the doctors' belief that Garfield's liver had been pierced was wrong. This diagnosis, the doctors later sheepishly admitted, came about after one of the phalanx of doctors treating Garfield just hours after the shooting stuck his finger in the bullet hole and made the pronouncement. The doctors then spent weeks attempting to find the Guiteau bullet; at one point they called

on Alexander Graham Bell, who provided a metal detector—
two electromagnets attached to a telephone receiver (of course)—
to find the stray shard, but the device did not work. There
might have been two reasons for this. The first was that, it was
later determined, Bell was looking for the bullet in the wrong
place; the second was that Garfield was lying on a mattress
filled with metal springs. Bell's wife, who watched all of this,
wrote to her mother that "Mr. Garfield himself is reported to
have said that he was much obliged, but did not care to offer
himself to be experimented on." Having been unable to find
the bullet, Garfield's doctors concluded that it would be too
difficult to remove it, so it was better to do nothing at all.

The autopsy showed otherwise. A competent surgeon could
have removed Guiteau's bullet and saved Garfield's life, the
report concluded, and such an operation should have been
attempted. Of course, Garfield might well have died anyway
(though the report most assuredly did not mention *that*), since
the use of antiseptics was then in its infancy and the now accepted routine of hand washing prior to an operation was
viewed with deep suspicion. One of the doctors present dismissed the notion that antiseptics were helpful, since to use
them it was "necessary that we should believe, or act as if
we believed, the atmosphere to be loaded with germs"—and
that, of course, was preposterous. When Garfield began to lose
weight, his doctors plied him with roast beef, eggs, potatoes,
and brandy, which he promptly vomited, which forced the
doctors to feed him again, with the same results. Garfield lost
eighty pounds in two months, despite being administered
sumptuous three-course meals followed by the routine application of morphine. Finally, Garfield was given a series of nutri-
tional enemas consisting of one egg, one ounce of bouillon, one
and a half ounces of milk, a half ounce of whiskey, and ten
drops of opium—a concoction that would be unwelcome to

anyone, perhaps, except a crazed drug addict. "Summing up the case from an allopathetic standpoint," one medical journal noted at the time, "the man is ignorantly or willfully blind who fails to see that President Garfield's case has been the most grossly mismanaged case in modern history, and his surgeons are guilty of a deliberate attempt to throw the burden of a glaring incompetence upon Providence, rather than leave it where it justly belongs."

The official autopsy report was also damaging, since it suggested that Garfield's doctors might well have been more successful if they had followed the instructions of one of the hundreds of Americans who wrote giving them advice: Just suspend Garfield by his heels, this citizen wrote, and let the bullet fall out on its own. The result of this scandal was that by the time of Grant's illness, doctors' reports were viewed with widespread skepticism; the public had concluded that they knew as much about treating illness as any team of physicians. In Garfield's case this might have been true, but in Grant's it was not. George Shrady was not only reasonable, credible, and careful in his profession, he was respected for his outspoken candor, a fact the public knew quite well from the Garfield autopsy commission that he headed. It was Shrady who noticed, on the morning of April 18, that Grant's cancer had spread from his tongue to the right side of his jaw and that his gums and the right side of his mouth were now filled with cancerous sores. Shrady's observation confirmed his earlier judgment, that any attempt to operate to excise the cancer would not have stopped its spread but only deepened the suffering of his patient.

Shrady must have been enraged by the newspaper reports that said Grant was recovering, not only because they repeated Senator Chaffee's ill-considered statement that Grant might not have cancer after all, but because they reignited the controversy over his profession that had followed the Garfield fiasco. But Shrady, dismissive of public criticism and mistrustful of reporters (and ministers), was wise enough to refuse to respond to questions about his diagnosis, an example he convinced his colleagues to follow. All agreed: They would not comment publicly on any criticism of their diagnosis but only continue to release the twice daily medical bulletins on Grant's condition. Shrady's determination to say nothing earned him and his team the unkind sobriquet "the silent men"—a phrase used by the World, in particular, to cast doubts on their professional abilities. And Shrady's well-considered policy of silence, intended to put an end to the rumors that Grant was recovering, only fed rumors that Grant's doctors were incompetent. Reports on their alleged incompetent treatment of the general began to be regular features in New York newspapers. The ever patient Grant was puzzled by this but hardly angered. Criticism was the price exacted on generals and politicians, he knew, so why not doctors. But Julia was enraged. She had first assumed that the optimistic newspaper reports reflected the views of Grant's doctors. When she was told otherwise, she clamped down hard on what reporters should and should not be told. As far as she was concerned, they should now be told nothing at all.

In the days and weeks that followed, only one exception was made to the rule of silence laid down by Shrady. He granted an interview to Whitelaw Reid's New York Tribune, primarily because it had refused to join the chorus of those who were now public critics of the medical profession. One of the Tribune's reporters approached Shrady and asked him for his views on Grant's health. As Grant's doctor, Shrady admitted, there was little he could do. He could relieve Grant's pain and lessen his suffering, he said, but that was all. The reporter pressed him: Grant had once seemed to be recovering, he said, and now seemed to have regained his strength. "Exhaustion and revival are characteristic of the disease," Shrady responded.

Grant's early April crisis followed by his recovery days later was not unusual. After the April 17 report of the *World*, Grant asked for Shrady's thoughts on what the newspapers were saying. Shrady was blunt: He was right and the newspapers were wrong, he said. To which Grant nodded his agreement, adding that he was satisfied with his treatment, and he was, "after all, the person with the most at stake." Grant then tried to salve Shrady's obvious bitterness at the unfair criticism he was receiving. He had once received such criticism himself, both as head of the Union armies and as president, he said. He took no account of "scribblers," he added, since their judgments were valueless. "If a man assumes the responsibility of doing a thing he naturally does it in his own way and the result is the only proof that he may be right or wrong," Grant added. "One does the work and the other does the guessing."

When some of Grant's friends advised that he change his doctors, if for no other reason than to lessen the public criticism, he refused and instructed that a statement be released expressing his confidence in their treatment. The statement reflected Grant's anger. "This paper, the *World*," he said, "is a reformer in medicines. It is an advertising medium for quack medicines prepared by ignorant people. If I were left to their treatment, I would die within a few days, suffering the extremist agony in the meantime. I would not have the entire faith in the four doctors attending me, unsupported by the judgment of anybody else. But they are all distinguished in their profession. They reject no treatment because it is not given at their own suggestion." He then concluded: "It is not true that they [the doctors] are experimenting on me with a single medicine about which they know little or nothing. It is not true they are persisting in a single treatment. With every phase of the disease, they have varied the treatment. The medicine alluded to as the one being 'experimented with' is, I presume Cocaine. That has never been given me as a medicine. It has only been administered as an application to stop pain. It is well known that it accomplishes that result without leaving injurious effects behind. It is only applied when much needed."

Ulysses S. Grant and his family celebrated his sixty-third birthday on April 27. For Grant, it was a day like any other, and he had appeared that morning well rested and intent on working on his memoirs—and on maintaining the disciplined schedule he had been keeping since the first week of April. Grant emerged from his home in the early afternoon for a ride in the park and then, returning, decided to take yet another ride. He wanted to take advantage of the warm, clear spring air; in Central Park the flowers were blooming. A carriage ride through New York, he believed, would be a fitting birthday present to himself. In the late afternoon he stood at attention in his upstairs window as New York's Seventh National Guard Regiment passed in review. He left the window open when he returned to his work. He was interrupted after a short time by General James Wilson, one of his former cavalry commanders, who called on him with a gift. Grant and Wilson talked about a number of Wilson's campaigns, and Grant gave his former comrade parts of his memoirs to read. After Wilson departed, a messenger delivered sixty-three roses, a gift of Andrew Carnegie. Grant's spirits were high, the pain in his throat seemed to have abated, and his work was going better than he could have expected. The routine and discipline of his work was particularly satisfying, as it took his mind off his illness and returned him to the days when he had commanded tens of thousands of men—the most challenging and fulfilling days of his life. That evening Julia decorated the dinner table with sixty-three candles.

FOR THE EDITORS of the *Century* magazine, 1885 provided a bounty of great American literature. January saw the publication not only of Mark Twain's "Jim's Investments and King Sollermun," the first in a series of excerpts from *Adventures of Huckleberry Finn*, but also of the first installment of William Dean Howells's masterpiece, *The Rise of Silas Lapham*. Like Twain, Howells was at the height of his literary powers and had embarked on a series of novels that deepened the public's understanding of the Gilded Age and probed the inequalities and injustices of America's race to affluence. *The Rise of Silas Lapham* opened a new chapter in American letters that Howells defined as "realism"—the unvarnished treatment of how Americans lived. "Let fiction cease to lie about life," he once said. "Let it portray men and women as they are, actuated by the motive and the passions in the measure we all know." Older than Twain, Howells encouraged his work and that of Henry James and built the *Atlantic* into the most widely read literary journal of its time. The January issue of the *Century* also contained George W. Cable's "The Freedman's Case in Equity." The essay ripped away America's post–Civil War tradition of racial silence. The next month the *Century* included a second installment of Howells's novel, a second installment of Cable's essay, another excerpt from *Adventures of Huckleberry Finn* ("Royalty on the Mississippi"), and General Grant's "The Battle of Shiloh." The February issue also contained the first installment of Henry James's novel *The Bostonians*.

Twain's assessment that the *Century* would benefit from the publication of Grant's work proved accurate; the magazine's subscriptions increased by 40 percent over a period of just sixteen months, providing Roswell Smith, Robert Johnson, and Richard Watson Gilder with a windfall of profits. Grant's Civil

War recollections were only one of the reasons for the magazine's success. Few magazines in American history could ever boast of publishing excerpts from three novels destined to remain a part of the nation's literary tradition. Even so, the works of Twain, James, Howells, and Grant serve as only part of the explanation for the *Century*'s unprecedented success. In 1885, the magazine showed that it could provide something for everyone, including a long-running series on dog breeds ("The Water-Spaniel," "The Collie," "The Fox Terrier," "The Scotch Deer Hound"), detailed reminiscences of the life of abolitionist William Lloyd Garrison, an essay on Samuel Taylor Coleridge, a photographic essay on the ancient city of Petra, a series of essays on the issue of providing pensions for ex-presidents (undoubtedly occasioned by the public discussion over Grant's bankruptcy), a debate on civil service reform, a summary account of the state of sculpture in England, more essays on dog breeds ("The Gordon Setter," "The American Setter," "The Irish Setter," "The Llewellin Setters," and "The Modern English Setter"), a short biography of Henry Clay (written by no less than George Bancroft, the giant of American historians), a series of self-help essays ("Impatience" by Alice Ward Bailey and "Humility" by Walter Learned), a set of regular poems from various hands, and an article from the frontier ("Still-hunting the Grizzly") by a little-known New York politician named Theodore Roosevelt.

In the midst of this bounty was dumped the "*Century* Series on the Civil War." The articles appeared in no particular order, which enhanced their popularity—as readers had no idea from month to month what would appear and who would be that month's author (neither did Richard Watson Gilder, who struggled to maintain the semblance of a private life while editing piles of articles from former commanders and common soldiers). The key to the enormous popularity of the *Century*'s series was not simply that it was able to induce Grant to be one of its major contributors, but that the magazine was thereby able to induce other commanders to follow him with accounts of their own. The result, unanticipated by Smith, Johnson, and Gilder, was the astonishing proliferation of unsolicited comments, criticisms, and counterclaims written by other commanders who believed their roles in the war were ignored, underestimated, or stained. The *Century* series provided the first publicly available firsthand chronicle of the war from the generation that had fought it—and the series remains one of the most valued primary sources on the American conflict.

Grant was gratified that his work was appearing alongside that of some of the most noted commanders in the war, including Generals William T. Sherman, James Longstreet, Fitz-John Porter, George B. McClellan, Ambrose Burnside, P. G. T. Beauregard, Oliver O. Howard, and John Bell Hood—an extraordinary roster of the great and near great. The series was accompanied by maps and drawings of the campaigns; civilian reminiscences and sketches of the Civil War years in Charleston, New Orleans, Vicksburg, and countless other cities; and commentaries from prisoners of war and presidential secretaries. The *Century* intended to make its series comprehensive, so great detail was paid to matching personal accounts with official records and, where the two diverged, hiring writers to comment on the differences. In all, the *Century* published four volumes of articles from hundreds of writers and dozens of artists and engravers. It was an extraordinary accomplishment that must have done much to salve Smith, Johnson, and Gilder's disappointment at their failure to win approval for the publication of Grant's memoirs. For Twain, the *Century* series must have also seemed like a perfect way to publicize Grant's work.

The literally dozens of canvassers were reporting that the public response to the prospective sale of Grant's work was surpassing even Twain's optimistic sales projections.

By mid-April, meanwhile, Grant had finally completed all the articles he had promised the *Century* (on Shiloh, Vicksburg, Chattanooga, and the Wilderness) and was plunging ahead in the race to complete his memoirs before the deterioration in his health made this impossible. He was now attempting to complete the last part of his work, from the end of the Wilderness Campaign to the surrender of Lee at Appomattox, which covered fully one-fourth of the material that finally appeared in his *Personal Memoirs*. This was the most difficult part of the book: It included detailed descriptions and commentaries on the Battle of Spotsylvania Court House, the investment of Richmond, Grant's attack south of Richmond on Petersburg, the siege of Richmond (which lasted nearly nine months), the pursuit of Lee to Appomattox, and Lee's eventual surrender. Grant would not be satisfied with this; he had planned to end his memoirs not only with a personal note on the meaning of the war, but with a section that focused on the importance of Lincoln (and his relationship with him), the capture of Confederate president Jefferson Davis, the last operations of the Union Army after Appomattox, his estimate of the command abilities of his military colleagues, and his account of the Grand Review of the Armies at Washington—a considerable goal, considering that the task not only would take three extra chapters and thousands of words, but might (considering Grant's failing health) not be completed at all.

Twain was philosophical about this. Grant had done so much work, and compiled so much material, that he viewed the memoirs as nearly complete. The maps for the final chapters of volume two were in order, the outline for the remaining battles was clear, and Grant had made detailed notes on enough of the remaining materials. Only a few minor shifts in Grant's daily routine marked the passage of the general's disease: Where before his writing had been strong, the letters of his words etched deeply in the unlined pages of his papers, now the letters were weakly shaped, the penmanship wavering, the pages lined in order to set out markers for Grant's failing eyes. Still, by the end of April Grant had made great progress and was about to embark on a recitation of his final campaign. No one could defeat Grant, Twain believed. Even if the worst came, Fred would finish his father's book, or Adam Badeau. Grant's name would still be on the cover of volume two, as it was on the cover of volume one, and it would be viewed by the public as his work—and no one else's.

ADAM BADEAU'S RESEARCH on the Civil War was indispensable to Grant. He corrected names and dates, suggested revisions in the text, and provided his own memory of the battles and campaigns that Grant commanded. But as Grant became more adept at passing his accounts onto paper, Badeau was consigned to the position of research clerk, fetching reports and maps when needed and encouraging Grant to continue writing when the task before him seemed almost overwhelming. Badeau could take some satisfaction in this work, but he had too often played the role of man behind the man, and by the late winter his opinions on Grant's narrative and his suggestions for revisions were becoming increasingly shrill. He disagreed with Fred, with Julia, and with Grant, and it was clear that he resented the more prominent role that Twain was taking as Grant's closest personal adviser. Badeau soon found himself in an unusual role: His work was appreciated, his opinions greeted respectfully, but he was no longer the indispensable man he had been during important portions of Grant's career. In March, when Grant's daughter, Nellie, arrived, Badeau moved out of his room at 66th Street. Already resentful of the role taken by others, Badeau now found himself sidelined by Grant himself.

On April 29, the *World* (whose reports had earlier caused Grant, his family, and his doctors such consternation) reported that Grant's memoirs were the work not of the ailing general, but of a ghostwriter. The *World* based its story on a report it had received from Colonel George P. Ihrie, who had served with Grant in Mexico. Ihrie had told a *World* reporter that "Grant is no writer," a statement that, Ihrie later protested, he had not known was going to end up on the front pages of New York's leading newspapers. Protest or not, the *World* story sparked a storm of controversy on Grant's work that was to be repeated in one form or another for the next generation. "The work upon his new book about which so much has been said is the work of Adam Badeau," the *World* went on to explain. "General Grant has furnished all of the material and all of the ideas in the memoirs, but Badeau has done the work of composition. The most the General has done upon the book has been to prepare the rough notes and memoranda for its various chapters. He is so great that he can well afford to have the exact truth told about him."

Twain was enraged by the *World*'s report and told friends that he would sue the newspaper. He directed Webster to retain Clarence Seward to bring the suit. Twain, who talked of suits endlessly and was prepared at any moment to threaten suit against any competitor, critic, or foreign government for any slight, real or imagined, was—this time—deadly serious. He described the *World* as "that daily issue of unmedicated closet paper" and immediately wrote of his plan to Fred Grant. "The General's work this morning is rather damaging evidence against the World's intrepid lie," he said. "The libel suit ought to be instituted at once. No compromise or apology will do. Press for punitive damages. Damages that will cripple—yes, *disable*—that paper financially." Fred was more circumspect, believing that the *World*'s story could easily be struck aside, while a lawsuit, he supposed, would mean that Grant would be faced with having to prove that his memoirs were actually his. He issued a statement shorn of threats. "My father is dictating the Appomattox Campaign," he said simply. "And from his dispatches and other data is enabled to give a perfectly straight and lucid account to a stenographer."

Three days after the *World* story appeared, Grant dictated a letter to Twain: "My attention has been called to a paragraph in the World newspaper of this city of Wednesday, April 29th of which the following is a part. 'The work upon his new book about which so much has been said is the work of General Adam Badeau. General Grant, I have no doubt, has furnished all of the material and all of the ideas in the memoirs as far as they have been prepared; but Badeau has done the work of composition. The most that General Grant has done upon this book has been to prepare the rough notes and memoranda for its various chapters.'" Grant then answered each of the claims ("I will divide this into four parts," he wrote, "and answer each of them") in turn:

> First—"The work upon his new book about which so much has been said is the work of General Adam Badeau."
>
> This is false. Composition is entirely my own.
>
> Second—"General Grant, I have no doubt, has furnished all of the material and all of the ideas in the memoirs as far as they have been prepared."
>
> This is true.
>
> Third—"but Badeau has done the work of composition."

The composition is entirely my own.

Fourth—"The most that General Grant has done upon this book has been to prepare the rough notes and memoranda for its various chapters."

Whatever rough notes were made were prepared by myself and for my exclusive use.

You may take such measures as you see fit to correct this report which places me in the attitude of claiming authorship of a book which I did not write and is also injurious to you who are publishing and advertising such a book as my work.

Twain read this response and circulated it, using a network of reporters he viewed as friends to strike down the Badeau claim. He also made certain that Grant's letter received front-page publicity, an easy enough task considering that every New York newspaper (and every national newspaper of prominence, for that matter) was intent to have a say in the controversy. This done, Twain decided that it would be far better to embarrass the World than sue it, a project that Grant had begun simply by writing his letter. Twain then, like Grant, began a quiet investigation of who had been the author of the rumors and for what purpose. Neither of them had to look too far: Both Twain and Grant settled on Badeau and knew there was good reason for doing so.

On the day that Grant sent his detailed response on the World report to Twain, Badeau handed a letter to Grant that contained a demand that the general increase his stipend, from the agreed-upon sum of $5,000 out of the first $20,000 of profits (and an additional $5,000 if the book made $30,000) to double that amount. Badeau included in his letter a summary of the personal sacrifices he had made on Grant's behalf, adding to these a list of personal grievances. He concluded by saying that he had continued to work for Grant "under very trying circumstances," which was a veiled reference to his view that Fred and Julia and Twain had eclipsed his role as Grant's primary aide and confidant. In the end, Badeau's complaints came down to one: Grant's book, when it was published, would be more important and get more attention than his. "Your book is to have a circulation of hundreds of thousands," he wrote, "and the larger its circulation the greater its importance—the more completely it will stamp out mine. Yours is not and will not be the work of a literary man, but the simple story of a great general. Proper for you, but not such as would add to my credit. Your name sells your work; your deeds are in its theme; your own story told by itself is what the people want. Under these circumstances I am willing to agree to complete the work from your dictation in the first person with all the supervision you are able to give but in any event to complete it; to claim, of course, no credit whatever for its composition but to declare as I have always done that you wrote it absolutely."

The letter was elegantly, if transparently, done. Badeau implied that he was the author of the book, though without explicitly claiming that he was. He did this presumably for posterity (for that is what he looked to) and in the sure knowledge that in saying that he "would take no credit whatever for [the book's] composition," people would come to the opposite conclusion: that his "great personal sacrifice" amounted to his selfless decision to give Grant all the credit, when no such credit was due. This was blackmail pure and simple, with the implication being that if Grant did not agree, then Badeau would stand aside, selflessly, and allow Grant to finish a book that was rightly his. He ended his missive by laying out his demands: He would receive $1,000 each month, to be paid in advance, until the work was completed and, thereafter, 10 percent of all of the profits. He would work under these conditions, he said, and would make Grant's memoirs "a monument such as no man ever put up to his own fame."

Grant was having none of it. He knew Badeau quite well. He had seen him at his worst. He admired his abilities and he valued his friendship, but Badeau's behavior, particularly his cross words with Julia, could not be forgiven. The article in the World, which Grant and Twain were now convinced was planted by him, was the last straw. It made him expendable. Grant did what he had always done during a crisis. He marshaled his forces and vowed not to retreat.

In a letter to Badeau written on May 6, Grant said that he understood what Badeau wanted, but he would not agree to it, and that therefore "you and I must give up all association so far as the preparation of any literary work goes which bears my signature." He then responded point by point to Badeau's claims, noting that Badeau had already profited a great deal from their relationship. He had even given Badeau full access to his personal papers, from which Badeau had written his own account of the war. He added that Badeau had not, as he claimed, kept up his part of his original agreement with Grant and had not added significantly to Grant's work on the Chattanooga or Wilderness articles (which were written by Grant without Badeau's help). Grant finished with a flourish: "You are petulant, your anger is easily aroused, and you are overbearing even to me. As an office holder you quarreled with your superiors until you lost your office. My name goes with the book and I want it my work in the fullest sense. I do not want a book bearing my name to go before the world which I did not write to such an extent as to be fully entitled to the credit of authorship. I do not want a secret between me and someone else which would destroy my honor if it were divulged. I cannot think of myself as depending on any person to supply a capacity which I am lacking. I may fail but I will not put myself in such a position." But this was not nearly enough.

I have to say that for the last twenty years I have been very much employed in writing. As a soldier, I wrote my own orders, plans of battle, instructions and reports. As President, I wrote every official document, I believe, usual for Presidents to write, bearing my name. All these have been published and widely circulated. The public has become accustomed to my style of writing. They know it is not even an attempt to imitate either a literary or classical style; that it is just what it is and nothing else. If I succeed in telling my story so that others can see as I do what I attempt to show, I will be satisfied.

Badeau—Uriah Heep–like (but not nearly so 'umble)—beat a retreat. But he remained unchastened. "As I have stated to you in my letter of Saturday I have no desire, intention or right to claim authorship to your book. The composition is entirely your own. What assistance I have been able to render has been in suggestion, revision or verification." In a subsequent letter, Badeau said that he would send for his trunk and personal possessions, which were still in the room set aside for him at 66th Street.

Grant was somewhat mollified, for this letter could always be put before the world as proof that even Badeau himself could not claim authorship to Grant's work. That seemed to end the matter, though Mark Twain remained suspicious and watched carefully for any stories that might be planted by Badeau. And while Twain could never prove it, Badeau was probably the person responsible for the rumors that soon began circulating in New York (and that gained some currency through the years) that in fact it was not Grant, or even Badeau, who wrote Grant's memoirs—but Mark Twain.

———— ❧ ————

GRANT MAY NOT have known it, but now, near the end of his life, he was as obsessed with words and their value as he had been as a young student at a private school in Kentucky. "They taught me that a noun was the name of a person, place or thing so often that I came to believe it," he had written in remembering his youth. Now, more than fifty years later, he focused on verbs. "A verb is anything that signifies to be; to do; or to suffer," Grant wrote in a note to Dr. John Douglas in mid-May 1885. "I signify all three." Since the crisis of April 1, Grant had dictated nearly all of volume two, save for two hundred pages of personal views that he was intent to add to his account of battles and campaigns, his views of his fellow commanders, and a short section on what he thought the war meant for the nation. The prodigious effort had exacted such an enormous physical cost that even Dr. Douglas, who had once argued that Grant should write as much as possible so as to relieve his mind of worry over his illness, was concerned that Grant was not getting enough rest. Grant's neck was now swollen, and he could barely speak. The cancer had spread into the back of his throat and into his jaw. It was, literally, eating him alive. But the pain he felt seemed to have the opposite effect on him that it had prior to April: It kept him awake—which meant that he now composed alone, through the night and into the early morning hours, when everyone else was asleep. Julia often found him now at dawn, dozing fitfully in his chair. "I could do better," he wrote in one note to Twain, "if I could get the rest I crave."

Grant began the final pages of his book during the third week of May, writing for four to five hours each night on the end of the siege of Petersburg and Lee's retreat to Appomattox. Grant's mind seemed more focused, though now he could barely swallow. He was required to communicate solely by writing short notes to his family. He wrote without major revisions until June 8, when he informed Twain that volume two had been completed, though only in rough draft. He would still be required, he said, to review all of the material, make certain it was in the proper chronological order, and add more details to some of the papers that he had presented only in skeleton form. "The General says he has made the book too long by 200 pages—not a bad fault," Twain confided in his journal. "A short time ago we were afraid we would lack 400 of being enough." The day after Grant's announcement, Twain released notice to his canvassers that volume two would soon be published. He contracted for the use of twelve more printing presses and seven more binderies, all of which combined would produce one set of memoirs every second. All of Twain's funds were now tied up in printing, marketing, and distributing Grant's memoirs.

But when Twain asked Grant for a final copy of volume two, hoping thereby to produce a final copy for the printers, Grant refused. There were still some odd details to iron out, he protested, and he wanted to make certain that he said everything in exactly the right way. Twain understood Grant's worries, for he had felt the same way in each of the books he had written: They seemed never to be finished. "He is going to stick in here and there no end of little plums and spices," Twain wrote proudly to Howells. In mid-June, the New York newspapers reported that Grant's doctors were recommending that the general leave the city for the summer. His disease had now progressed to the point where the heat of the city might increase his suffering. But this recommendation was not the result simply of Douglas's or Shrady's concern for Grant's comfort. That year, Dr. Edward Livingston Trudeau had reported that the cooler mountain air of the Adirondacks helped to treat tuberculosis—the nineteenth century's most vicious and misunderstood killer. Trudeau established the first sanatorium for tuberculosis patients at Saranac Lake, New York, and early reports suggested that Trudeau's treatment might actually defeat the disease. Shrady and Douglas took note of this and began looking for a rural community that would host Grant until his death.

There were a number of options, for hotel and resort proprietors were anxious to increase their profits by hosting the nation's most famous military and political figure. The locale that Shrady, Douglas—and now Fred Grant and Julia—eventually fixed on, however, was a small cottage at Mt. McGregor, which was adjacent to the Balmoral Hotel, twelve miles from Saratoga, in upstate New York. The cottage was owned by Joseph W. Drexel, the Philadelphia financier and philanthropist, who was also a part owner of the Balmoral. Drexel admired Grant, but this was not the sole reason that he offered the use of his summer home: He also believed that Grant's final days on Mt. McGregor might make the area (in which he was a primary investor) a popular resort, bringing visitors to the Balmoral from Boston, New York, and Philadelphia. "That is just the place I have been looking for," John Douglas said of the Drexel cottage. "There is little heat there, it is on the heights, it is free from vapors, and above all it is among the pines, and the pure air is especially grateful to patients suffering as General Grant is suffering."

Douglas and Shrady made all of the medical arrangements. Douglas would be in constant attendance of Grant during the summer, and Shrady would be close by. This was important to

Grant, who sensed that his last physical crisis was now imminent. "So anxious was he that nothing would interfere with such an understanding that he questioned me concerning my whereabouts and my future plans," Shrady later recounted. "On learning that my summer home was my farm on the Hudson near Kingsbridge, he was particular to learn how long it would take me to reach him in response to an urgent message."

Reassured that Shrady would be close by, Grant approved the move to Mt. McGregor, and the family began to pack their belongings. Grant personally oversaw the transport of his beloved manuscript, which he worked on now (adding "plums and spices") with increasing intensity for several hours each day. Twain was anxious; Grant claimed that he was not yet finished. But he would be done in time, he said—and certainly by September 15, when he planned to return to New York. That was characteristically optimistic of Grant, though certainly his doctors and family knew the truth. He would be dead by then.

EIGHT

◉

"THE ME IN ME"

The train that took Ulysses S. Grant from New York to Mt. McGregor was provided by William H. Vanderbilt. It had a locomotive, a dining car, and Vanderbilt's private coach, in which workmen placed Grant's two large leather chairs. Grant would be seated in one of these for the journey, surrounded by his wife, his son Fred and Fred's wife, his daughter, Nellie, his five grandchildren from both these marriages, and N. E. Dawson, his indefatigable transcriber. Harrison Tyrrell, Henry McQueeney (a nurse recommended to Grant by his doctors), and John Douglas were assigned to Grant to take care of his medical needs. As word spread early on the morning of June 16, 1885, that Grant would be leaving the city, a crowd gathered outside his home. At a little after eight A.M. Grant emerged, nodded to the knot of well-wishers, and was helped into a carriage by Harrison for the short trip to Grand Central Station.

It was a sultry and humid day, and the temperature would soon be hovering near one hundred. But Grant was bundled up for the journey; he wore a long coat and top hat, and his neck was swaddled in a scarf. Douglas was happy that Grant was leaving, believing that the pain in his throat would worsen in the New York City summer. Douglas's most recent examination showed that the cancer had spread even farther into Grant's throat and his neck was more swollen than Douglas had yet seen it. Grant could barely talk and spent most of his time communicating by writing short notes. While his condition had improved for a short while in April, and there had been no crises after his near death on April 1, the disease's inroads were debilitating, with the cancer eating away at his tongue and mouth. Grant was now enfeebled and appeared aged well beyond his sixty-three years. His beard, once jet black, was fully white. He was barely able to walk without support. Because he could not swallow, Douglas knew, he was literally starving to death.

The train moved ponderously through the Hudson Valley, lush with summer foliage. Crowds of people stood along the track to catch a glimpse of Grant, and here and there aging veterans stood at attention when his train passed. Grant dozed in Vanderbilt's coach, his chair turned south, away from the smoke of the locomotive—which threw sparks and cinders into the air. At West Point, Julia woke her husband so that he could glimpse the academy, parts of which seemed to tower over the river below. Almost exactly five hours after leaving New York, "the Grant train" came to a stop at Saratoga. An honor guard awaited his arrival and hoped for his inspection, but the trip had weakened him to such a degree that all Grant could do was raise his cane and nod. He walked weakly from the Vanderbilt coach across the tracks to a car of the Saratoga, Mt. McGregor & Lake George Railroad. Behind him, Fred and Harrison wrestled with Grant's chairs, hefting them across the tracks and onto the new train. This new train traveled on smaller-gauge rails, and its engine—"the J. W. Drexel"—was dwarfed by the massive Vanderbilt locomotive. The "Drexel" would pull Grant the final twelve miles to Mt. McGregor, where a welcoming committee awaited the arrival of him and his entourage—enlarged now by the presence of Joseph Drexel, his wife, the manager of Mt. McGregor's Balmoral Hotel (within walking distance of the Drexel cottage), the board of directors of the Mt. McGregor Corporation, and two local constables.

The trip to Mt. McGregor was uneventful, though the pace of the journey was even more ponderous, with the "J. W. Drexel" laboring up the mountainside. The railroad station at Mt. McGregor was within walking distance of the cottage, and a gurney awaited Grant, but he waved it aside and gamely struggled up the railroad embankment, across a short road, and onto the cottage grounds. Dr. Douglas and one of Saratoga's constables, however, were required to carry Grant the last few yards up the steep hill and into the cottage.

He was pleased with the two-story home; it was large and airy, was painted a pleasing light brown, and had a spacious open porch that encircled the house on three sides. Grant's own room, just off the porch near the front, had large windows. The surrounding hills were thick with northern pines, and after the cacophony of New York, the green woods seemed virtually silent. Harrison helped Grant with his coat and brushed away the cinders from his hair and face. Fifteen minutes after his arrival, he appeared on the porch, sternly surveying his surroundings and seemingly unconcerned about the curious crowd that had gathered, just yards away, to see him. Less than one-quarter of a mile through the woods stood the Balmoral, built in 1881 by Drexel, W. J. Arkell, and a number of their business partners in the hopes that the hotel's view and its proximity to New York, Boston, and Philadelphia would attract vacationers. The railroad up the mountain to the Balmoral was constructed in 1882.

The Balmoral seemed like a good investment to Drexel and

his syndicate. The three-sided, four-story hotel was large and well constructed and boasted an exceptional restaurant. With access to Saratoga's nearby "springs" and a stunning view of the Adirondacks, Drexel believed that it was only a matter of time before Balmoral became as popular as, say, Long Branch, New Jersey. Drexel's plan included an expansion of the hotel and an extension of the railroad, which would deliver vacationers as far north as Lake George. A previous owner of the property, Duncan McGregor, had the same idea as Drexel and had prospered for a time as an innkeeper, but he did not have the funds to enlarge his holdings. That was certainly not true of Drexel or his partners. The only hurdle they now faced was making certain that Americans able to afford the luxury of the Balmoral actually heard about it, which was one of the reasons Drexel and his primary business partner, W. J. Arkell, agreed that Grant should spend his last days at the resort. "I thought if we could get him to come here to Mt. McGregor, and if he should die there, it might make the place a national shrine—and incidentally a success," Arkell, apparently a man who gave little thought to what he said, later admitted.

The cottage itself was perfect for the Grants, with opulent settings of china and crystal, an open and spacious dining room, and bedrooms set well away from one another, as they had not been on 66th Street. While Mt. McGregor was certainly new to the general, he felt immediately at home, setting up his two large chairs in his room and arranging his Civil War research materials on a large table nearby—in nearly the order they had appeared in New York. While visibly weakened by his illness, he immediately fell into his usual routine, though now he simply wrote or edited on his own. Because Grant's voice was so weak, Dawson no longer transcribed what he dictated; instead he would read portions of the manuscript to Grant, who would recommend changes. In the evenings the entire Grant family left the cottage to dine at the hotel, unless Grant was too weak to join them. That was more and more often the case through much of June, when Grant was forced to subsist on tea and soft fruit. While the hotel was not yet officially open for the summer season, a battalion of reporters (many of the same ones who had kept their post outside the Grant home in New York) had already established their headquarters in the hotel dining room—with the result that the Grants dined in one of the smaller private dining rooms that looked out on a porch. Mt. McGregor appealed to Grant, as Douglas had hoped it would. On his first night at the cottage, the temperature fell into the low fifties, and Grant enjoyed the first full night of rest in many weeks.

The next morning, Grant decided he would explore his surroundings and directed Harrison to accompany him to a nearby knoll, which provided a celebrated view of the countryside. He seated himself on a wooden bench at the height and looked out across the valley to Saratoga, where Horatio Gates had once accepted the surrender of "Gentleman" Johnny Burgoyne during the Revolutionary War. He took in the view and returned to the cottage, but it was clear that the effort of climbing had been exhausting. Turning to Harrison, he asked for a pencil and some papers. Harrison, believing he was going to once again turn his attention to his book, stood waiting for further instructions, but Grant waved him aside. He wrote three letters. The first was to Dr. John Douglas:

Dr., since coming to this beautiful climate and getting a complete rest for about ten hours, I have watched my pains, and compared them with those of the past few weeks. I can feel plainly that my system is preparing for dissolution in three ways; one by hemorrhage; one by strangulation; and the third by exhaustion. The first and second are liable to come at any moment to relieve me of my earthly sufferings. The time of the arrival of the third can be computed with almost mathematical certainty. With a decrease of daily food, I have fallen off in weight and strength very rapidly for the last two weeks. There cannot be hope of going far beyond this period. All my physicians, or any number of them can do for me now is to make my burden of pain as light as possible. I do not want any physician but yourself, but I tell you, so that if you are unwilling to have me go without consultation with other professional men, you can send for them. I dread them however, knowing that it means another desperate effort and suffering.

He wrote a second letter to his son Fred:

I have given you the directions about all my affairs except my burial. We own a burial lot in the cemetery at St. Louis and I like that city, as it was there I was married and lived for many years and there three of my children were born. We also have a burial lot in Galena, and I am fond of Illinois, from which state I entered the Army at the beginning of the war. I am also much attached to New York, where I have made my home for several years past, and through the generosity of whose citizens I have been enabled to pass my last days without experiencing the pains of pinching want. It is possible my funeral may become one of public demonstration, in which event I have no particular choice of burial place; but there is one thing I would wish you and the family to insist upon and that is that wherever my tomb may be, a place shall be reserved for your mother.

He wrote a third, shorter, letter to Julia and tucked it inside his coat pocket.

~∞~

WHILE THE ILLNESS of his friend Ulysses S. Grant saddened him, it had been a good year for Mark Twain. The "Twins of Genius" tour that he had conducted with Cable netted him over $46,000—an extraordinary sum that helped to offset his mounting bills. In addition, sales from *Adventures of Huckleberry Finn* continued to be strong, and it now looked as if the book would outsell both *Tom Sawyer* and *The Innocents Abroad*, his two previous profitable successes. While the official date of the publication of *Huckleberry Finn* was December 1884, it had not been until February that Twain's nephew-in-law announced that forty thousand copies had been sold by subscription. Another forty thousand followed within three months. While the public and his critics had yet to comprehend the brilliance of his work, intimations of its future as perhaps the greatest novel written in the American language were beginning to appear. It was, oddly, most appreciated in England, at least at first, where almost all the reviews were positive. Twain was proud of *Huckleberry Finn* and proud too that it, like *Uncle Tom's Cabin*, was for obvious reasons largely unread in the South. On the eve of Grant's move to Mt. McGregor, Twain could hardly believe his good fortune. "I am frightened at the proportions of prosperity," he wrote to a friend. "It seems to me that whatever I touch turns to gold."

Now that *Tom Sawyer* and *Huckleberry Finn* had proven profitable, Twain began to explore ways to expand their popularity.

He returned to a manuscript he had begun the summer before about Huck and Tom and their adventures in the West, playing off his own experiences in Nevada. Over the next five years he worked diligently on a story called "Huck Finn and Tom Sawyer Among the Indians." But he never felt comfortable with the story's plot or the evolving characters of his two protagonists. Tom and Huck were fine as boys, but they worked less well as young men. In many ways, Twain decided "Huck Finn and Tom Sawyer Among the Indians" was even more difficult to write than the last part of *Adventures of Huckleberry Finn*, in spite of the treasure of stories on the West collected for him by Webster. Eventually he put the story aside. A second idea occurred to him that same summer of 1885, inspired by "the slathers of ancient friends, and such worlds of talk, and such deep enjoyment of it." His plan was to have Huck and Tom and Jim's deaf daughter take a steamboat to New Orleans and "so put the great river and its bygone ways into history in form of a story." Yet another idea occurred to Twain that summer—to put Tom and Huck together in Twain's old rebel outfit, the Marion Rangers, during the Civil War. The story was to reach its culmination, Twain said, when a "Union soldier accosts Tom and says his name is U. S. Grant."

Only one of these great plans ever reached fruition. In 1893, Twain published *Tom Sawyer Abroad*—which took Tom to Europe. But with the sole exception of that 1893 book (which the author himself, it seems, would have rather forgotten), Twain never could find a way to transform Tom and Huck into respectable adults. "I conceive that the right way to write a story for boys," he argued, "is to write so that it will not only interest boys but will strongly interest any man who has ever been a boy. That immensely enlarges the audience." Twain was stuck: Huck could certainly interest boys, but the nuances and power of Huck's message was meant for adults. In the misty silences of the Mississippi Valley, Huck had explored the meaning of slavery and issued not-so-subtle comments on a populace comprising "robbers, horse thieves and counterfeiters" who were impressed by men with false titles, fraudulent histories, and phony manners. Huck, speaking for Twain, admits that he does not mind this so much: "If they wanted us to call them kings and dukes, I hadn't no objections, 'long as it would keep peace in the family." But, of course, that was precisely Twain's point. All of those "sham grandeurs, sham gauds, and sham chivalries" had *not* kept "peace in the family." They had caused the Civil War.

Taking Huck now, when the war was over, back down the Mississippi would mean having Huck discover what Twain discovered in 1882—that the river he knew as a boy had vanished. Twain realized this, finally, near the end of his life: "There was another of these half-finished stories. I carried it as far as thirty-eight thousand words four years ago, then destroyed it for fear I might some day finish it. Huck Finn was the teller of the story and of course Tom Sawyer and Jim were the heroes of it. But I believe that that trio had done work enough in this world and were entitled to a permanent rest." Twain had not made that decision yet, in 1885, but nearly so. There was something about Huck Finn that could never be replicated. While Twain did not know it yet, the publication of *Huck Finn* was to mark the end of the most important part of his creative life. In the years ahead he rarely returned to the Mississippi, and while he continued to be obsessed with America, he had now become a Connecticut Yankee. Huck was abandoned but not forgotten. Through the years Twain would reflect on the meaning of the book. But it was only in the last years of his life that he realized it was Jim, and not Huck, who was at the center of his story. Twain wrestled with Jim and with his own feelings about African Americans.

All the negroes were friends of ours, and with those of our own age we were in effect comrades. I say in effect, using the phrase as a modification. We were comrades and yet not comrades; color and condition interposed a subtle line which both parties were conscious of and which rendered complete fusion impossible. We had a faithful and affectionate good friend, ally and adviser in "Uncle Dan'l," a middle-aged slave whose head was the best one in the negro quarter, whose sympathies were wide and warm and whose heart was honest and simple and knew no guile. He has served me well these many, many years. I have not seen him for more than half a century and yet spiritually I have had his welcome company a good part of that time and have staged him in books under his own name and as "Jim," and carted him all around—to Hannibal, down the Mississippi on a raft and even across the Desert of Sahara in a balloon—and he has endured it all with the patience and friendliness and loyalty which were his birthright. It was on the farm that I got my strong liking for his race and my appreciation of certain of its finer qualities. This feeling and this estimate have stood the test of sixty years and more and have suffered no impairment. The black face is as welcome to me now as it was then.

If this seems presumptuous, clichéd, perhaps even tinged with prejudice, if Twain's words seem uneasily written and uncomfortably stated—it is because they were. Twain was no different from any American of his time: He had yet to sort out his racial views and struggled to do so. He knew that racism was still a virulent infection in the nation's soul, but like so many people of his time, he did not believe it infected *his.* While he excoriated slavery, he put on "black face" and pranced and prattled in his own private minstrel shows, much to the delight of his Hartford guests. But he grew. Late in his life he became embittered by America's silence on racial matters, calling the nation "the United States of Lyncherdom" and excoriating "the damned human race."

Discomfiting as the questions of race and slavery were to Twain, he returned to them again and again, writing and rewriting his own views and viewing and reviewing his slave-infested Missouri childhood. In *The Tragedy of Pudd'nhead Wilson* (which takes place in a small Missouri town called Dawson's Landing—"a slaveholding town"), Twain puts the question of race at the center of a folk tale in which two infants are switched at birth: the slave child becoming the master and the master's child a slave. The book was a watershed for Twain—the first time he could look at Hannibal (and St. Petersburg) from the outside, as southern towns. Twain then started and discarded three separate stories that featured children of mixed relationships. He could never settle on a proper poignant ending for these stories, perhaps because he could never fully bring himself to write (even in *Pudd'nhead Wilson*) of what southerner Mary Chesnut called "a thing we can't name." As the author of *Pudd'nhead Wilson*, Twain must have agreed with her judgment: "God forgive us, but ours is a monstrous system. Like the patriarchs of old, our men live all in one house with their wives and their concubines; and the mulattos one sees in every family partly resemble the white children. Any lady is ready to tell you who is the father of all the mulatto children in everybody's household but her own. Those, she seems to think, drop from the clouds."

Having attempted and failed, Twain discarded his half-finished manuscripts and came at the issue, a few years later in *Following the Equator*, by indirection. The book, an account of his travels in Asia, is meant as a companion to *The Innocents Abroad*, but Twain is no longer innocent and his subjects are no longer farcical foreigners with strange habits. They are human beings just like us. In a vivid scene he recounts an incident in India where a white master publicly beats his native slave.

> I had not seen the like of this for fifty years. It carried me back to my boyhood, and flashed upon me the forgotten fact that this was the usual way of explaining one's desires to a slave. I was able to remember that the method seemed right and natural to me in those days, I being born to it and unaware that elsewhere there were other methods; but I was also able to remember that those unresented cuffings made me sorry for the victim and ashamed for the punisher.

But something happens then, in the midst of an otherwise innocent travelogue, that had not happened to Twain since *Huckleberry Finn*: He returns to his boyhood, to the Mississippi, and to his father's "cuffing" of a slave—and Twain literally and figuratively crosses his own personal equator. "It is curious—the space-annihilating power of thought," he wrote. "For just one second, all that goes to make the me in me was in a Missourian village, on the other side of the globe, vividly seeing again these forgotten pictures of fifty years ago, and wholly unconscious of all things but just those; and in the next second I was back in Bombay, and that kneeling native's smitten cheek was not done tingling yet! Back to boyhood—fifty years; back to age again, another fifty; and in a flight equal to the circumference of the globe—all in two seconds by the watch!"

Later, in looking back on his life, Twain admitted what he had discovered about himself in India: that the central and singular fact that had shaped his time and shaped him was the question of slavery—that "bald, grotesque and unwarrantable usurpation" of human freedom that "stupefied humanity." And at the heart of slavery was the question of race, of racism—which is what made slavery possible. Race was present, for Twain, everywhere he turned: in his Missouri childhood, in his recollections of "Uncle Dan'l," in the face of Tom Lewis at Quarry Farm, in the strange behavior of his next-door neighbor Harriet Beecher Stowe, and in his own writing. It was "the me in me." It was this, the question of race, that so attracted Twain to Grant. In Grant's struggles Twain saw his own. Like Twain, Grant turned the question of slavery, and race, over and over in his own mind and was faced with it each and every day. Raised by an abolitionist, he employed his father-in-law's slaves, remained silent when his wife defended the institution, and assiduously ignored the calls for racial equality when he was president. Grant condemned slavery and fought against it, and he abhorred racism. But he could not overcome it. Like Twain, he believed the nation's soul was infected by racism, but not *his*. Why?

Why was it that after the loss of more than six hundred thousand Americans in a catastrophic civil conflict, men like Twain and Grant could not complete the victory sealed at Appomattox? Why, deep into their own century, could they not stay the hand of southern (and American) injustice, which freed the slaves to be citizens but then denied them their rights? Books, theses, and endless monographs would be written on the subject in the decades following the passing of Twain's generation, but the simplest answer might well have been uttered by Sam Grant as a commander in Tennessee. One day, observing the lines of the thousands of former slaves following his army, he turned to John Rawlins, one of his closest aides. "I don't know these people," he said.

The author of *Uncle Tom's Cabin* and Twain's Hartford neighbor, Harriet Beecher Stowe. *Courtesy The Harriet Beecher Stowe House, Hartford, Connecticut*

Isabella Beecher Hooker. *Courtesy The Harriet Beecher Stowe House, Hartford, Connecticut*

The *Century* magazine's
Robert Underwood Johnson—
who first approached Grant
about his memoirs.
Courtesy Library of Congress

The Reverend
John Philip Newman.
Courtesy Library of Congress

Mark Twain with John T. Lewis—
the model for "Jim"—at Quarry Farm.
Courtesy Library of Congress

William Tecumseh Sherman
in retirement. *Courtesy Library
of Congress*

Ulysses S. Grant at Mt. McGregor, checking the manuscript of his memoirs. Drs. Douglas and Shrady are at left, with unidentified members of Grant's family. *Courtesy Library of Congress*

Ulysses S. Grant with his family at Mt. McGregor. Left to right: Mrs. Jesse Grant, Nellie Grant Sartoris, Jesse Grant's daughter, Grant, Col. Fred Grant's daughter, Col. Fred Grant's son, Dr. John Douglas, Fred Grant, and Fred Grant's wife. *Courtesy Library of Congress*

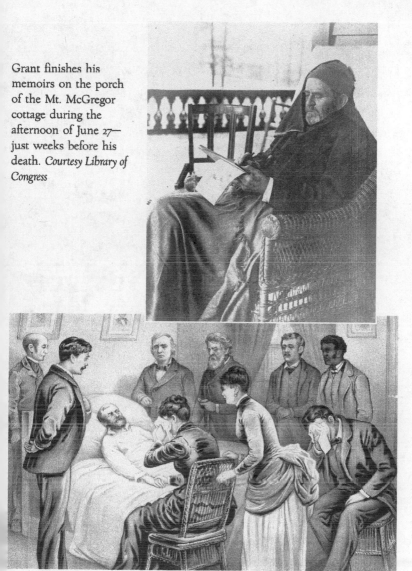

Grant finishes his memoirs on the porch of the Mt. McGregor cottage during the afternoon of June 27—just weeks before his death. *Courtesy Library of Congress*

An artist's rendition of Grant's final moments. Left to right: his nurse, Henry; Buck Grant; Rev. Newman; Julia Dent Grant; Dr. John Douglas; Nellie Grant; Jesse; Harrison; and Col. Fred Grant. *Courtesy Library of Congress*

Grant's funeral procession moves down Broadway in New York. *Courtesy Library of Congress*

Grant's Tomb, in Riverside Park. *Courtesy Library of Congress*

Mark Twain in his last years.
Courtesy Library of Congress

Mark Twain in his bath chair
in 1910. *Courtesy The Mark Twain
Project, Bancroft Library, Berkeley,
California*

E.W.Kemble.

THE END. YOURS TRULY, HUCK FINN.

—∞—

MARK TWAIN RETURNED to Quarry Farm just after Grant arrived at Mt. McGregor. The first volume of Grant's memoirs was now in page proofs, with the second volume yet to be typeset. Twain had spent the days prior to Grant's move to Mt. McGregor visiting the general at his home on 66th Street. While a constant visitor, Twain now seemed to be hovering over the general, hoping to snatch volume two from his hands so that it could be prepared for publication. Grant would not cooperate; he had yet to add some pages to the second volume, he said. Twain had heard this before. When Grant said that he had finished the book, he had really meant to say that he had finished the final draft of volume one. When he said that he had finally finished volume two, what he had meant to say was that he had finished the first draft of volume two. And when he said that he had finally finished that, he added that he wanted to keep the manuscript in order to add just a bit, here and there, those "plums and spices" that were absolutely essential.

Twain was impatient. Grant, he heard, was adding sections to the page proofs of volume one—material that he thought was important to the book. These were not minor changes, and because they were being made to the proofs, they cost Twain money. The entire first volume, Twain feared, would have to be retypeset. Through all of early June Grant worked on his memoirs, editing, rewriting, and sometimes adding as many as twenty pages to sections of the book that were already in proof.

Each day now, Grant added more and more to his memoirs. His most productive day was June 21, when he spent hours sitting on his porch while N. E. Dawson read out large sections of the second volume. From time to time, Grant interrupted Dawson's reading to suggest a change, an edit, or an addition.

Days later, his voice apparently regaining some of its old strength, Grant sat with Dawson and completely rewrote his chapter on Lee's surrender at Appomattox. "During his last days, the General worked almost continually on his book," Dawson later remembered. "I saw that he was sinking fast and suffering intensely, and [I] worked all the time to try and ease his discomfort."

The efforts Grant made to get his book exactly as he wished it—adding, editing, excising, and then redictating huge portions of it—sapped the last of his strength. "I have worked off all I had notes of," he scribbled to Douglas, "and which kept me thinking at night. I will not press to make more notes for the present."

As always, there were constant interruptions. People from all over the nation suddenly turned up at the Balmoral just to be near Grant. One of these visitors was a gray-haired acquaintance who knew Grant before the war and sat with the general on his porch for three hours. When he left, Grant scribbled Douglas a note: "Mr. N is a Texan, but before he went to Texas in '44, he was a great admirer of Mr. Clay. In the contest of '44 between Clay and Polk, he took a vow never to cut his hair until Mr. Clay was President." Other visitors were not so polite, the more intrusive actually attempting to gain Grant's attention by yelling at him from the gallery of visitors that congregated on the cottage lawn.

Grant's condition continued to worsen, and now the cocaine treatments he received to ease his pain became more frequent. As time went on they became increasingly less effective. "I feel worse this A.M. than I have for some time," he wrote to Douglas one day. "My mouth hurts me and cocaine ceases to give me the relief it once did. If its use can be curtailed I hope it will soon have its effect again."

At the end of June, Grant welcomed the addition of a "bath" chair to the cottage's furnishings. The chair, a kind of rickshaw, allowed the general a change of scenery, as it could be pulled to the Balmoral, saving Harrison, Dawson, and Fred from having to carry Grant up the hill to the hotel when he wanted to leave the cottage (and sparing Grant the indignity). The bath chair was pulled to the hotel by Harrison one day, with the help of a group of neighborhood boys. When Grant returned to the cottage, a crowd of spectators watched as Dawson moved him to a large chair on the porch and fluffed his pillows so that he could rest. It was clear to all that he was reaching the end.

One of the most welcome visitors to Grant was Charles Wood of Lansingburgh, that same veteran who had sent him $1,000 "on account of . . . services" and which Grant had returned just after Congress had reinstated him on the retired list. Grant greeted Wood affably, and the aging veteran proved to be as gracious in person as he was in giving Grant the $1,000. He understood that Grant could not speak, so he recounted his own time in the Union Army, reviewed some of its battles, and then left—understanding that Grant was easily tired by long visits. He took with him a note from his old commander: "I am glad to say that while there is much unblushing wickedness in this world, yet there is a compensating goodness of the soul."

During the last week of June, Grant focused on his memoirs, and on June 27—believing that he was within pages of finishing—he sent a note to Mark Twain asking him to come to Mt. McGregor. The note reached Twain on the evening of June 27 and he left immediately to see Grant, arriving at the cottage the next evening. When he arrived, Grant handed him the Century's edited version of his article on the Vicksburg Campaign. Richard Watson Gilder had edited the article and now wanted Grant to add a number of appropriate transition sentences and paragraphs to key sections of the piece—to make it more coherent. Twain and Fred went immediately to work:

The edits were simple to understand, and Grant's notes on the campaign were detailed. Twain was intent that the changes to the article be reflected in Grant's memoirs, so he and Fred worked through the night of June 28 and into the next morning.

Twain hoped that this would be the final edit for volume two and that when he left Mt. McGregor he could take the completed manuscript back with him to Quarry Farm. Grant had other ideas. "If I could have two weeks of strength," he wrote to Twain, "I could improve it very much. As I am, however, it will have to go as is, with verifications by the boys and by suggestions which will enable me to make a point clear here and there." Grant made it clear that he would continue to add to his book. Twain was defeated, though he later admitted that Grant's final efforts on the manuscript made a huge difference. During his short time at Mt. McGregor, Grant wrote a five-hundred-word preface—one of the strongest sections of the book. A part of the preface, dated July 1, was sent to the papers, where it received front-page attention.

Twain's work was done, but he waited at Mt. McGregor to see Jesse Grant, one of the general's sons. Jesse and Twain were involved in a prospective business deal to build a railroad from Constantinople to the Persian Gulf—a franchise given to Jesse by Leland Stanford after Stanford's son (who was to be the president of the company) died. Nothing came of the business arrangement, of course, but Grant was happy to see his son, especially now that it was clear he had very few days remaining.

Simon Bolivar Buckner, Grant's old West Point friend who had once loaned him $50—and the commander of Confederate forces at Ft. Donelson (Grant's first great victory)—visited Grant in late June, just as Twain was set to depart. Buckner reminisced as Grant nodded thoughtfully, smiling easily now in remembering their early days in the army. Buckner was an exceptional commander, retrieving his honor after his surrender at Ft. Donelson by commanding forces at Chickamauga, the great rebel victory in the West. After the war he became editor of the *Louisville Courier* and in 1888 became the governor of Kentucky. Twain sat with the two men and listened to Buckner's stories and then escorted Buckner when he left the cottage grounds. "I have my full share of admiration and esteem for Grant," Buckner said to Twain. "It dates back to our cadet days. He has as many merits and virtues as any man I am acquainted with but he has one deadly defect. He is an incurable borrower and when he wants to borrow he knows of only one limit—he wants what you've got. When I was poor, he borrowed $50 from me; when I was rich, he borrowed 15,000 men."

Twain left then, without Grant's manuscript, and returned to Elmira. "General Grant had no enemies, political or sectional, in these last days," he wrote to his friend Albert Bigelow Paine. "The old soldier battling with a deadly disease yet bravely completing his task, was a figure at once so pathetic and so noble that no breath of animosity remained to utter a single word that was unkind."

When George Shrady arrived at Mt. McGregor, Grant gave him all of his attention. He was fading fast now, Shrady could see, but there was at least a small chance that he could live for several more months. Believing this possible, he ordered Grant to stop using his voice—if even for a short time. He examined Grant and made no comment. The disease had progressed to a fatal point. "I do not suppose," Grant wrote in a note to him, "I will ever have my voice back again at all." Shrady made no comment.

When Grant had trouble breathing that same evening, Shrady gave him morphine, though Grant objected because the drug clouded his mind and made it impossible for him to write. But he had no choice: Each day brought new coughing fits, which usually ended only when Grant, choking on his own blood, was able to vomit and clear his breathing passages. Shrady was intent on reassuring the dying general that while he was now in deep discomfort, his death would be free of pain. Shrady also told Grant that he might well live to the end of the summer and might even be able to return to New York. But, Shrady insisted, Grant must conserve his strength. "It is postponing the final event," Grant wrote to Shrady. "A great number of my acquaintances who were well when the papers commenced announcing that I was dying are now in their graves. They were neither old nor infirm people either. I am ready now to go at any time. I know there is nothing but suffering for me while I live."

The Reverend John Philip Newman, sensing that these were Grant's last days, arrived at Mt. McGregor to visit with him and to comfort Julia. Grant accepted his presence and made him feel at home, but Shrady always attempted to be elsewhere when Newman was in attendance. Grant had Newman read to him from the Book of Matthew, which he enjoyed, and he listened from his porch when Newman conducted Sunday services at the Balmoral. The sound of raised voices singing Christian hymns came clearly through the forest to him as he dozed in his porch chair. In early July, Grant wrote a flurry of notes to Fred about the last chapters of his book and began to write out his final words, intended to close both his writing and his life. When Grant learned that Robert Johnson of the *Century* magazine was at Mt. McGregor to retrieve his Vicksburg article, he summoned him to his cottage and sat with him for a time. "I could hardly keep back the tears as I made my farewell to the great soldier who saved the Union for all its people and to the man of warm and courageous heart who had fought his last long battle for those he so tenderly loved."

Grant spent an uneventful July 4, celebrating Independence

Day by reviewing the work he had done and rewriting again the very end of the book. He was concerned, he told Fred, about the chapter he had written on the battles around Petersburg at the end of the war. He worked diligently through the next week. Shrady, uncertain about Grant's end, left Mt. McGregor. Before he left, Douglas pulled him aside. "I fear the worst the day the General completes his book," he said.

On the afternoon of July 19, as Grant was seated, bundled in his chair, he put down his pencil and looked at Dawson. He smiled a bit, looked back down at his paper, and then handed it to the transcriber. The book was finished, he said. He had done as much as he could. "The dictation for him was painful and his voice got lower and lower as he went on," Dawson recounted. "At last it was a mere whisper and then it stopped altogether. I shall never forget his joy at the completion of his book. He was so afraid in the last weeks that he couldn't finish it or revise it." Several hours after finishing the book, Grant wrote his last message to Douglas.

After all that however the disease is still there and must be fatal in the end. My life is precious of course to my family and would be to me if I could entirely recover. There never was one more willing to go than I am. I know most people have first one and then another little something to fix up, and never quite get through. This was partially my case. I first wanted so many days to work on my book so the authorship would be clearly mine. It was graciously granted to me, after being apparently much lower than since, and with a capacity to do more work than I ever did in the same time. My work has been done so hastily that much was left out and I did all of it over from the crossing of the James River in June/64 to Appomattox. Since then I have added as much as fifty pages to the book, I should think. There is nothing more I should do to it now, and therefore I am not likely to be more ready to go than at this moment.

On the morning of July 20, Grant said that he wanted to visit the nearby knoll one last time. Douglas agreed, and Dawson and Harrison pulled and twisted and pushed the bath chair through the cottage's undergrowth and up the mountainside. It was a difficult climb, and Grant alighted from the chair at key moments to allow Fred and Dawson to move it over the most difficult obstacles. Grant was pale and weak on the summit of the mountain, but he enjoyed the view and the clear, clean air. When Fred suggested they return to the cottage, he agreed. The day was hot and the evening humid. Grant was uncomfortable and had difficulty breathing. Douglas administered two small doses of morphine. When Grant fell asleep, McQueeney suggested they move him to a more airy room. His chair was moved while Grant, nearby, swayed uneasily on his feet. Douglas took his temperature, which had risen throughout the day. His family stayed with him, talking on the porch.

Douglas believed the end was near, and Fred telegraphed Buck in New York City that their father was dying. Shrady arrived the next morning, took the general's pulse, and told the family that Grant was nearing the end. Grant remained conscious throughout that day and into the evening. When asked if he wanted anything, he said, "Water," and it was brought. Still in his chair, Grant rose late in the evening and said he wanted to lie down. This was his surrender. It was the first time in many months that he had not slept in his chair. Julia sat beside him into the early hours of July 22. Newman sat behind her. Late on the evening of July 22, Douglas ordered them to get some sleep, and as the sun rose, he took a walk through the nearby woods. When he returned, Grant's breathing was shallow, feeble, and troubled. He awakened the family. Julia was at her husband's side, with Fred, Buck, Jesse, Nellie, and Douglas nearby. McQueeney, at the head of the bed, gently fanned his face. Ulysses S. Grant died at 8:08 A.M. on the morning of July 23, 1885.

⊶⊷

MARK TWAIN WAS AT Quarry Farm when Grant died. "I then believed he would live several months," he remembered. "He was still adding little perfecting details to his book, and preface, among other things. He was entirely through a few days later. Since then the lack of any strong interest to employ his mind has enabled the tedious weariness to kill him. I think his book kept him alive several months. He was a very great man and superlatively good."

In New York, the newspapers bordered their headlines in black, and the city was nearly silent in mourning. Within one hour of Grant's death, the flags of the city were at half-mast. In Washington, aides to President Grover Cleveland struggled to shape a public message. Julia was past consolation but attempted to busy herself with making the arrangements for her husband's burial. She was given a last note from her husband.

Look after our dear children and direct them in the paths of rectitude. It would distress me far more to hear that one of them could depart from an honorable, upright and virtuous life than it would to know that they were prostrated on a bed of sickness from which they were never to rise alive. They have never given us any cause for alarm on this account, and I trust they never will. With these few injunctions and the knowledge I have of your love and affection and the dutiful affection of all our children, I bid you a final farewell, until we meet in another and, I trust, better world. You will find this on my person on my demise.

John Douglas expressed his own sense of Grant in a long letter to a reporter.

Nine months of close attention to him have only endeared him to me. I have learned to know him as few can know him. The world can know him as a Great General, as a successful politician; but I know him as a patient, self-sacrificing, gentle, quiet, uncomplaining sufferer, looking death calmly in the face and counting almost the hours in which he had to live, and those hours were studied by him that he might contribute something of benefit to some other fellow-sufferer. If he was great in his life, he was even greater in death. Not a murmur, not a moan, from first to last. He died as he had lived, a true man.

Douglas and Shrady concluded that starvation was the cause of death, brought on by complications arising from cancer. A special coffin of polished oak was purchased for Grant. It arrived at the cottage three days after his death—his body being preserved by ice until its arrival. Grant was prepared for burial, and Julia insisted that he be buried in the Prince Albert coat he favored. Fred told an emissary sent to the family from President Cleveland that they did not want a military funeral but that they had not yet decided on a burial place. A local lodge of the Grand Army of the Republic, constituted of Union veterans from Saratoga, served as a temporary honor guard at the cottage until Grant could be moved. A number of offers were then given for a burial place, though Fred had decided that his father would not be buried in Ohio or Illinois—since he had spent the last years of his life in the East. He wired the mayor of New York City that the family was considering an appropriate burial ground in the city. Fred traveled to New York City on July 25, and he and a delegation of officials toured prospective sites. On July 28, Fred decided that his father should be interred at a temporary tomb in Riverside Park overlooking the Hudson. The city architect drew up plans for the tomb (a brick vault with a semicircular roof), closed by a large barred door embossed with the letter G. Formal plans for the funeral were completed during the last week of July.

On August 4, Grant's body was taken from the cottage and, after a long service (which included a ninety-minute peroration from the Reverend John Philip Newman), was transported by rail to Albany. It was accompanied by General Winfield Scott Hancock, a classmate of Grant's, at the head of the U.S. Army's Fourth Infantry—Grant's old unit. The military unit was accompanied by a group of ministers and dignitaries, including William T. Sherman, Joseph Drexel, and Hamilton Fish. Wherever Grant's remains now resided, they were accompanied by a riderless horse with boots reversed—an honor accorded presidents. In Albany, Grant lay in state in the Capitol building for twenty-four hours. On August 6, Grant's casket was put aboard another train for the trip to New York City. The trip took six hours. Crowds of people stood, hushed, as it traveled through the Hudson Valley. As it passed West Point, Grant's train slowed as the assembled Corps of Cadets, ramrod straight, saluted his passing. Tens of thousands of people awaited Grant's arrival in New York City. His casket was transported to City Hall, where it lay in state for another twenty-four hours. Nearly three hundred thousand people passed through City Hall to pay their respects.

On the early morning of August 8, after hundreds of hours

of preparation and coordination, a funeral procession honoring Grant began to assemble at City Hall. General Hancock once more escorted the casket. Hundreds of thousands of people had arrived in the city over the previous days, streaming across the city's bridges and crowding aboard steamboats. They now packed the sidewalks along the route of the procession. In the first line of marchers were eight senior military commanders, including Fitzhugh Lee, Robert E. Lee's nephew. Behind the military came the ministers and behind them Grant's family and close friends, including John Douglas and George Shrady. The funeral car that bore the casket was pulled by twenty-four black stallions. The rank of march was in descending order—from honor guard, military officers, ministers, family, and friends to representatives of the federal, state, and local governments. It was the longest funeral procession in American history to that time, and it moved "like a river" from City Hall up Broadway to 57th Street, then west again to Broadway, then onto 72nd Street, and then north on Riverside Drive to 122nd Street.

The funeral march was well planned, with units and dignitaries joining the procession at assigned spots. In all, and not counting the thousands of dignitaries, sixty thousand members of the U.S. military had been assigned by President Cleveland to march in the funeral procession. In addition to these thousands, General Daniel Sickles, who had lost a leg at Gettysburg, rode at the head of eighteen thousand members of the Grand Army of the Republic. At Julia's request, President Cleveland appointed Generals Joe Johnston and Simon Bolivar Buckner to be two of Grant's honorary pallbearers—representing the Confederacy. William T. Sherman and Philip Sheridan, Grant's old comrades in arms, walked with them. Thousands jammed the route. Nearly every building was hung with black. What color there was came from the flags—thousands of them in red, white, and blue that were hung, waved, and carried by nearly every man, woman, and child. Grant's picture, his well-trimmed beard, his face expressionless, adorned almost every major building.

At precisely 2:30 P.M., Grant's catafalque, escorted by General Hancock, his aides, the members of the Fourth Infantry, the family and ministers to Ulysses S. Grant, the president and secretary of state—and then the thousands who had marched behind them—began to file into Riverside Park. Hancock's appearance was signaled from a nearby palisade to a fleet of warships anchored in the Hudson, and the ships began to boom out their homage. Two hours later, after a short service, Grant's casket was officially interred in the temporary mausoleum. The temporary pallbearers placed the casket on its short pedestal and stood aside as Hancock intoned: "God of battles, Father of all. Amidst this mournful assembly we seek Thee with whom there is no death."

MARK TWAIN WAS NOT a part of the funeral. Instead, early that morning, he took up his position in the window of his publishing firm overlooking Union Square to watch the funeral procession. He stood there for five hours watching the procession as it snaked its way north through Manhattan. When it was finished, Twain returned to his work. He had plans for a new book that needed to be written. He had great hopes for a new typesetting machine that he believed would transform the printing industry and make him a rich man. But he knew that the man interred that day, his good friend, had forever changed his life.

Over the years that followed, Twain returned to mull over this relationship in his notebooks and autobiography. He spent hundreds of hours and thousands of words summarizing his feelings for the man and attempting to plumb the meaning of their relationship. His greatest homage to Grant, a man he could never bring himself to call "Sam"—no matter how close they had become—may well have already been penned, however, in the opening words of *Huckleberry Finn*. This "Notice" was not a dedication. Indeed, it was more of an afterthought, having been written after the book was completed. In it, Twain recognized the central role of Jim by calling his story a "narrative"—akin to the slave narratives that had told of innumerable flights to freedom. And in the next line, Twain came as close as he was ever to come in recognizing how Grant had helped him finish his book.

NOTICE.

Persons attempting to find a motive in this narrative
will be prosecuted; persons attempting to find a moral
in it will be banished; persons attempting to
find a plot in it will be shot.

BY ORDER OF THE AUTHOR
Per G.G., CHIEF OF ORDNANCE.

Twain never unwrapped the riddle of this passage, nor did he ever hint at who "G.G." might be. But the "G.G." of *Huckleberry Finn* can only refer to Twain's true "chief of ordnance" and his good friend, a man he always referred to out of respect as "General Grant."

"MANY A DEEP REMORSE"

The first volume of the *Personal Memoirs of U. S. Grant* was published on December 10, 1885. On February 27 of the next year, Twain presented Julia Grant with a check for $200,000. To that time it was the largest royalty payment ever made in U.S. publishing history. Grant had won his race and Twain had won his bet. Over the course of the next decade, Twain presented Julia with several more checks. In all, she received nearly $450,000 from the sale of her husband's book. Twain's publishing firm enjoyed an appreciable profit from the sales of Grant's *Memoirs*, even after he had added up the cost of publicity and printing. Twain was overjoyed. But he soon learned that his firm was deeply in debt and within a few years it was struggling to stay alive. In all, he intimated to friends, the Grant enterprise had netted him $200,000. The American people received much more. For millions of them, the final words of Grant's *Memoirs* came to symbolize the lesson of a war that divided a nation and cost six hundred thousand lives. "Let us have peace," Grant wrote. They were the last words of his book.

Writing in *Patriotic Gore* one century later, Edmund Wilson noted, "The thick pair of volumes of the *Personal Memoirs* used to stand, like a solid attestation of the victory of the Union forces, on the shelves of every pro-Union home." Grant's *Memoirs* was more than a publishing triumph. It may well be the most powerful military memoir in print, vying with Julius Caesar's commentaries as (in Wilson's words) "the most remarkable work of its kind." The British poet and essayist Matthew Arnold was another of Grant's admirers: "I found a language all astray in its use of *will* and *shall*, *should* and *would*, an English employing the verb to conscript and the participle *conscripting*, and speaking in a dispatch to the Secretary of War of having *badly whipped* the enemy; an English without charm and without high breeding." Twain took great umbrage at this, not understanding that Arnold's point was that the writing's lack of "high breeding" was its great strength. "There is one striking thing about Grant's orders: no matter how hurriedly he may write them on the field, no one ever had the slightest doubt as to their meaning, or ever had to read them over a second time to understand them," said George Meade, Grant's fellow commander, during the war. That was true of Grant's *Memoirs*.

Wilson extolled Grant's memoirs by grounding them in Grant's personality. "This capacity for inspiring confidence," he said, "this impression Grant gave of reserves of force, comes through in the *Personal Memoirs* without pose or premeditation. Grant faltered a little in the later chapters—sometimes repeating himself—when his suffering blurs the text; but, in general, the writing of the *Memoirs* is perfect in concision and clearness, in its propriety and purity of language. Every word that Grant writes has its purpose, yet everything seems understated." Wilson then added: "These literary qualities, so unobtrusive, are evidence of a natural fineness of character, mind and taste; and the *Memoirs* convey also Grant's dynamic force and the definiteness of his personality. Perhaps never has a book so objective in form seemed so personal in every line, and though the tempo is never increased, the narrative, once we get into the war, seems to move with the increasing momentum that the soldier must have felt in the field."

Ernest Hemingway once wrote that "all modern American literature comes from one book by Mark Twain called *Huckleberry Finn*." That may well be true for American fiction, but it is not true for American nonfiction, which is our nation's most lasting and important gift to the world. Americans love nonfiction—we are a nation consumed by politics and history. If Twain, as Hemingway supposes, wrote the quintessential American novel, then Grant, his friend, wrote the single most important work of nonfiction in our literature: It ranks with *Walden* as a symbol of the American character. Grant's book is not simply a profound narrative written with "dynamic force"; it is, as Twain rightly described it, "a literary masterpiece." Grant attempted to tell *our* story to *us*—and he succeeded.

❦

JULIA GRANT CONTINUED to live in New York City until the end of her life. She wrote her memoirs, participated in the women's suffrage movement, and spoiled her twelve grandchildren. She became good friends with Varina Davis, the widow of former Confederate president Jefferson Davis. She died in 1904 and was interred in Riverside Park, next to her husband.

Fred also remained in New York City, where he became president of the American Wood Working Company. He was involved in politics—and was mentioned as a potential vice presidential nominee for the 1888 Republican Party ticket. He served as ambassador to the Austro-Hungarian Empire, was a high-ranking officer during the Spanish-American War, and commanded a brigade in the Philippines, fighting the local insurrection. He died in New York in 1912 and was buried, a major general, at West Point. Fred's son, Ulysses S. Grant III, graduated from West Point in 1903, served in World War I, and retired a major general.

Nellie Grant finally divorced "Algie" after her father's death and returned to the United States. She lived with her mother in New York City. She rarely spoke of her father. Fred's two brothers, Jesse and Buck, did not follow in their father's footsteps: They opened the profitable U. S. Grant Hotel in San Diego, and later in his life Buck became a respected genealogist.

William Tecumseh Sherman, irascible to the last, died in New York City in 1891. Joe Johnston was one of his pallbearers, as he had been for Grant. Johnston contracted pneumonia during Sherman's funeral and died one month later.

Roswell Smith continued in his role as one of the early titans of New York publishing. He was the owner of Scribner's and remained, for many years, an arbiter of America's literary tastes. His disciple Richard Watson Gilder also exerted considerable influence on American arts and letters. He and his wife's Friday evening dinners in New York City became a gathering place for writers. He died, after a long illness, in 1909. Robert Underwood Johnson succeeded Gilder as editor of the Century and was a noted poet and anti-imperialist. Johnson wrote "The White Man's Burden"—a powerful condemnation of racism. He died, having lived a life of great usefulness, in 1937.

What is the White Man's burden
That weighs upon his sleep?

> To hear the hundreds dying?
> To see the thousands weep?
> Oh, wanton war that haunts him!
> Oh, seed that he must reap!

William Henry Vanderbilt and Senator Jerome Chaffee joined Grant in death in 1885. Dr. George Shrady died in 1908 after a long and distinguished career. He was noted as a reformer in his profession and successfully lobbied the New York legislature to pass a law requiring that doctors be tested and licensed. An empiricist and believer in science, Shrady died believing there were no such things as germs.

Dr. John Douglas fell on hard times. To make ends meet, his wife opened a boardinghouse in Bethlehem, Pennsylvania. His great contribution to history was his extensive and detailed recounting of the last days of Ulysses S. Grant. He died in penury.

The year after Grant's death, Adam Badeau published *Grant in Peace*—a biography of his former commander's last years. He argued with Fred Grant, and in March 1888 they went to court over money that Badeau claimed he was owed. Badeau accepted a payment of just over $11,000 from Fred. He continued to be widely published. He died, quietly, in 1891.

Karl Gerhardt reentered the life of the Grant family, casting the general's death mask. But he refused to turn it over to the family until he was paid $17,000. Julia Grant was enraged by this demand and refused. Twain was embarrassed. To resolve the issue, he paid Gerhardt $10,000 from his own funds. The last Twain heard of Gerhardt, he was an itinerant minister, preaching fire and brimstone in revivals staged in rural Louisiana, where he died.

James Fish and Ferdinand Ward each spent six years in

prison for their role in the scandal surrounding the bankruptcy of Grant & Ward. A broken man, Ward died in his hometown in upstate New York.

———— ✺ ————

AFTER GRANT'S DEATH, Mark Twain wrote and published *A Connecticut Yankee in King Arthur's Court, The American Claimant, The Tragedy of Pudd'nhead Wilson, Personal Recollections of Joan of Arc, Tom Sawyer, Detective, Following the Equator, The Mysterious Stranger, What Is Man?*—and innumerable essays and short stories. None of them were as popular as *Adventures of Huckleberry Finn*.

Twain's last years were filled with tragedy. The publishing firm he founded with Charles Webster was beset by debts and infighting. Under constant threats and pressures from Twain, Webster collapsed from exhaustion and died a young man. Twain expended all of the profits he had gained from *Huck Finn* and Grant's *Memoirs*—sinking most of the money into the development of the Paige Typesetting Machine, which he believed would revolutionize publishing. It bankrupted him. Twain gamely attempted to recover his fortunes by returning to his work with new fervor, but none of his writing projects reached his expectations.

Aging and bankrupt, Twain retreated to Europe, then embarked on another speaking tour. It was a success and allowed him to pay some of his debts. But in the midst of his celebration—in August 1896—he learned that his beloved daughter Susy had died of a mysterious fever. "In my age as in my youth," he wrote, "night brings me many a deep remorse. I realize that from the cradle up I have been like the rest of the race—never quite sane in the night." The death of Susy stayed with him forever, but he continued to fight, turning most of his attention to political questions. He condemned racism and lynching, imperialism and war. He wrote as prolifically as he had as a young man. Most of it was brilliant—but the best of what he wrote in his last years would not be published in his lifetime.

Twain knew and understood death. But it was still a shock when Livy died, during a trip to Europe, in 1904.

A respected and celebrated icon of American literature, Twain was feted constantly by his friends and admirers in New York. While he never lost his public humor, the death of Susy and Livy embittered him. He accepted an honorary degree from Oxford University, then returned to the United States and lived at his new home, Stormfield, in Redding, Connecticut. When he traveled he was pushed and pulled in what looked like a replica of Grant's bath chair—and his neck was swaddled in a scarf to keep away the cold. His health began to fail. He died at 6:22 in the evening of April 21, 1910. Services were held in New York. One of the mourners was William Dean How-ells, who wept. Howells succumbed to pneumonia at the age of eighty-three, in 1920.

The author acknowledges those previous works on the final years and death of Ulysses S. Grant by historians Richard Goldhurst (*Many Are the Hearts: The Agony and Triumph of Ulysses S. Grant*) and Thomas M. Pitkin (*The Captain Departs: Ulysses S. Grant's Last Campaign*). While Mark Twain's friendship with Grant during the general's last days is not the primary focus of their work, Pitkin and Goldhurst provided an essential starting point for this book.

Grant never commented in writing on his relationship with Twain, but his family and friends did—in numerous letters and reminiscences. Twain himself was the friendship's key chronicler. He devoted hundreds of pages to his relationship with Grant, though he remained largely silent on the extent of Grant's illness. That Twain was a "Grant-intoxicated man" is clear from his own writing in the extensive notebooks and letters that he left behind. He continued to talk and write about his relationship with Grant until his death.

The University of California's three volumes of Twain's journals were an indispensable aid in this study. The Mark Twain Papers at the University of California, Berkeley, represent the largest holding of Twain papers in the nation. The scholars, archivists, and historians at Berkeley's "Mark Twain Papers and Project" have built an impressive and unparalleled repository for the study of Twain's life and work.

The manuscript of *Adventures of Huckleberry Finn* is in the Buffalo and Erie County Public Library in Buffalo, New York. I commend to the reader *The Annotated Huckleberry Finn*, edited and with an introduction by Michael Patrick Hearn, as the most detailed study of how Twain wrote *Huckleberry Finn*. The annotations in the manuscript are an invaluable line-by-line guide to the manuscript.

The most widely accepted and comprehensive edition of *Huckleberry Finn* was published by Random House in 1996, soon after the rediscovery of the original first half of the manuscript. While *Huckleberry Finn* has been published in various formats by dozens of publishers through the years, for the purposes of this book I have used the most accessible and popular modern paperback edition, published by the Modern Library.

The letters of Ulysses S. Grant, his manuscripts, presidential papers, wartime dispatches, and battle reports, are scattered throughout the nation. The most extensive collections of Grant's papers are at the Library of Congress, the New York Public Library, and the Chicago Historical Society. The most extensive collection of Grant's wartime dispatches is contained in *The War of the Rebellion: The Official Records of the Union and Confederate Armies*. Over 125 volumes in length, the *Official Records* are the best testimony of Grant's clarity of thought and style.

Personal Memoirs of U. S. Grant was published by Charles L. Webster in 1885 in two volumes. The most accessible edition of the *Memoirs* was published by the Modern Library in 1999 and is based precisely on Grant's manuscript. All citations in this work from the *Memoirs* come from that edition. My appreciation also goes to to a little-known but invaluable Web site on Grant: www.mscomm.com/~ulysses/.

No book on Grant could ever be complete without a detailed reading of the work of his prodigious and talented biographers, particularly Lloyd Lewis, Bruce Catton, William S. McFeely, Brooks D. Simpson, and Jean Edward Smith. I commend the reader to these works and that of Adam Badeau, Grant's first and most controversial biographer. His work has stood the test of time. The depth and breadth of work on Grant is paralleled by that done on Twain. The two most outstanding biographies of the writer were completed by Albert Bigelow Paine and Justin Kaplan. Kaplan's work is still a hallmark of scholarship and insight. However, in terms of the story told in this book, the work of a number of Twain scholars remains paramount. The articles and insights of James Cox, Shelley Fisher Fishkin, Michael Hoffman, Myra Jehlin, Leo Marx, and Neil Schmitz (whose works are noted in the bibliography) were of inestimable help.

Finally, Drs. George F. Shrady's and John H. Douglas's service to Ulysses S. Grant was completed only when they made their notes and thoughts available to the public. If Grant and Twain were remembered solely for the loyalty of their friends, their reputations would ring through history.

NOTES

⬤⬤⬤

PROLOGUE: "HE FIGHTS"

xiii   Girth did not come with fame: *Grant: A Biography*, William S. McFeeley, Norton, New York, 1981, p. 13. See also *Personal Memoirs of Ulysses S. Grant*, Ulysses S. Grant, Modern Library, New York, pp. 15–16.

xiv   The tanner's son had a hard-nosed quality: Ibid., p. 17. See also *Ulysses S. Grant: Triumph over Adversity*, Brooks D. Simpson, Houghton Mifflin, Boston, 2000, pp. 31 32 (hereafter Simpson).

"He fights": *Abraham Lincoln and Men of War-Times*, Alexander K. McClure, Times Publishing, Philadelphia, 1892, p. 111. See also *Grant*, Jean Edward Smith, Simon & Schuster, New York, 2001, p. 178 (hereafter Smith).

"He looks as if he meant it," the private said: *The Civil War: A Narrative*, vol. 3, Shelby Foote, Random House, New York, 1974, p. 148.

"He habitually wears an expression": Ibid., p. 6.

xv   "We must make up our minds to get into line of battle": Ibid., p. 123.

"Ulysses don't scare worth a damn": *Patriotic Gore*, Edmund Wilson, W. W. Norton & Co., New York, 1962, p. 134.

xvi   Ulysses S. Grant's financial partner Ferdinand Ward: *Grant: A Biography*, p. 149. See also *Many Are the Hearts: The Agony and Triumph of*

Ulysses S. Grant, Richard Goldhurst, Reader's Digest Press, New York, 1975, pp. 5–9, and *The Captain Departs: Ulysses S. Grant's Last Campaign*, Thomas M. Pitkin, Southern Illinois University Press, Carbondale, 1973, pp. 10–13.

xvi　While less dashing than the evanescent Ward: *Grant: A Biography*, p. 460.

xvii　"There's millions in it": *The Gilded Age*, Mark Twain, Modern Library, New York, 2002, p. 88.

"Some men worship rank," Twain had once written: *Mark Twain's Notebooks and Journals*, vol. 1, Frederick Anderson, Michael B. Frank, and Kenneth M. Saunderson, eds., University of California Press, Berkeley, 1975, p. 334. See also *The Quotable Mark Twain: His Essential Aphorisms, Witticisms and Concise Opinions*, Kent Rasmussen, ed., Contemporary Books, New York, 1998, p. 184.

xviii　Buck borrowed $100,000 from his father-in-law: *Many Are the Hearts*, p. 9.

Within three years, Grant's initial investments were worth $750,000: Ibid., p. 4.

xix　Ward arrived at the Grant home at midmorning on May 4: *The Captain Departs*, p. 4.

xx　That afternoon, Grant visited the home of an old friend: *Many Are the Hearts*, p. 3.

"I care nothing for the Marine Bank, General Grant": Ibid., p. 4. See also *Grant: A Biography*, pp. 492, 508. Vanderbilt was privately critical of Grant for not being more careful with his money—and attributed the habit to Grant's having too much of it too soon. He said that while there was much sympathy for Grant, there was also "much fault-finding."

xxi　He told Buck that they should pay a visit to Mr. Ward: *Many Are the Hearts*, pp. 5–6.

"We'll wait," Elkins said: Ibid., p. 6. The specific events of the Grant-Ward confrontation were given by Buck to *The New York Times* (in an article dated July 8, 1884) and the *New York Tribune* (in an article dated May 8, 1884). From May 8 to May 13, *The New York Times* and the *New York Tribune* printed no fewer than one dozen articles on the bankruptcy of Grant & Ward.

"The whole thing is suspicious," he said: Ibid., p. 6.

An angry crowd gathered at the bank: Ibid., p. 7.

xxii　"The Marine Bank closed this morning": "Grant & Ward Bankrupt," *The New York Times*, May 10, 1884, p. 1.

xxiii   It was to be a grand event, national in scope: *The Autobiography of Mark Twain*, Mark Twain (Charles Neider, ed.), Harper & Row, New York, 1959, p. 234.

"He has taught me to abhor and detest the Sabbath-day": *Mr. Clemens and Mark Twain: A Biography*, Justin Kaplan, Simon & Schuster, New York, 1966, p. 266. See also Introduction to *The Annotated Huckleberry Finn*, Michael Patrick Hearn, W. W. Norton & Co., New York, 2001, p. liii.

he was "a Grant-intoxicated man": Ibid., pp. 223–24.

xxiv   "My father and I," Clemens wrote, "were always on the most distant terms": *The Autobiography of Mark Twain*, p. 28.

"I shook hands and then there was a pause and silence": Ibid., p. 317.

As Grant sat, impassively, listening: Ibid., pp. 317–20.

xxv   "I fetched him up," he wrote to his wife: "Letter to Olivia Langdon Clemens," in the Mark Twain Papers, vol. 3, University of California Library, Berkeley, p. 222 (hereafter Mark Twain Papers). See also *Mark Twain's Letters*, vol. 2, Albert Bigelow Paine, Harper & Brothers, New York, 1917, pp. 370–73.

xxvi   Howells was suitably grateful, but Grant was modest: *Many Are the Hearts*, pp. 126–27.

"I argued that the book would have an enormous sale," he recounted: *The Autobiography of Mark Twain*, p. 310.

xxvii   IS GRANT GUILTY?: "Is Grant Guilty?" *New York Post*, May 5, 1884, p. 1.

xxviii   "Now that I am at liberty to treat these things as my own": *Many Are the Hearts*, p. 24. See also "The Last Days of General Grant," Adam Badeau, *Century* magazine 30 (October 1885), p. 153.

xxix   In the midst of his financial crisis, Charles Wood: *Many Are the Hearts*, pp. 21–22.

An old friend closer to Grant, Mexican ambassador Mathias Romero: Ibid., p. 22.

CHAPTER ONE: "A MAN WITH FIRE"

3   That was not true of his father, Jesse: *Grant: A Biography*, pp. 5–8.

Hannah Simpson was a strong-willed Pennsylvania woman: Ibid., p. 7.

The house was sparsely furnished, as Hannah insisted: Ibid., p. 10.

But Jesse was not well liked: Smith, p. 22.

5   Jesse Grant was proud of his son Ulysses and showed him off: Ibid., p. 23.

5   Throughout his life, Grant had an affinity for horses: Ibid.

When his mother was warned that her three-year-old son: *Many Are the Hearts*, p. 31. There were persistent reports among some of Grant's colleagues that his mother was "simple-minded," a rumor mentioned in McFeeley's seminal biography of the general. But he, and other biographers, have since noted that Hannah Grant prized education—pushing her own husband to read more frequently and insisting that her son Ulysses do well in school. Interestingly, Hannah Grant was a loyal Democrat and believed it a national tragedy when the Republicans were elected in 1860. When her son, a Republican, was elected president, she never visited the White House.

6   "Well, Ulysses, you've become quite a great man": *Many Are The Hearts*, p. 32.

"I'll work at it though, if you wish me to": Ibid., p. 33.

He bore the casual hooting and indiscreet bullyings: *Personal Memoirs of Ulysses S. Grant*, p. 11.

7   He worked diligently: Ibid., p. 10.

His only truly unique and eccentric quality: *Many Are the Hearts*, p. 111. Grant recognized this quality. In his later years he carried this obsession to unusual lengths, refusing to acknowledge to anyone that he was ever lost. It nearly cost him his life during the Battle of the Wilderness, where rather than turn back through a thickly wooded area, he insisted that his staff follow him straight ahead—where they ran into a Confederate patrol. Grant barely escaped.

8   Jesse made enough money to enroll his son: *Personal Memoirs of Ulysses S. Grant*, p. 10.

White expected his pupils to teach themselves: Ibid., p. 11.

"They taught me that a noun was the name of a person": Ibid., p. 8.

Jesse Grant's son had big ideas: Ibid., p. 9.

9   While Jesse had campaigned for Hamer: Ibid., p. 13.

"I received your letter": *Many Are the Hearts*, pp. 36–37.

"My father said he thought I would": *Personal Memoirs of Ulysses S. Grant*, p. 12.

10   It was then, and still is, a tradition at West Point: Ibid., 14.

He stood barely five feet one: *Grant: A Biography*, p. 13.

11   Grant finished his first year near the bottom of his class: Ibid., p. 16. Grant never claimed to be a good student: "I did not take hold of my studies with avidity," he later wrote. "In fact, I rarely read over a lesson the second time during my entire cadetship."

11   a "breeding ground for snobbery and a waste of money": *Many Are the Hearts*, pp. 38–39.

12   "very wearisome and uninteresting": *Personal Memoirs of Ulysses S. Grant*, p. 15.

"The subject was so easy to me as to come almost by intuition": Ibid.

"I do love the *place*": "U. S. Grant to R. M. Griffith," September 22, 1839, in *The Papers of Ulysses S. Grant*, vol. 1, John Y. Simons, ed., Southern Illinois University Press, Carbondale, 1991, pp. 4–8.

13   He struggled in French: *Many Are the Hearts*, p. 40.

as if "man and beast had been welded together": Ibid., p. 39.

14   The class of 1846: See *The Class of 1846: Stonewall Jackson, George McClellan and Their Brothers*, John G. Waugh, Warner Books, New York, 1994.

While he graduated twenty-first in his class: *Personal Memoirs of Ulysses S. Grant*, p. 17.

15   Grant did the best he could to keep his mind focused on his work: *Grant: A Biography*, p. 20.

The large Dent family was led by the imposing: Ibid., pp. 22–23.

16   There was a small herd of cattle and dozens of chickens: Ibid.

"That young man will be heard from some day": *Many Are the Hearts*, pp. 46–47. See also *Captain Sam Grant*, Lloyd Lewis, Little, Brown & Co., Boston, 1950, p. 105.

17   "His cheeks were warm, and round, and rosy; his hair was fine and brown": Ibid.

"You are too young and the boy is too poor": Ibid., p. 47. See also *Captain Sam Grant*, p. 112. Colonel Dent did not say this directly to his future son-in-law, rather pleading that his daughter Julia's health was too frail for that of an army wife.

18   "Colonel Dent, I want to marry your daughter Julia": *Captain Sam Grant*, p. 112.

19   "In going away now I feel as if I had someone else than myself": "U. S. Grant to Julia Dent (undated)," in *The Papers of Ulysses S. Grant*, vol. 1, p. 101.

"Evry thing looks beliggerent to a spectator": Ibid., p. 109.

"Don't fear for me my Dear Julia": Quoted in full in *Captain Sam Grant*, p. 156.

"It was a terrible sight to go over the ground the next day": "Ulysses S. Grant to Julia Dent," in *The Papers of Ulysses S. Grant*, vol. 1, pp. 148–50. See also Simpson, p. 39.

20   "Wherever there are battles a great many must suffer": *The Papers of Ulysses S. Grant*, vol. 1, pp. 148–50.

21   Grant showed his mettle as a soldier: *Grant: A Biography*, pp. 33–34.

"getting very tired of his war": "Ulysses S. Grant to Julia Dent," in *The Papers of Ulysses S. Grant*, vol. 1, p. 163. See also Simpson, p. 39.

"While it was a most inspiring sight": *Personal Memoirs of Ulysses S. Grant*, p. 53.

"You could not keep Grant out of battle": *Many Are the Hearts*, p. 53.

22   "There goes a man with fire": Simpson, p. 44.

"If you were here I should never wish to leave Mexico": "Ulysses S. Grant to Julia Dent," in *The Papers of Ulysses S. Grant*, vol. 1, p. 164.

23   "He came out of his shell in her presence": *Many Are the Hearts*, p. 47.

"You can get a leave of absence once or twice a year": Ibid., p. 54. See also *Grant: A Biography*, p. 43.

24   Grant was crestfallen: *Personal Memoirs of Ulysses S. Grant*, p. 107.

"We sail directly for the Isthmus": "U. S. Grant to Julia Dent Grant," in *The Papers of Ulysses S. Grant*, vol. 1, August 3, 1851, pp. 211–12.

He bought a farm, but it washed away: *Grant: A Biography*, pp. 48–50.

"I am doing all I can to put up a penny": "U. S. Grant to Julia Dent Grant," in *The Papers of Ulysses S. Grant*, vol. 1, February 10, 1852, pp. 232–33.

"Liquor seemed a virulent poison to him": Simpson, p. 58.

In the fall of 1853, Grant: Ibid., p. 60.

25   "You never complain of being lonesome": "U. S. Grant to Julia Dent Grant," in *The Papers of Ulysses S. Grant*, vol. 1, March 6, 1854, p. 322.

"Whoever hears of me in ten years": Ibid., p. 324.

Grant booked passage on a ship to New York: Simpson, p. 62.

26   "Evry [sic] day I like farming better": "U. S. Grant to Jesse Grant," in *The Papers of Ulysses S. Grant*, vol. 1, December 28, 1856, pp. 134–35.

"He was no hand to manage negroes," a neighbor recalled: In "A Slave Talks About Grant," an interview with Mary Robinson, in Ulysses S. Grant home page www.mscomm.com/~ulysses/.

"I could tell you enough about Mr. Grant": Ibid.

27   So at the age of thirty-eight: *Grant: A Biography*, p. 56.

28   The townspeople of Galena outfitted the recruits: Ibid., p. 79.
Even Illinois governor Richard Yates thought Grant unimpressive: Simpson, p. 82.

28   In his first command in Missouri: Ibid., pp. 86–87.

29   "I was received with so little cordiality": *Personal Memoirs of Ulysses S. Grant*, p. 147.

But Fort Donelson, deep in the Tennessee woods: *The Civil War: A Narrative*, vol. 1, pp. 194–209.

"Sir: Yours of this date proposing Armistice": Ibid., p. 212.

30   "I gave up all idea of saving the Union": *Personal Memoirs of Ulysses S. Grant*, p. 193.

"one of the most brilliant in the world": *The Civil War: A Narrative*, vol. 2, p. 639.

31   "He's a little 'un," he said: Ibid., vol. 3, p. 24.

"This is a crisis that cannot be looked upon too seriously": Ibid., p. 185.

32   Ulysses S. Grant's "Forty Days": Ibid., pp. 146–317.

33   Grant's two terms as president: *Grant: A Biography*, pp. 400–49.

34   On May 26, Ferdinand Ward returned to New York: *Many Are the Hearts*, p. 19.

CHAPTER TWO: "A WOUNDED LION"

36   Samuel Langhorne Clemens, the sixth child of John Marshall: *Mr. Clemens and Mark Twain*, p. 18. See also *Mark Twain: A Biography*, Albert Bigelow Paine, IndyPublish.com, McLean, Virginia, 1994 (reprint), pp. 6–9.

described by Clemens as "a child's paradise": *The Autobiography of Mark Twain*, p. 5.

"A pilot, in those days": Ibid., p. 128. See also *Mark Twain: An Illustrated Biography*, Geoffrey C. Ward, Dayton Duncan, and Ken Burns, Alfred A. Knopf, New York, 2001, p. 24.

"Two things seemed pretty apparent to me," he later wrote: Ibid.

37   "For forty-eight hours I labored at the bedside": Ibid., p. 20.

"When I retired from the rebel army in '61": Ibid., p. 27.

"I succumbed and grew as frenzied as the craziest": Ibid., p. 35.

38   "I began to get tired of staying in one place so long": Ibid., p. 36.

"I am tired of being a beggar," he wrote to Orion: Ibid.

39   "The foremost among the gentlemen of the California press": Ibid., p. 55.

"of the western character of ludicrous exaggeration": *Mr. Clemens and Mark Twain*, p. 34.

40   "We wish to learn all the curious, outlandish ways" *Mark Twain: An Illustrated Biography*, p. 63.

41   Charles Dudley Warner, the editor of the *Hartford Courant*: Ibid., pp. 54–56. See also *Mr. Clemens and Mark Twain*, pp. 203–04.

"I'll harass that girl and harass that girl": *Mark Twain: An Illustrated Biography*, p. 75.

"They said with one accord that I got drunk oftener than was necessary": Ibid., p. 77.

42   *The Innocents Abroad* sold one hundred thousand copies: *Mr. Clemens and Mark Twain*, pp. 57, 98.

On February 2, 1870, Livy Langdon and Mark Twain were married: *Mark Twain: An Illustrated Biography*, p. 78.

"The fountains of my great deep are broken up": Ibid., p. 79.

In 1870, Livy gave birth to a son, Langdon: Ibid., p. 86.

43   ("the most detestable lecture campaign that ever was"): Ibid.

"Susy is bright & strong & we love her so": Ibid.

"the quietest of all quiet places": Ibid., pp. 96–97. In all, the Clemens family spent twenty summers at Quarry Farm. Twain thought it "the quietest of all quiet places" because, in part "we have no neighbors."

44   "I begin to write incidents out of real life": Ibid., p. 105.

"Mr. Clemens was never so good and loveable as he is now": Ibid., pp. 117–18.

45   "The Clemenses are whole-souled hosts": *Mr. Clemens and Mark Twain*, p. 144.

"The study is a wonderful study of the boy-mind" *Mark Twain: An Illustrated Biography*, p. 101. See also *Writing Huck Finn*, Victor A. Doyno, University of Pennsylvania Press, Philadelphia, 1991, and *Dangerous Water*, Ron Powers, Basic Books, New York, 1999. The fullest account of the writing of *Huckleberry Finn* can be found in Michael Patrick Hearn's *An Introduction to The Annotated Huckleberry Finn*, Michael Patrick Hearn, ed., W. W. Norton & Company, New York, 2001.

"Just think of this going on all day long": Ibid., p. 135. It was mostly Twain's fault. Ward, Duncan, and Burns catalog the incessant parties, masquerades, and dinners that Twain insisted his family hold for their friends and his colleagues.

46   "old Mississippi days of steamboating glory": *Mr. Clemens and Mark Twain*, p. 184.

"What a virgin subject": Ibid.

46   "The piece about the Mississippi is capital": Hearn, p. 101.
"another boy's book": Ibid., p. 117.

47   "So this is the little lady that caused this Civil War": *Harriet Beecher Stowe: A Life*, Joan D. Hedrick, Oxford University Press, New York, 1994, pp. 299–300. As Hedrick herself notes, the story of the meeting of Lincoln and Harriet Beecher Stowe, while repeated and quoted through the years, is probably apocryphal.

"You can have no idea of the pleasure of being admired": *Mr. Clemens and Mark Twain*, pp. 157–58.

48   The stammering but handsome Henry Ward Beecher: Ibid., p. 160.

"bullets to kill men with": *Harriet Beecher Stowe: A Life*, p. 106.

Henry Ward Beecher was discovered: Ibid., pp. 374–78.

49   that "virago," that "griffon"—as the press pilloried her: Ibid., p. 375.

"This nation is not reflected in [Massachusetts abolitionist] Charles Sumner": "Samuel L. Clemens to Orion Clemens," *Mark Twain Papers*, vol. 2, p. 542.

50   "the human being is a stupidly-constructed machine": *Mr. Clemens and Mark Twain*, p. 158.

she would "slip up behind a person": *Mark Twain: A Biography*, vol. 2, p. 224.

51   "In my schoolboy days I had no aversion to slavery": *The Autobiography of Mark Twain*, p. 8.

"In the small town of Hannibal, Missouri, when I was a boy": Ibid., p. 9.

"Began another boy's book": *Mr. Clemens and Mark Twain*, p. 197. Twain's letters to William Dean Howells are contained in *Mark Twain–Howells Letters*, Henry N. Smith and William M. Gibson (eds.), 2 vols., Harvard University Press, Cambridge, 1960.

52   The morning of June 2, 1884, found Ulysses S. Grant: *Many Are the Hearts*, p. 141.

53   Childs was one of Long Branch's most important investors: Ibid., pp. 108–110.

54   On Thursdays of each summer, Grant and Julia: Ibid., p. 109.
After another moment he howled in pain: Ibid.

55   Da Costa examined Grant: Ibid.
"No combination of Wall Street sharpers": Ibid., p. 110.

56   They had first approached Grant: Ibid., p. 111. In his own account of the *Century's* efforts, Twain did not cite the *Century's* first offer
to Grant but alluded to it by noting that Grant had already been
writing for Johnson, Watson, and Gilder. See also *The Captain Departs*,
pp. 14–18. Both Goldhurst's and Pitkin's treatments of Grant's illness
and his decision to write his memoirs were the first attempts to provide a coherent explanation of how Grant's illness pushed him to the
decision to write his memoirs. The difference in viewpoints between
their accounts and mine may seem minor, but they are significant and
suggestive. In Goldhurst and Pitkin, Grant's throat pain in Long Branch
was preceded in the text by the visit from the *Century* editors, when, in
fact, in strict chronological terms the visit from the *Century* editors followed Grant's "peach incident"—a significant difference that suggests,
as I do, that Grant may have suspected that the pain he felt (and which
worsened) was a sign of his deteriorating health. The conclusions are
the same, however: If Grant had not known he was dying, it is highly
unlikely he would have written his memoirs.

"I have frequently started to go places": *Many Are the Hearts*, p. 111.

"Grant's recent election to the Army of the Potomac position": Ibid.,
p. 112.

57   "He gave me the impression of a wounded lion": Ibid., p. 113.

Grant set to work on the Shiloh article: "The Last Days of General
Grant," p. 157.

58   "Hurrah for Grant": *Many Are the Hearts*, p. 116. See also *The Captain Departs*, p. 113. The articles submitted by Grant to the *Century* were
written in rough chronological order: Shiloh, Vicksburg, Chattanooga,
and the Wilderness. After the completion of Grant's *Memoirs*, the *Century* reprinted sections of Grant's work as sidebars to some of its other
feature articles.

During their several meetings together Johnson applauded this: *Remembered Yesterdays*, Robert U. Johnson, Little, Brown & Co., Boston, p. 92.

"I told him that what was desirable for the success": Ibid., p. 93.

59   "We were moving along the northern edge of a clearing": *Personal Memoirs of Ulysses S. Grant*, p. 232.

60   "Never had a father a more devoted son": Ibid., p. 233.

61   "I said we do not want Grant's book unless he wants us to
have it": Ibid.

"I have now been writing on the Vicksburg Campaign two weeks":
The Captain Departs, p. 41.

62   "Mr. Johnson understands the book situation, evidently with thoroughness": *Many Are the Hearts*, p. 117.

63   "Do you really think anyone would be interested in a book by me?": Ibid., p. 119.

"His ideas agree with ours—to make a good book": Ibid., p. 121.

CHAPTER THREE: "THE SMALL ROOM AT THE HEAD OF THE STAIRS"

64   In 1884, the Republican Party candidate for president: *What Happened When*, Gorton Carruth, Penguin Books, New York, 1991, p. 506. Less than two weeks after Burchard's speech: Ibid.

65   Douglas was something of a medical genius: *The Captain Departs*, pp. 24–25.

"Is it cancer?" Grant asked him: "Records of the Last Days of the Magnanimous Soldier U. S. Grant," John Hancock Douglas Papers, Library of Congress (undated, with no page numbers). The notes are an authoritative account, apparently passed on in his lifetime to Badeau and others. They have been widely quoted in nearly every account of Grant's illness since his death.

"General," he said, "the disease is serious" Ibid. See also *Many Are the Hearts*, p. 143.

66   Douglas applied a muriate of cocaine to the swollen area: Ibid. See also *Many Are the Hearts*, p. 143.

He wanted to spare Julia and his children: "The Last Days of General Grant," p. 157.

67   While in Long Branch, he had drafted, redrafted, and then rewritten: Ibid.

Grant told Smith that he wanted to write: *The Captain Departs*, p. 24.

"General Grant has just been in," he noted: Ibid., p. 15. Pitkin points out that while other writers, including Badeau, have highlighted only a few visits between Grant and the editors of the *Century*, there were at least half a dozen and perhaps more, stretching over a period from June 1884 until October 22, 1884.

68   He told Grant that the Century Company would offer him: Ibid. Over a period of two weeks: "The Last Days of General Grant," p. 157. See also *Many Are the Hearts*, pp. 142–47.

"This specimen comes from the throat": "General Grant's Last Days," Dr. George F. Shrady, *Century* magazine 76 (July 1908), p. 80.

69   "The wisdom of such a decision": Ibid., p. 81.

69   George Frederick Shrady was not simply well known in his profession: *The Captain Departs*, pp. 31–32.

70   Shrady always listened closely to Grant: Ibid., p. 32.

"It was always the idea to do it with the least suffering": "General Grant's Last Days," p. 81.

"It would hardly have been possible to recognize Grant": Ibid., p. 92.

71   "Gentlemen," Grant said, "this is the last cigar I will ever smoke": *Many Are the Hearts*, pp. 148–49.

72   Grant also solicited the help of an old friend, Adam Badeau: Ibid., p. 150.

73   "Badeau," Adams wrote, "was stout; his face was red": *The Education of Henry Adams*, Henry Adams, Modern Library, New York, 1999, p. 263.

At the end of the summer, Badeau: "The Last Days of General Grant," p. 154.

74   "The proposition was a great blow to me": Ibid.

What he intended to do, Grant told Badeau: Ibid., p. 155.

"There will be a room for you": *Many Are the Hearts*, p. 118.

75   "My family is American" *Personal Memoirs of Ulysses S. Grant*, p. 3.

76   Grant worked at a small desk: "The Last Days of General Grant," p. 154. See also *Many Are the Hearts*, pp. 153–54.

Grant wrote out his memoirs in his own hand: Ibid., p. 154. A careful viewing of the manuscript shows that, in fact, not *all* of the manuscript was written in his hand; on occasions—as I have recounted in this work—Grant's words were transcribed by N. E. Dawson. Even so, considerable marginalia show that none of the manuscript was written in any other voice than Grant's.

"The small room at the head of the stairs": Ibid., pp. 154–55.

77   Harrison Tyrrell, an unappreciated and virtually unknown figure: "Records of the Last Days of the Magnanimous Soldier U. S. Grant." While undated and appearing without page numbers, Douglas's remembrances are the best account we have of Tyrrell's character. Even so, the historical record of this dedicated friend of Grant's is very sparse.

79   Grant's illness took an immediate toll on his family: *Many Are the Hearts*, pp. 154–56.

80   "Mrs. Grant never could bring herself to believe": "The Last Days of General Grant," p. 157.

81   Shrady noted that Grant's physical fortitude was unique: "General Grant's Last Days," p. 88.

81   "Pretend you are a boy again": "Interviews with Grant's Doctor," George F. Shrady, *The Saturday Evening Post*, September 9, 1901.

82   "One night in the first week of November": *The Autobiography of Mark Twain*, p. 310. In fact, this was the last night of the "Twins of Genius" tour. It was a propitious moment, and not simply because Twain "overheard" a conversation on Grant's memoirs. Free now from his tour, he could give his full attention to Grant's work. In *Mr. Clemens and Mark Twain*, Justin Kaplan notes that Twain had not only been positioning himself as Grant's publisher, he had even implied to Gilder and Johnson that he did not want the memoirs and, furthermore, he derided the idea of "subscription" publishing to them—commenting that those who engaged in it were "scalawags." During the entire period, we may justifiably surmise, Twain had been plotting to publish Grant's memoirs himself and offer them to the public "by subscription."

83   "We want the Century's warbook": *Mr. Clemens and Mark Twain*, p. 261.

Over dinner, Gilder confirmed that the *Century*: Ibid.

84   "The thing which astounded me": *The Autobiography of Mark Twain*, p. 312.

"I found him in his library with Col. Fred Grant, his son": Ibid., p. 310.

85   "Of course this was nonsense": Ibid., p. 311.

"I pointed out that the contract": Ibid.

86   "The General was immovable and challenged me to name the publisher": Ibid., p. 312.

88   "There's many a woman in this land": *Mr. Clemens and Mark Twain*, p. 262.

"Sherman told me that his profits on that book": *The Autobiography of Mark Twain*, p. 314.

89   "Sell *me* the memoirs, General": Ibid., p. 315.

"Give me the book on the terms which I have already suggested": Ibid., p. 316.

CHAPTER FOUR: "TURN HIM LOOSE!"

91   We are told that all of the bad things that happen to Huck: Schmitz, "Banned in Concord: Adventures of Huckleberry Finn and Classic American Literature," pp. 93–115. See also "A Hard Book to Take," James M. Cox, in *Modern Critical Interpretations: Mark Twain's Adventures of Huckleberry Finn*, Chelsea House Publishers, New York, 1986, pp. 87–108.

91   what the critic Neil Schmitz calls "a large and suspicious reef": "Huckspeech," Neil Schmitz, in *Modern Critical Interpretations*, p. 63.

92   "The first significant rift in the manuscript occurs here": Ibid. "I dived—and I aimed for the bottom, too": *Adventures of Huckleberry Finn*, Mark Twain, Modern Library, New York, 2001, p. 80.

93   Twain was spending as much in one month on household expenses: *Mr. Clemens and Mark Twain*, pp. 99–100. See also *Mark Twain: An Illustrated Biography*, p. 134.

94   He was loud, ribald, scathingly small-minded, and intemperate: *Mark Twain: An Illustrated Biography*, p. 110.

95   "It is unquestionably the best book he has ever written": Ibid., p. 117.
"He is a contemptible cur, and I want nothing more to do with him": *Mr. Clemens and Mark Twain*, p. 241.

96   "It isn't good journalism": Ibid.
He began to plot his revenge, telling Charley Webster: Ibid., p. 242.
He filled his notebooks with his ravings: *Mark Twain's Notebooks and Journals*, vol. 3, pp. 282–85.

97   "What the devil could those friends of mine have been thinking about?": *Mr. Clemens and Mark Twain*, p. 242.
"When I come to write the Mississippi book, then look out!": "Samuel L. Clemens to Olivia Langdon," *Mark Twain's Letters*, vol. 1, p. 119.

98   "I am sorry Osgood is with you": *Mr. Clemens and Mark Twain*, p. 243.
They arrived in St. Louis: *Mark Twain's Notebooks and Journals*, vol. 2, p. 521.
"Mike Gavin is dead. Strother Wiley is alive": Ibid., pp. 527–28.
("Sam was ever making notes in his memorandum book"): *Mr. Clemens and Mark Twain*, p. 244.

99   "To-night when some idiot approaching Cairo didn't answer our whistle": *Mark Twain's Notebooks and Journals*, vol. 2, pp. 530–31.
"When we got down below Cairo": Ibid., p. 532.

100   The real-life feud: *The Annotated Huckleberry Finn*, pp. 188–92. The feud appeared in a number of guises throughout Twain's work—not only in *Huckleberry Finn*, but also in *Life on the Mississippi*. Twain also featured the feud in a number of his lectures. The Mark Twain Project at the University of California provides the most extensive record of the actual feud.

100   "He dodged among the wood piles": *Mark Twain's Notebooks and Journals*, vol. 2, pp. 567–69.

"some rhymes about the little child": Ibid., p. 570.

101   "Well, sah, my ole man—dat's my husband": Ibid., p. 572.

"The rugged truth of the sketch": *Mr. Clemens and Mark Twain*, p. 181.

"The town (2000 inhab.) used to be where the river now is": *Mark Twain's Notebooks and Journals*, vol. 2, p. 539.

102   "Col. Grangerford was a gentleman, you see": *Adventures of Huckleberry Finn*, p. 89.

"made every gentleman in the South a Major": *Life on the Mississippi*, Mark Twain, Library of America, New York, 1982, p. 501. We can assume that Twain did not mention his dislike of Scott to Ulysses S. Grant, who was a great fan of his novels—and spent considerable time reading them as a cadet at West Point. He noted this in his *Memoirs*, saying that he should have been studying.

103   Vicksburg was "now a country town": *Mark Twain's Notebooks and Journals*, vol. 2, p. 471.

"Rode to National Cemetery": Ibid., p. 472.

Twain arrived in New Orleans on April 28: Ibid., p. 460.

104   "Clergyman then lined a hymn": Ibid.

"I did the steering myself": Ibid., p. 467.

"The river is so thoroughly changed": Ibid.

105   "What a splendid moon": Ibid., p. 469.

"People talk only about the war": Ibid.

106   Grant made eight attempts to capture Vicksburg: *The Civil War: A Narrative*, vol. 2, pp. 336–37.

107   "They hain't no right to shut him up!": *Adventures of Huckleberry Finn*, p. 240.

"The romance of boating is gone now": *Mark Twain's Notebooks and Journals*, vol. 2, p. 478.

108   "Alas! Everything was changed in Hannibal": Ibid., p. 479.

"Arrived per Minneapolis at St Paul & put up at the Metropolitan": Ibid., p. 480.

109   Twain was pleased to be finished with the book: *Mr. Clemens and Mark Twain*, pp. 248–49.

"Charley, if there are any instructions to be given" Ibid., p. 249.

The sales from a book "in trade": Ibid., p. 250. Books sold by subscription generally cost more than those sold "in the trade"—in bookstores. But the returns were also greater. After a book was "fully subscribed" (a number established to reflect what a publisher thought he could sell—a guess, really), the book could then be offered "in the trade." What Twain is saying here is that a book sold in subscription rarely sold thereafter in a bookstore.

110   "I have never for a moment doubted that you did the very best": Ibid., p. 250.

"Never mind about the play": Ibid., p. 253.

111   "I haven't piled up MS so in years": "Samuel L. Clemens to William Dean Howells," *Mark Twain Letters*, vol. 1, p. 435. See also *The Annotated Huckleberry Finn*, p. xvii.

"I haven't had such booming working-days for many years": *Mr. Clemens and Mark Twain*, p. 251.

112   Twain gave it to his wife to read: *The Annotated Huckleberry Finn*, p. xxvi.

"Ever since papa and mama were married": Ibid., pp. xxvi–xxvii.

"For my own amusement and to enjoy the protests of the children": Ibid., p. xxvii.

113   Twain gave Webster the manuscript in mid-1884: Ibid., p. xliii.

114   "My book is draining me day by day": "Samuel L. Clemens to William Dean Howells," *Mark Twain Letters*, vol. 1, p. 532.

115   Canvassing for the book was begun by Webster in November: *The Annotated Mark Twain*, p. lix.

"We have the book," Twain told Webster at the end of November: *The Captain Departs*, pp. 21–22.

116   After Twain left Grant's home on November 20, Grant talked about Twain's offer: Ibid., p. 21.

117   By early December, Childs was convinced: *Many Are the Hearts*, pp. 157–59.

"Experience provides that the man who obstructs a war": *Personal Memoirs of Ulysses S. Grant*, pp. 96–97.

118   "I do not think there was ever a more wicked war": *Many Are the Hearts*, p. 48.

"Give the book to Twain," he said: *The Autobiography of Mark Twain*, p. 316.

"If these chickens should really hatch": *Mark Twain, Businessman*, Samuel C. Webster, Little, Brown & Co., Boston, 1946, p. 302.

119   Twain had put aside $10,000 as an advance: *The Autobiography of Mark Twain*, pp. 315–16.

119   "It was a shameful thing," he later recounted: *Many Are the Hearts*, p. 131.

"The General, who knew nothing of the customs or etiquette": *Remembered Yesterdays*, pp. 213–15.

CHAPTER FIVE: "THEY HAVE EXPELLED HUCK"

121   By mid-December, the pain that had been throbbing in his throat: "General Grant's Last Days," p. 82. See also a series of interesting letters from Grant to his daughter on his own condition at this time: "USG to Nellie Sartoris," November 18, 1884, and February 16, 1885, Ulysses S. Grant Papers, Chicago Historical Society.

"The cannon did it," he shouted one night: *Many Are the Hearts*, p. 151.

122   Julia wrote to Grant's old friend and fellow commander: Ibid., p. 150.

This was typical of Grant, Sherman wrote: Ibid., p. 151. Due to his closeness to Grant and his lifetime association with him, Sherman realized that his colleague was dying. His letter to Julia should be read as his attempt to express his sympathy about Grant's condition—not his rejection of his illness.

123   "My tears blind me," Julia wrote: Ibid., p. 150.

It could be, Douglas believed, that Grant's descent into depression: Ibid., pp. 143–44. See also George F. Shrady, "The Surgical and Pathological Aspects of General Grant's Case," *New York Tribune*, July 31, 1885, p. 3.

124   "The General is cheerful and comfortable," they said: Ibid., p. 157.

125   If Sherman noticed any deterioration in Grant's health: *The Captain Departs*, p. 114.

126   So on December 28, Sherman arranged for a meeting: *Many Are the Hearts*, pp. 166–69. General William T. Sherman's papers, including his extensive correspondence, much of which in this period covers his knowledge of Grant's illness, is housed at the University of Missouri.

"Through the press and otherwise": Ibid., pp. 135–36.

127   "War is hell," he said: *Memoirs of General William T. Sherman*, General William T. Sherman, Library of America, New York, 1990, pp. 580, 585. See also *The Civil War: A Narrative*, vol. 3, p. 14; vol. 2, p. 602.

When war broke out, Sherman became a colonel of volunteers: *The Civil War, A Narrative*, vol. 3, pp. 196–200.

128   "How far your advice and suggestions have been of assistance": Ibid., p. 427.

"one class of men makes war": Ibid., p. 149.

129   Grant said that he would "hold the cat": *The Civil War: A Narrative*, vol 3, pp. 18–19. This was one of Grant's favorite sayings; he would use it to express his overriding belief that if only the Union could participate in "continuous operations" against the rebels, the preponderance of northern numbers could finally be brought to bear.

"I can make that march and make Georgia howl": Ibid., pp. 614–15.

"Madam," he said, "my soldiers have to subsist themselves": Ibid., pp. 602–03.

130   "I will not accept if nominated and will not serve if elected": *What Happened When*, p. 510.

131   At Sherman's urging, George Edmunds of Vermont: *Many Are the Hearts*, p. 167.

Arthur vetoed the bill on a technicality: Ibid., p. 168.

132   "The action of Congress in refusing to pass the bill": Ibid., p. 166.

133   "Thus," *The New York Times* editorialized, "four Confederate brigadiers": "Ulysses S. Grant" (editorial), *The New York Times*, February 17, 1885.

134   the "Twins of Genius" tour: *Mr. Clemens and Mark Twain*, pp. 265–68. See also *The Annotated Huckleberry Finn*, pp. lii–liv. For background on the Twain-Cable relationship, see *Mark Twain and George W. Cable*, Arlin Turner, University of Michigan Press, East Lansing, 1960. The Mark Twain Papers at the University of California contain almost all of Twain's correspondence on the tour.

"the pitifulest human louse": *Mr. Clemens and Mark Twain*, p. 267.

"See here, Cable," he said, "we'll have to cut this part of the program out": Ibid. See also *Mark Twain: A Biography*, vol. 2, p. 189.

135   "With his platform talent": *Mr. Clemens and Mark Twain*, p. 267.

136   Early in the tour, when Cable and Twain: Ibid., p. 266.

137   "He keeps his programs strung out to one hour": Ibid., p. 265. See also *Mark Twain: A Biography*, vol. 2, p. 189.

"I miss a good many faces": Ibid., p. 265.

"Cable, why do you sit in here?": Ibid., p. 264.

Twain returned to New York on February 21: *Many Are the Hearts*, p. 157.

138   "I mean you shall have the book": *Mark Twain's Notebooks and*

Journals, vol. 3, pp. 96–97. The first half of the third volume of *Mark Twain's Notebooks and Journals* is filled with entries on Grant—a prodigious amount of information. Paradoxically, though Twain now rarely saw Harriet Beecher Stowe, the entries have occasional references to *Uncle Tom's Cabin*—with special attention paid to the number of copies that book sold.

139   "a case of chronic superficial inflammation": "General Grant's Condition," *New York Tribune,* February 21, 1885.

"I took for granted the report": *Mark Twain: A Biography,* vol. 2, p. 203.

140   As an afterthought, Twain agreed with Grant that he should hire a stenographer": Ibid., 204.

141   Within twenty-four hours of announcing: Ibid., p. 205.

"Clemens was boiling over with plans for distribution": Ibid.

142   "It would be very hard for me to be confined to the house": "USG to Nellie Sartoris," February 25, 1885, Ulysses S. Grant Papers, Chicago Historical Society.

143   "The book is to be issued when a big edition has been sold": *The Annotated Huckleberry Finn,* p. lxiv.

"Had the first edition been run off": Ibid., p. lxiii.

144   "I am not able to see anything that can save Huck Finn": Ibid., p. lxv. Twain seemed less concerned with the comments in early reviews than with the opinions of his friends. Despite his justified fear of pirating (and Howells's admonition that he not give any advance copies to anyone, even his family), Twain made certain that a handful of friends, including Oliver Wendell Holmes, received advance copies. Their responses were mixed.

"The announcement that Mark Twain": *Many Are the Hearts,* p. 160.

"is very much the same character": "Huck Finn," *San Francisco Examiner,* March 9, 1885.

"Anyone who has ever lived in the Southwest": Untitled, *Sunday Chronicle,* March 6, 1885.

145   "Everybody will want to see Huckleberry Finn": "Mark Twain's New Book," *Hartford Courant,* March 9, 1885.

"Who on earth except Mark Twain": Untitled, *New York Sun,* February 15, 1885.

"cheap and pernicious stuff": "Mark Twain's Huck Finn," *New York World,* March 2, 1885.

146   "vulgar and abhorrent": "Huckleberry Finn," *Boston Herald,* January 18, 1885.

146   In one of the few times he completely misjudged his audience:
"Twain at the Whittier Dinner," *The New York Times*, December 20, 1877.
"They had been drinking—I could see that": Ibid.
"singularly flat, stale, and unprofitable": "Huckleberry Finn," *Evening
Traveler*, March 5, 1885.
"wearisome and labored": "Huckleberry Finn," *Advertiser*, March 12,
1885.

147   "While I do not wish to state it as my opinion": "Louisa
May Alcott Speaks Out on Huckleberry Finn," *St. Louis Globe Democrat*,
March 17, 1885. See also *The Annotated Huckleberry Finn*, pp. lxxvi–lxxix,
and *Mark Twain: An Illustrated Biography*, p. 122. For the implications of the
controversy for Twain's legacy, see "Banned in Concord: Adventures of
Huckleberry Finn," Myra Jehlen, *The Cambridge Companion to Mark Twain*,
Forrest G. Robinson, ed., Cambridge University Press, Cambridge, 1995,
pp. 93–115.
"cannot be said to have a very high moral tone": "Mark Twain's
Huckleberry Finn," *Springfield Daily Republican*, April 3, 1885.

148   "If Mr. Clemens cannot think of something better": *Mr. Clemens
and Mark Twain*, p. 268. Michael Patrick Hearn, in his *An Introduction to
the Annotated Huckleberry Finn*, points out that Twain had little regard for
Alcott. He wrote *The Gilded Age*, in part, as a response to her *Little Women*.
"If the Concord people are not in league with Mark Twain": "The
Concord Decision," *Sacramento Daily Record-Union*, April 20, 1885.
"Dear Charley," he wrote to Webster: *Mr. Clemens and Mark Twain*,
pp. 268–69.

CHAPTER SIX: "HE WAS JUST A MAN"
149   GRANT IS DYING: "Grant Is Dying," *New York Herald*, March 1, 1885.
By the evening of March 2: *Many Are the Hearts*, p. 172.
Harrison Tyrrell took the lead: Ibid., p. 173.

150   There was some disagreement: Ibid., pp. 174–175.
The debate did not divide the family: Ibid., p. 175.

151   At the end of the first week of March: *The Captain Departs*, p. 30.

152   A small group of them: Ibid.
One man came to pray: *Many Are the Hearts*, p. 177.
Another well-wisher made it past the police barricade: Ibid.
"He's my former commander and I love him": Ibid., p. 178.

153   Thomas L. Crittenden, a Union corps commander: Ibid., p. 177.
Biographies of Union and Confederate commanders are from *Historical*

Times Illustrated Encyclopedia of the Civil War, Patricia L. Faust, ed., Harper-Collins Publishers, New York, 1986.

153   Roscoe Conkling and Benjamin Bristow: *Many Are the Hearts,* p. 177.

In early March, Grant took the family carriage: Ibid., p. 183.

154   General John A. "Blackjack" Logan visited: Ibid., p. 178.

Logan went on to spend twenty years in the House of Representatives: *Historical Times Illustrated Encyclopedia of the Civil War,* p. 443.

155   "His physical suffering seems to have nerved his mind": *Many Are the Hearts,* p. 178.

Porter had been one of Grant's closest comrades: *Historical Times Illustrated Encyclopedia of the Civil War,* p. 594.

"To see him wasting and sinking in this way": *Many Are the Hearts,* pp. 178–79.

"In the history of the United States": *The Autobiography of Mark Twain,* pp. 327–28.

156   "He has organized victory from the beginning": Simpson, p. 284.

157   "Mr. Childs, you know during the last day of a session": *Many Are the Hearts,* p. 169.

158   With that done, at precisely eleven A.M.: Ibid., p. 170. See also the account in Simpson, pp. 624–25.

But at the last minute, Wilson rose from his chair: *Many Are the Hearts,* p. 170.

159   At the front of the Senate chamber, a clerk scaled a ladder: Ibid., p. 171.

"I am grateful the thing has passed," he said: Ibid., p. 170.

"Every face there betrayed strong excitement": *The Autobiography of Mark Twain,* pp. 328–29. See also *Mark Twain: A Biography,* p. 206.

160   But Lincoln demurred, saying that that duty: *Many Are the Hearts,* p. 171.

"The law," he told him, "is to date the commission from the time one accepts": Ibid., p. 172.

Wood received Grant's payment: Ibid., p. 171.

162   "The General had a good army library": Dawson's views of Grant, "Grant's Last Days," can be found at www.mscomm.com/~ulysses/page60.html.

163   "General Grant was a sick man," he later wrote in *The Autobiography of Mark Twain,* p. 331.

"It kills me these days to write half of that": Ibid., p. 208.

163   "Then I have fulfilled my contract to them": *Many Are the Hearts*, p. 178.

165   Irritated by Twain's presentation: Ibid., p. 162.

"It was easily demonstrable they were buying ten-dollar gold pieces": Ibid.

166   "Well, sir, it was perfectly charming": *Mark Twain: A Biography*, p. 207. See also *Many Are the Hearts*, pp. 164–66.

167   Twain agreed to provide for Gerhardt during his education: *Mark Twain, A Biography*, p. 207.

168   "You are those poor little people's god": "Mark Twain and Karl Gerhardt," Barbara Schmidt, *Mark Twain On-Line*, www.twainquotes .com.

"You have behaved miserably": Ibid.

169   "One marked feature of General Grant's character is his exceeding gentleness": *The Autobiography of Mark Twain*, p. 330.

"I've been reading what you wrote this morning": *Mark Twain: A Biography*, pp. 208–10.

170   But on March 25 Grant suffered a choking fit: *The Captain Departs*, p. 33. See also *Many Are the Hearts*, p. 180.

"The truth is the disease has gotten away from the doctors": *Many Are the Hearts*, pp. 181, 184–85.

171   "It is doubtful if the General's health could stand another choking attack": Ibid., p. 181.

"He was a far greater man": "Sheridan's Views of Grant," *New York Tribune*, March 26, 1885.

"Let him die in peace": Ibid.

"When General Grant dies": Ibid.

172   "General, we propose to keep to this line if it takes all summer": John Hancock Douglas Papers, Library of Congress.

173   "My marks will not be seriously important": *Mark Twain: A Biography*, pp. 208–09.

174   "Whenever galley proofs or revises went to General Grant": *The Autobiography of Mark Twain*, p. 330.

175   Fred suggested that it might be good for Grant: Ibid.

"I was as much surprised as Columbus's cook would have been": Ibid.

"By chance I had been comparing the memoirs with Caesar's 'Commentaries' ": Ibid.

176   "I learned afterward that General Grant was pleased": Ibid., p. 331.

"I am very much touched and grateful": *Many Are the Hearts*, p. 184.

CHAPTER SEVEN: "THE COMPOSITION IS ENTIRELY MY OWN"

178   "blow the Federal and the Gospel trumpets": *Many Are the Hearts*, p. 181.

Newman toured the world at government expense: Ibid., p. 187.

179   Grant, he believed, was a gentle man of God: "A Sudden Change for the Worse," *The New York Times*, April 8, 1881.

Newman counseled Grant to cease his Sabbath labors: Ibid. Newman was not always so self-centered in his comments. In one *New York Times* piece, he noted: "The way the man faces death is absolutely marvelous. It is a remarkable instant of pure will power. He knows there is no hope. He simply awaits the end patiently, calmly, without complaint, in great suffering. His mind is clear, his energies composed and his soul at perfect peace. All of this is wholly in keeping with the splendid greatness of his life."

"God will not reward us," Cooke said: *Many Are the Hearts*, p. 189.

"A great sufferer is passing away": "A Sudden Change for the Worse."

180   an overly loud "Amen": *Many Are the Hearts*, p. 190.

"As I began to pray," Newman later recalled: *The Captain Departs*, p. 69.

181   "If you doctors know how long a man can live under water": *Many Are the Hearts*, p. 190.

Prayers had saved Grant's life, he said: Ibid.

"They mourned his death two weeks ago": "A Talk with Reverend Dr. Newman," *The New York Times*, April 8, 1885.

182   "There's been a good deal of nonsense in the papers": "General Grant Holds His Own," *The New York Times*, April 19, 1885.

"Thrice have I been in the valley of death": *Mark Twain's Notebooks and Journals*, vol. 3, p. 136.

"Preachin's my line, too": *Adventures of Huckleberry Finn*, p. 103.

"Ten cents to a thousand dollars": *Mark Twain's Notebooks and Journals*, vol. 3, p. 136. Twain thought so little of Newman, there is only a single notation in his notebooks on Newman's time with Grant—and that was to call his statement "posh." This entry was then followed, very quickly, by another: "See if there is any patent for indenting a waffle mould in asphalt pavement." He was ever the inventor.

182   "The doctors are responsible three times for my being alive": *Many Are the Hearts*, p. 191.

183   "Oh, how grieved I was for God's cause": "A Talk with Reverend Dr. Newman."

"I believe you will be raised up": *Many Are the Hearts*, p. 192.

"Can he cure cancer?" he asked: Ibid.

"I do not care how much praying goes on": Ibid., p. 193.

184   "The diagnosis of the doctors might be wrong": "Astonishing His Family," *The New York Times*, April 18, 1885.

"The people rejoice that their great soldier Grant": "Not Cancer After All," *New York World*, April 19, 1885.

185   "It appears the doctors have been mistaken," the *Tribune* concluded: "General Grant Recovering," *New York Tribune*, April 21, 1885.

For a time the public believed that Garfield: *The Assassination of James A. Garfield*, Robert Kingsbury, Rosen Publishing Group, New York, 2002, p. 130.

An independent autopsy showed that the doctors' belief: Ibid., p. 157.

186   "Mr. Garfield himself is reported to have said that he was much obliged": Ibid., p. 199.

One of the doctors present dismissed the notion: *Many Are the Hearts*, p. 176. That doctor was George Frederick Shrady.

187   "Summing up the case from an allopathetic standpoint": "Garfield II: A Lengthy Demise," History House (Internet site), www.historyhouse.com. See also *Garfield: A Biography*, Allan Peskin, Kent State University, Kent, 1978, and *The Murder of James A. Garfield*, James C. Clark, McFarland & Company, New York, 1993.

It was Shrady who noticed, on the morning of April 18: "General Grant's Last Days," p. 91.

189   "Exhaustion and revival are characteristic of the disease": Ibid., p. 92.

"after all, the person with the most at stake": *Many Are the Hearts*, p. 185.

"If a man assumes the responsibility of doing a thing": Ibid., p. 186.

"This paper, the *World*," he said, "is a reformer in medicines": "General Grant's Response," *New York World*, April 25, 1885.

191   "Let fiction cease to lie about life": "A Critical Introduction to a Hazard of New Fortunes," Arthur Schlesinger Jr., in *A Hazard of New Fortunes*, Modern Library, New York, 1976, p. xxix.

193   In all, the *Century* published four volumes of articles: "The

Century Magazine," in "Making of America," Cornell University Library, Cornell, New York. The "Making of America" is a digital library of historical documents that can be found at www.htl.umich.edu/m/moagrp/

195 He disagreed with Fred, with Julia, and with Grant: *The Captain Departs*, p. 40.

196 Ihrie had told a *World* reporter that "Grant is no writer": *Many Are the Hearts*, p. 194.

"The work upon his new book": "Who Is Writing Grant's Book?" *New York World*, April 19, 1885.

He directed Webster to retain Clarence Seward: *Mark Twain, Businessman*, p. 310.

"that daily issue of unmedicated closet paper": *Many Are the Hearts*, p. 195. Twain did not seem to hold a grudge against Badeau, for he later considered having Webster publish his book *Grant's Last Days*.

197 "My father is dictating the Appomattox Campaign": Ibid.

"My attention has been called": "General Grant Responds." See also *The Captain Departs*, pp. 42–43.

198 Badeau handed a letter to Grant: *Many Are the Hearts*, p. 196.

200 "you and I must give up all association": Ibid.

201 "As I have stated to you in my letter of Saturday": Ibid., p. 187.

202 "A verb is anything that signifies to be": "A Doctor Talks," George F. Shrady, *The Saturday Evening Post*, September 9, 1901.

"I could do better," he wrote in one note to Twain: *Mark Twain: A Biography*, vol. 2, p. 212. See also *Many Are the Hearts*, p. 202.

203 "The General says he has made the book too long": *Mark Twain's Notebooks and Journals*, vol. 3, pp. 123–25.

"He is going to stick in here and there": Ibid., p. 97.

204 "That is just the place I have been looking for": *Many Are the Hearts*, p. 204.

205 "So anxious was he that nothing would interfere": "A Doctor Talks."

CHAPTER EIGHT: "THE ME IN ME"

206 The train that took Ulysses S. Grant: "The Last Days of General Grant," p. 31.

At a little after eight A.M. Grant emerged: Ibid.

207 The train moved ponderously through the Hudson Valley: *Many Are the Hearts*, pp. 210–11.

208   He was pleased with the two-story home: *The Captain Departs*, p. 48.

209   Drexel's plan included an expansion: Ibid., pp. 48–51.

"I thought if we could get him to come here to Mt. McGregor": "Grant Coming to Saratoga," *Albany Evening Journal*, June 19, 1885.

210   "Dr., since coming to this beautiful climate": John Hancock Douglas Papers, Library of Congress. See also *Many Are the Hearts*, p. 213.

211   "I have given you the directions about all my affairs": "General Grant's Last Wish," *New York Herald*, July 12, 1885. "U. S. Grant to Fred Grant," July 11, 1885, Grant Family Papers, Chicago Historical Society. See also *Many Are the Hearts*, pp. 213–14.

212   "I am frightened at the proportions of prosperity": *Mr. Clemens and Mark Twain*, p. 279.

213   "the slathers of ancient friends, and such worlds of talk": *The Annotated Huckleberry Finn*, p. 275.

"I conceive that the right way to write a story for boys": Ibid., p. cii.

214   "If they wanted us to call them kings and dukes": *The Adventures of Huckleberry Finn*, p. 106. Readers of *Huckleberry Finn* will note that on p. 106 cited above, the reality of what Twain was doing demanded an explanation—or, as the duke says: "Goodness sakes, would a runaway nigger run *south*?" Huck's explanation is so convoluted that the duke simply lets it drop.

"There was another of these half-finished stories": *The Autobiography of Mark Twain*, p. 349.

215   "All the negroes were friends of ours": Ibid., p. 7.

216   "The United States of Lyncherdom," *Mr. Clemens and Mark Twain*, p. 364. The essay was originally intended for *The North American Review*. It can now be found in *The Complete Essays of Mark Twain* (ed. Charles Neider), Da Capo Press, New York, 1991, p. 673.

In *The Tragedy of Pudd'nhead Wilson: The Tragedy of Pudd'nhead Wilson*, Library of America, New York, 1992.

"a thing we can't name": *A Diary from Dixie*, Mary Boykin Chesnut (Ben A. Williams, ed.), Houghton Mifflin, Boston, 1961, pp. 21–22.

"God forgive us, but ours is a monstrous system": Ibid., p. 22.

217   "I had not seen the like of this for fifty years": *Following the Equator*, Mark Twain, Boondocks Press (www.boondocks.com), chapter LVIII.

"It is curious—the space-annihilating power of thought": Ibid., chapter XXXVIII.

218   "bald, grotesque and unwarrantable usurpation": *Huck Finn and Tom Sawyer Among the Indians*, Mark Twain, University of California Press, Berkeley, 1989, p. 256.

"I don't know these people," he said: *Grant*, pp. 259–60. See also Simpson, pp. 162–63.

220   "During his last days" N. E. Dawson, "Grant's Last Days," at www.mscomm.com/~ulysses/page60.html.

"I have worked off all I had notes of": John Hancock Douglas Papers, Library of Congress. See also *The Captain Departs*, p. 67.

"Mr. N is a Texan": *Many Are the Hearts*, p. 216.

"I feel worse this A.M. than I have for some time": Ibid., p. 218.

222   "If I could have two weeks of strength": "A Note to Dr. Douglas" (undated), John Hancock Douglas Papers, Library of Congress.

223   "I have my full share of admiration and esteem for Grant": *The Autobiography of Mark Twain*, p. 331.

"General Grant had no enemies, political or sectional, in these last days": *Mark Twain: A Biography*, p. 212. These words, penned by Twain, were originally written to Henry Ward Beecher. The letter is not contained in any of Twain's correspondence, but is quoted by Paine.

"I do not suppose," Grant wrote in a note to him: "A Doctor Talks."

224   "It is postponing the final event," Grant wrote to Shrady: Ibid.

"I could hardly keep back the tears": *Many Are the Hearts*, p. 221.

225   "I fear the worst the day the General completes his book": "A Doctor Talks."

"The dictation for him" N. E. Dawson, "Grant's Last Days," at www.mscomm.com/~ulysses/page60.html.

"After all that however the disease is still there": "Longing for Real Rest," *The New York Times*, July 4, 1885.

227   Ulysses S. Grant died at 8:08 A.M.: "A Hero Finds Rest. Ulysses S. Grant's Painless, Peaceful Death. The End Coming in the Early Morning," *The New York Times*, July 24, 1885.

"I then believed he would live several months": *Mark Twain: A Biography*, p. 212.

"Look after our dear children": "Grant's Last Letters to Julia," June 29, 1885, Ulysses S. Grant home page, www.mscomm.com/~ulysses/.

228   "Nine months of close attention to him": John H. Douglas Papers, Library of Congress.

229   On July 28, Fred decided that his father: *The Captain Departs*, p. 94.

231   "God of battles, Father of all": "General Grant Is Buried," *New York Tribune*, August 5, 1885. See also "The Honored Dead," *Frank Leslie's Illustrated Newspaper*, August 8, 1885.

232   "Persons attempting to find a motive in this narrative": *Adventures of Huckleberry Finn*, p. 2.

EPILOGUE: "MANY A DEEP REMORSE"

233   On February 27 of the next year: *Mark Twain's Notebooks and Journals*, vol. 3, p. 312.

234   "The thick pair of volumes of the *Personal Memoirs*": *Patriotic Gore*, Edmund Wilson, W. W. Norton & Co., New York, 1962, p. 132.

"I found a language all astray": Ibid., p. 139.

"There is one striking thing about Grant's orders": Ibid., p. 143.

235   "These literary qualities, so unobtrusive: Ibid.

"all modern American literature": *Green Hills of Africa*, Ernest Hemingway, Scribner & Sons, New York, 1935, p. 123.

"a literary masterpiece": in the Mark Twain Papers, "Notebook 22," University of California, Berkeley.

Julia Grant continued to live in New York City: *The Personal Memoirs of Julia Dent Grant*, Mrs. Ulysses S. Grant (John Y. Simon, ed.), G. P. Putnam's Sons, New York, 1975.

Fred also remained in New York City: Ibid., pp. 85–86.

236   Nellie Grant finally divorced "Algie": Ibid., p. 324.

William Tecumseh Sherman: *Historical Times Illustrated Encylopedia of the Civil War*, pp. 681–82.

Roswell Smith continued in his role: *Remembered Yesterdays*, p. 212.

His disciple Richard Watson Gilder: "Richard Watson Gilder," chapter X, "Later Poets," www.bartleby.com.

"What is the White Man's burden": *Remembered Yesterdays*, p. 213.

237   William Henry Vanderbilt and Senator Jerome Chaffee: *Many Are the Hearts*, p. 253.

Dr. George Shrady died in 1908: Ibid.

The year after Grant's death: Ibid.

James Fish and Ferdinand Ward: Ibid.

238   Aging and bankrupt, Twain retreated to Europe: *Mr. Clemens and Mark Twain*, pp. 336–58.

"In my age as in my youth" Ibid., p. 341.

239   He died at 6:22 in the evening of April 21, 1910: Ibid., p. 388.

Howells succumbed to pneumonia: "William Dean Howells," *A Hazard of New Fortunes*, p. viii.

BIBLIOGRAPHY

❦

ARTICLES AND MONOGRAPHS

Badeau, Adam, "The Last Days of General Grant," *Century* magazine 30 (October 1885): 151–63.

Cox, James M., "A Hard Book to Take," Harold Bloom, ed., in *Modern Critical Interpretations* (New York: Chelsea House, 1986).

Current, Richard N., "Grant Without Greatness," *Review in American History* 9, no. 4 (1981): 507–09.

Dickson, John N., "The Civil War Years of John Alexander Logan," *Journal of the Illinois State Historical Society* 56, no. 2 (1963): 212–32.

Dorsett, Lyle W., "The Problem of Ulysses S. Grant's Drinking During the Civil War," *Hayes Historical Journal* 4, no. 2 (1983): 37–48.

Douglas, Dr. John H., "Records of the Last Days of the Magnanimous Soldier U. S. Grant," John Hancock Douglas Papers, Library of Congress.

Fuller, Alfred M., "Grant's Horsemanship: An Incident," *McClure's* magazine 8 (April 1897): 501–03.

Giberson, N. S., "Captain Grant's Old Post, Fort Humboldt," *Overland Monthly* 8, 2nd series (1886): 22–25.

Gold, Charles H., "Grant and Twain in Chicago: The 1879 Reunion of the Army of the Tennessee," *Chicago History* 7, no. 3 (1978): 150–60.

Grant, Frederick D., "A Boy's Experience at Vicksburg," in Military
    Order of the Loyal Legion of the United States, *Personal Recollections of*
    the War of the Rebellion, 3rd series (New York: 1907), pp. 86–90.
Grant, Ulysses S., "The Battle of Shiloh," *Century* magazine 29 (February 1885): 593–613.
———, "Chattanooga," *Century* magazine 31 (April 1886): 128–45.
———, "General Grant on the Terms of Vicksburg," *Century* magazine 34
    (October 1887): 617–31.
———, "Preparing for the Campaigns of '64," in Clarence C. Buel and
    Robert U. Johnson, eds., *Battles and Leaders of the Civil War*, vol. 4 (New
    York: Century, 1884).
———, "Preparing for the Wilderness Campaign," *Century* magazine 31
    (April 1886): 573–82.
———, "The Siege of Vicksburg," *Century* magazine 31 (October 1885):
    276–303.
Harris, Neil, "The Battle for Grant's Tomb," *American Heritage* 36, no. 5
    (1985): 70–79.
Hoffman, Michael J., "Huck's Ironic Circle," in Harold Bloom, ed., *Modern Critical Interpretations* (New York: Chelsea House, 1986).
Jehlen, Myra, "Banned in Concord: *Adventures of Huckleberry Finn* and
    Classic American Literature," in *The Cambridge Companion to Mark*
    Twain (New York: Cambridge University Press, 1995).
Keise, Thomas J., "The St. Louis Years of Ulysses S. Grant," *Gateway*
    Heritage 6, no. 3 (1985–1986): 10–21.
Leslie, Leigh, "Grant and Galena," *Midland Monthly* magazine 4 (September 1895): 195–215.
Mahan, D. H., "The Cadet Life of Grant and Sherman" (letter of March
    8, 1866), *Army and Navy Journal* 22 (March 31, 1866): 507–09.
Marx, Leo, "Mr. Eliot, Mr. Trilling, and Huckleberry Finn," in Harold
    Bloom, ed., *Modern Critical Interpretations* (New York: Chelsea House,
    1986).
Morrison, James L., Jr., "Educating Civil War Generals: West Point,
    1833–1861," *Military Affairs* 38 (1974).
Porter, Horace, "Personal Traits of General Grant," *McClure's* magazine 2
    (May 1894): 507–32.
Rice, Allen Thorndike, "Sherman on Grant," *North American Review* 142,
    (January–June 1886): 111–13.
Russell, Henry M. W., "The Memoirs of Ulysses S. Grant: The Rhetoric
    of Judgment," *Virginia Quarterly Review* 66, no. 2 (1990): 189–209.

Schmitz, Neil, "Huckspeech," in Harold Bloom, ed., *Modern Critical Interpretations* (New York: Chelsea House, 1986).

Sharp, Thomas, "Colonel Dent of Whitehaven: The Father-in-Law of General Grant," *McClure's* magazine 9 (May 1897): 667.

Sherman, W. T., "Sherman's Estimate of Grant," *Century* magazine 35 (February 1888): 78–92.

Shrady, George F., "A Doctor Talks," *The Saturday Evening Post*, September 9, 1901.

———, "General Grant's Last Days," *Century* magazine 76 (July 1908).

———, "The Surgical and Pathological Aspects of General Grant's Case," *New York Tribune*, July 31, 1885.

BOOKS

Adams, Henry, *The Education of Henry Adams* (New York: Random House, 1999).

Anderson, Frederick, Lin Salamo, and Bernard L. Stein, eds., *Mark Twain's Notebooks and Journals*, vol. 1 (1855–1873) (Berkeley: University of California Press, 1975).

———, *Mark Twain's Notebooks and Journals*, vol. 2 (1877–1883) (Berkeley: University of California Press, 1975).

———, *Mark Twain's Notebooks and Journals*, vol. 3 (1883–1891) (Berkeley: University of California Press, 1975).

Badeau, Adam, *Grant in Peace, from Appomattox to Mount McGregor: A Personal Memoir* (Hartford: D. Appleton, 1881).

Bearss, Edwin Cole, *The Campaign for Vicksburg*, vols. 1–3 (Dayton: Morningside Press, 1985).

Bloom, Harold, ed., *Modern Critical Interpretations* (New York: Chelsea House, 1986).

Budd, Louis J., *A Listing of and Selections from Newspaper and Magazine Interviews with Samuel L. Clemens, 1874–1910* (Arlington: University of Texas at Arlington Press, 1977).

Carruth, Gorton, *What Happened When* (New York: Penguin Books, 1991).

Catton, Bruce, *Grant Moves South* (Boston: Little, Brown & Co., 1960).

———, *Grant Takes Command* (Boston: Little, Brown & Co., 1968).

Chesnut, Mary Boykin, *A Diary from Dixie*, Ben A. Williams, ed. (Boston: Houghton Mifflin, 1961).

———, *Mary Chesnut's Civil War*, C. Vann Woodward, ed. (New Haven: Yale University Press, 1981).

Clark, James C., *The Murder of James A. Garfield* (New York: McFarland & Company, 1993).

Clemens, Samuel, *Mark Twain's Autobiography* (New York: Harper & Brothers, 1924).

Dana, Charles A., *Recollections of the Civil War* (Hartford: D. Appleton, 1899).

Dana, Charles A., and James H. Wilson, *The Life of Ulysses S. Grant, General of the Armies of the United States* (Springfield: Gordon Bill, 1868).

DeVoto, Bernard, *Mark Twain's America* (Lincoln: University of Nebraska Press, 1997).

Doyno, Victor A., *Writing Huck Finn: Mark Twain's Creative Process* (Philadelphia: University of Pennsylvania Press, 1991).

Dupuy, Ernest R., *Men of West Point: The First 150 Years of the United States Military Academy* (New York: Sloane, 1951).

Faust, Patricia L., ed., *Historical Times Illustrated Encyclopedia of the Civil War* (New York: HarperCollins Publishers, 1986).

Fishkin, Shelley Fisher, *Lighting Out for the Territory* (Oxford: Oxford University Press, 1998).

———, *Was Huck Black?* (Oxford: Oxford University Press, 1993).

Foote, Shelby, *The Civil War: A Narrative*, vols. 1–3 (New York: Random House, 1958–1974).

Gilder, Richard Watson, *The Letters of Richard Watson Gilder* (London: Harrap, 1931).

Goldhurst, Richard, *Many Are the Hearts: The Agony and Triumph of Ulysses S. Grant* (New York: Reader's Digest Press, 1975).

Grant, Jesse R., and Henry Francis Granger, *In the Days of My Father, General Grant* (New York: Harper & Brothers, 1925).

Grant, Julia Dent, *My Life Here and There* (New York: Harper & Brothers, 1921).

Grant, Mrs. Ulysses S., *The Personal Memoirs of Julia Dent Grant*, John Y. Simon, ed. (New York: G. P. Putnam's Sons, 1975).

Grant, Ulysses S., *Personal Memoirs of Ulysses S. Grant* (New York: Charles L. Webster, 1885).

———, *Personal Memoirs* (New York: Modern Library, 1999).

Green, Horace, *General Grant's Last Stand: A Biography* (New York: Charles Scribner's Sons, 1936).

Hearn, Michael Patrick, ed., *The Annotated Huckleberry Finn* (New York: W. W. Norton & Co., 2001).

Hedrick, Joan D., *Harriet Beecher Stowe: A Life* (New York: Oxford University Press, 1994).

Hemingway, Ernest, *Green Hills of Africa* (New York: Scribner's & Sons, 1935).

Holmes, Oliver Wendell, Jr., *Touched with Fire: Civil War Letters and Diary of Oliver Wendell Holmes, Jr.* (Cambridge: Harvard University Press, 1946).

Howells, William Dean, *A Hazard of New Fortunes* (New York: Modern Library, 2002).

Johnson, Robert U., and Clarence C. Buel., eds., *Battles and Leaders of the Civil War*, vols. 1–4 (New York: Century, 1884–1888).

Johnson, Robert U., *Remembered Yesterdays* (Boston: Little, Brown & Co., 1923).

Kaplan, Justin, *Mr. Clemens and Mark Twain* (New York: Simon & Schuster, 1966).

Kingsbury, Robert, *The Assassination of James A. Garfield* (New York: Rosen Publishing Group, 2002).

LeMaster, J. R., and James D. Wilson, eds., *The Mark Twain Encyclopedia* (New York: Garland Publishing, 1993).

Leone, Bruno, *Readings on the Adventures of Huckleberry Finn* (San Diego: Greenhaven Press, 1998).

Lewis, Lloyd, *Captain Sam Grant* (Boston: Little, Brown & Co., 1950).

Lewis, Thomas S., *To Be, to Do, to Suffer: The Memoirs of Ulysses S. Grant* (Saratoga Springs: Skidmore College Press, 1985).

Machlis, Paul, *Union Catalog of Clemens Letters*, vol. 1 (Berkeley: University of California Press, 1986).

——, *Union Catalog of Clemens Letters*, vol. 2 (Berkeley: University of California Press, 1992).

Mauck, Jeffrey, *The Education of a Soldier: Ulysses S. Grant and the War with Mexico* (Steamboat Springs, Colo.: American Kestrel Press, 1996).

McFeely, William S., *Grant: A Biography* (New York: W. W. Norton & Co., 1981).

Neider, Charles, ed., *The Complete Essays of Mark Twain* (New York: Da Capo Press, 1963).

Paine, Albert Bigelow, *Mark Twain: A Biography*, vol. 1 (McLean, Va.: IndyPublish.com, undated).

——, *Mark Twain: A Biography*, vol. 2 (McLean, Va.: IndyPublish.com, undated).

——, *Mark Twain: A Biography*, vol. 3 (McLean, Va.: IndyPublish.com, undated).

——, *Mark Twain: A Biography*, vol. 4, (McLean, Va.: IndyPublish.com, undated).

——, *Mark Twain: A Biography*, vols. 5 and 6 (Mark Twain's Letters) (McLean, Va.: IndyPublish.com, undated).

Peskin, Allan, *Garfield: A Biography* (Kent: Kent State University, 1978).

Pitkin, Thomas M., *The Captain Departs: Ulysses S. Grant's Last Campaign* (Carbondale, Ill.: Southern Illinois University Press, 1973).

Powers, Ron, *Dangerous Water: A Biography of the Boy Who Became Mark Twain* (New York: Basic Books, 1999).

Rasmussen, R. Kent, ed., *The Quotable Mark Twain* (Lincolnwood, Ill.: Contemporary Books, 1995).

Ringwalt, J. Luther, *Anecdotes of General Ulysses S. Grant Illustrating His Military and Political Career and His Personal Traits* (Philadelphia: J. B. Lippincott Co., 1886).

Robinson, Forrest G., *The Cambridge Companion to Mark Twain* (Cambridge: Cambridge University Press, 1995).

Ross, Ishbel, *The General's Wife: The Life of Mrs. Ulysses S. Grant* (New York: Dodd, Mead, 1959).

Sherman, William T., *Letters from General William Tecumseh Sherman to General Ulysses S. Grant and William McPherson in the Collection of W. K. Bixby of Saint Louis* (Boston: Merrymount Press [privately printed], 1919).

——, *Memoirs of William T. Sherman* (New York: Library of America, 1999).

Shrady, George, *General Grant's Last Days* (New York: De Vinne, 1907).

Simon, John Y., ed., *The Papers of Ulysses S. Grant* (Carbondale, Ill.: Southern Illinois University Press, 1967).

Simpson, Brooks D., *Ulysses S. Grant: Triumph over Adversity, 1822–1865* (Boston: Houghton Mifflin, 2000).

Smith, Jean Edward, *Grant* (New York: Simon & Schuster, 2001).

Turner, Arlin, *Mark Twain and George W. Cable* (East Lansing, Mich.: University of Michigan Press, 1960).

Twain, Mark, *Adventures of Huckleberry Finn* (New York: Modern Library, 2001).

——, *Adventures of Huckleberry Finn*, in *Mississippi Writings* (New York: Library of America, 1982).

——, *The Adventures of Tom Sawyer*, in *Mississippi Writings* (New York: Library of America, 1982).

——, *The American Claimant*, in *The Gilded Age and Later Novels* (New York: Library of America, 2002).

———, *The Autobiography of Mark Twain* (New York: Harper & Row, 1959).

———, *Collected Tales, Sketches, Speeches, and Essays* (New York: Library of America, 1992).

———, *A Connecticut Yankee in King Arthur's Court*, in *Historical Romances* (New York: Library of America, 1982).

———, *Following the Equator* (Boondocks Press, www.boondocks.com, 2002).

———, *The Gilded Age*, in *The Gilded Age and Later Novels* (New York: Library of America, 2002).

———, *Huck Finn and Tom Sawyer Among the Indians* (Berkeley: University of California Press, 1989).

———, *The Innocents Abroad* (New York: Library of America, 1984).

———, *Joan of Arc*, in *Historical Romances* (New York: Library of America, 1982).

———, *Life on the Mississippi*, in *Mississippi Writings* (New York: Library of America, 1982).

———, *My Autobiography: "Chapters" from the North American Review* (Mineola, N.Y.: Dover Publications, 1999).

———, *No. 44, the Mysterious Stranger*, in *The Gilded Age and Later Novels* (New York: Library of America, 2002).

———, *The Prince and the Pauper*, in *Historical Romances* (New York: Library of America, 1982).

———, *Roughing It* (New York: Library of America, 1984).

———, *Tom Sawyer Abroad*, in *The Gilded Age and Later Novels* (New York: Library of America, 2002).

———, *Tom Sawyer, Detective*, in *The Gilded Age and Later Novels* (New York: Library of America, 2002).

———, *The Tragedy of Pudd'nhead Wilson*, in *Mississippi Writings* (New York: Library of America, 1982).

Wallace, Lew, *Ben-Hur: A Tale of the Christ* (New York: Harper & Brothers, 1887).

———, *Lew Wallace: An Autobiography* (New York: Harper & Brothers, 1896).

Ward, Geoffrey C., Dayton Duncan, and Ken Burns, *Mark Twain: An Illustrated Biography* (New York: Knopf, 2001).

Warner, Charles Dudley, *My Summer in a Garden* (New York: Modern Library, 2002).

Waugh, John G., *The Class of 1846: Stonewall Jackson, George McClellan and Their Brothers* (New York: Warner Books, 1994).

Webster, Samuel C., *Mark Twain, Businessman* (Boston: Little, Brown & Co., 1946).

Wilson, Edmund, *Patriotic Gore* (New York: Farrar, Straus, Giroux, 1962).

Wilson, James Grant, *General Grant* (New York: D. Appleton & Co., 1913).

Young, John Russell, *Around the World with General Grant: A Narrative of the Visit of General U. S. Grant, Ex-President of the United States* (New York: American News, 1879).

COLLECTIONS

"The *Century* Magazine," in "The Making of America," Cornell University Library, New York. Copies of each article in every issue of *Century* magazine can be viewed at cdl.library.cornell.edu.

Ulysses S. Grant Papers, Chicago Historical Society, Chicago, Illlinois.

General William T. Sherman's Papers, University of Missouri, Columbia.

John H. Douglas Papers, Library of Congress.

The Mark Twain Project and the Mark Twain Papers, University of California, Berkeley.

NEWSPAPER REPORTS

"Twain at the Whittier Dinner," *The New York Times*, December 20, 1877.

"Ulysses S. Grant" (editorial), *The New York Times*, February 17, 1885.

"General Grant's Condition," *New York Tribune*, February 21, 1885.

"Grant Is Dying," *New York Herald*, March 1, 1885.

"Mark Twain's Huck Finn," *New York World*, March 2, 1885.

"Huckleberry Finn," *Evening Traveler*, March 5, 1885.

"Huck Finn," *San Francisco Examiner*, March 9, 1885.

"Mark Twain's New Book," *Hartford Courant*, March 9, 1885.

"Huckleberry Finn," *Advertiser*, March 12, 1885.

"Louisa May Alcott Speaks Out on Huckleberry Finn," *St. Louis Globe Democrat*, March 17, 1885.

"Sheridan's Views of Grant," *New York Tribune*, March 26, 1885.

"Mark Twain's Huckleberry Finn," *Springfield Daily Republican*, April 3, 1885.

"A Sudden Change for the Worse," *The New York Times*, April 8, 1885.

"A Talk with Reverend Dr. Newman," *The New York Times*, April 8, 1885.

"Astonishing His Family," *The New York Times*, April 18, 1885.

"General Grant Holds His Own," *The New York Times*, April 19, 1885.

"Who Is Writing Grant's Book?" *New York World*, April 19, 1885.

"Not Cancer After All," *New York World*, April 19, 1885.

"The Concord Decision," *Sacramento Daily Record-Union*, April 20, 1885.

"General Grant Recovering," *New York Tribune*, April 21, 1885.

"General Grant's Response," *New York World*, April 25, 1885.

"Grant Coming to Saratoga," *Albany Evening Journal*, June 19, 1885.

"Longing for Real Rest," *The New York Times*, July 4, 1885.

"General Grant's Last Wish," *New York Herald*, July 12, 1885.

"A Hero Finds Rest. Ulysses S. Grant's Painless, Peaceful Death. The End Coming in the Early Morning," *The New York Times*, July 24, 1885.

"General Grant Is Buried," *New York Tribune*, August 5, 1885.

"The Honored Dead," *Frank Leslie's Illustrated Newspaper*, August 8, 1885.

INDEX

GRANT

and

TWAIN

A Reader's Guide

MARK PERRY

To print out copies of this or other
Random House Reader's Guides,
visit us at www.atrandom.com/rgg

1. Ulysses S. Grant was not the only president to write his memoirs. Dwight D. Eisenhower and Lyndon Johnson wrote theirs also. Can you think of others? How do they measure up to Grant's writing? How are they different?

2. Only one president is generally considered a better writer than Ulysses S. Grant. In fact, he won a Pulitzer Prize for his writing. Do you know who this is? How does his work differ from that of Grant's work?

3. How did Grant and Twain's views of slavery, African Americans, and the problem of racism differ? How were they the same? How do they differ from our own attitudes?

4. Ulysses S. Grant served two terms as president of the United States, yet he never once wrote about his experiences in the Oval Office. Why do you think he focused on his war experiences?

5. There is some disagreement over why Grant wrote his memoirs. Some historians believe that he simply needed the money. Others say that he wanted to revisit his experiences in the war. Still others say he was influenced by his friend General William T. Sherman. Why do you think he wrote his memoirs? What factors in his life influenced his decision?

6. Literary critics say that Mark Twain's *Adventures of Huckleberry Finn* was his best book—and that he never wrote anything to compare with it. Do you agree? Why do you think that Twain was never able to equal the greatness contained in *Adventures of Huckleberry Finn*? What other later works by Twain might be considered its equal?

7. Mark Twain is thought of as a southern writer. He grew up in Missouri, in a slave society. Yet he spent most of his life in Connecticut and some of his best work (*A Connecticut Yankee in King Arthur's Court*) deals with being a Yankee. Which was he: a southerner or a Yankee? How would he have viewed himself?

8. Women played a major role in the lives of both Twain and Grant. It is doubtful that either could have finished their work without the help of their wives. How has the role of women changed since the 1880s and 1890s? Is the domestic tranquility enjoyed by both Twain and Grant necessary for great writing to emerge?

9. American writer Ernest Hemingway said that all of American literature "comes from one book—*Huckleberry Finn*." What do you think Hemingway meant? Do you agree?

10. *Adventures of Huckleberry Finn* is now viewed in some parts of our country as a controversial book, primarily because Mark Twain used the "N" word to describe Jim. Some schools have even banned the book. Do you think the book should be banned? How should we think of Twain's use of the word? Is Twain's use of the word simply a product of his time, which we should ignore, or is it a reflection of his own feelings about African Americans?

11. There have been significant political, social, and cultural shifts in America's treatment of minorities over the last hundred years. Do you think Grant or Twain had anything to do with these shifts? Can you find in their work any evidence of the deep doubts over the question of race that have been the focus of so much of our recent history? What, for instance, do you think that the Reverend Martin Luther King, Jr., or Malcolm X, or other civil rights leaders thought of Twain's work?

12. Ulysses S. Grant was once considered a poor general and a great president. Then, for a time, he was considered a great general and a poor president. Now some historians who have studied his presidency say that he was a much better political leader than we have given him credit for. What particular historical or political trends might have caused these changes in judgment? Do you believe that historians are influenced in their judgments by their own times?

PHOTO: NINA MIKHALEVSKY

MARK PERRY is the author of *Conceived in Liberty: Joshua Chamberlain, William Oates, and the American Civil War* and *Lift Up Thy Voice: The Grimke Family's Journey from Slaveholders to Civil Rights Leaders.* He lives in Arlington, Virginia.